WAR
AND
PEACE
IN
THE
SPACE
AGE

Books by James M. Gavin:

WAR AND PEACE IN THE SPACE AGE

AIRBORNE WARFARE

WAR AND PEACE IN THE SPACE AGE

Harper & Brothers, Publishers – New York

LT. GENERAL

JAMES M. GAVIN

WAR AND PEACE IN THE SPACE AGE

Copyright © 1958 by Harper & Brothers

H-H

LIBRARY OF CONGRESS CATALOG CARD NUMBER: 58-11396

For Jean

Contents

CONTENTS

MAPS

Preface

In writing this book I have sought to be realistic in examining our current and past situation, and in looking to the future. In doing so I have tried to avoid calling names and pointing a finger of guilt, for all of us, myself included, are responsible for where we now stand. And it is not the time for name calling, it is a time to close ranks and as a united people meet the danger that confronts us. But where deficiencies have been apparent in our organizational structure and shortcomings have been evident in our defense policies I have tried to point them out. Only in this manner can we take corrective action and prepare ourselves for the greater challenges of tomorrow.

During the past ten years I have been closely associated with the development of national defense policy, as a member of the Weapons Systems Evaluation Group, Department of the Army staff, and in the search for tactical innovations in field commands. I have written a number of books and articles during that time, *Airborne Warfare*, "Tactical Use of Nuclear Weapons," "Cavalry and I Don't Mean Horses," "Pushbutton Warfare," "Why Missiles," etc. Each treated with a separate problem in national defense but the over-all problem has never been considered as a whole. The purpose of this book is to do just this, to treat the national problem as an entirety, in terms of space, of the earth, and of the role of all services and the defense establishment that controls them. It is quite an order, and perhaps beyond the capability of anyone to do well. Nevertheless it must be done.

The subject of war and peace is like an iceberg in the sense that most of it—for reasons of security—may not be exposed to public view. This book therefore is based upon that portion of the information which can be made visible to the public eye. However, I can state confidently that the important lines of this book would only be strengthened by the material which for security reasons is denied to us.

We Americans must devote more attention to our problem of national survival. And we must learn to think of the earth as a tactical entity and of space as the next great strategic challenge—space and the mind of man. This book is a modest effort to do this very thing.

I have but one regret: that I have not had more time for its writing. It has taken a great deal of my thoughts for the last several years and all of my working hours for the past couple of months. If it can make a contribution to the defense of this country, and of the West, against the menacing encroachment of Communism, it will have been well worth while.

Wellesley Hills, June, 1958

JAMES M. GAVIN

WAR
AND
PEACE
IN
THE
SPACE
AGE

1

"The Most Significant Event
of Our Time"

December 13, 1957, was a cold and wintry day in Washington. It was late in the afternoon, and as I looked out of my office window Arlington National Cemetery was barely visible through the swirling snowflakes. It had been on a day such as this that the 82nd Airborne Division launched its counteroffensive in the Battle of the Bulge. I had a picture of a soldier in that battle on the wall of my office. He was running forward, wearing little equipment, carrying a submachine gun in one hand and ammunition magazines in the other. It was a moment of loneliness for him. He was doing what he knew had to be done and he was on his own.

I felt now as he must have, for momentarily I expected the phone to ring summoning me to appear before the congressional committee investigating our missile-satellite readiness. For the past four years, I had been closely associated with our missile and satellite programs. I knew what we had done, and I realized what we should have done. It was in the nation's interest that we be honest with ourselves and that we be frank with Congress. In the technical battle in which we were joined with the Soviets, it was our nation's survival that was at stake. I was aware that the risks in being forthright were great, but the stakes were high, and if, in a sense, it was to be a moment of no return, then the moment was to be welcomed for its challenge, and not avoided.

The phone rang. I was told that the committee was waiting for me at the Capitol. I called to my colleague, Major General Jack Daley, to accompany me and I remember now saying to him as we went up the hall:

"Jack, this is just like going into combat. We have searched our souls for answers to our problems and we have made all of our preparations; now we are going in."

You were born to be free. You were also born with a responsibility to contribute to our common defense. For as long as a trace of avarice exists in the hearts of men, there will be a need for the defense of men and their established institutions.

The purpose of this book is to look into that defense. Since I have spent over thirty years in the United States Army, twenty of them in a search for tactical innovations and in the development of tactical doctrine, I would like to draw upon that experience. As most boys do, I grew up living for tomorrow. I learned early in life, in competition, the need to anticipate coming events. I learned later, in combat, that one's very survival depends upon one's ability to anticipate events. And, as with an individual, so the life of a nation depends upon its ability to foresee the challenges of the future. No longer does any nation enjoy the luxury of a shield of space or time. These are the things that I would like to write about, and in doing so I would like to make specific recommendations in the related fields of tactics, strategy and organization. The period of greatest concern is the Decade of Decision—1955 to 1965.

We are now almost three years into that decade. Its significance first became apparent when the Soviets made startlingly clear their progress in the fields of missiles, nuclear weapons and jet aircraft—several years, at least, in advance of the West. It was the time of the rape of Budapest and the frustrations of Suez, the time when the Soviets showed the meaning of an imbalance of power in their favor through rather heavy-handed rocket diplomacy.

Early in the decade, as part of our nation's contribution to the International Geophysical Year, which was to end December 31, 1958, we agreed to undertake a satellite program. Our commitment was based upon a completely new program, optimistically labeled the "Vanguard." It was at best a marginal program and offered little assurance of our being the first into space. At the time, in a memorandum to the Assistant Secretary of Defense for Research, the risks of psychological damage if the Soviets were first to launch were pointed out, but this aspect of it was not taken seriously. Even after Sputnik I the administration's party line seemed to be that it didn't amount to much anyway, but the public and the world at large knew better as the widespread reaction made clear. The year in which Vanguard was approved, 1955, was the year in which a decision was made not to initiate an IRBM[1] program because of its cost. The early decade was a time in which we reaffirmed our reliance upon massive retaliation although there was already some evidence that we were beginning to doubt its adequacy. The frustrations of Indo-China, Quemoy and Matsu, Hungary and Suez, all seemed to be related to a single-weapons-system strategy. And finally, as the prospects and dangers of the missile age became real, the proposal to look into the possibilities of developing an anti-missile missile, a missile to protect our country against Soviet missile attack, met with skepticism and delay. It was dismissed as "not worth trying" at the time.

Now, several years later, most informed people agree that the Soviets are ahead of us technologically, and some believe that they are ahead of us militarily. I believe that they are, and I believe that the broad spectrum of their capabilities, as

[1] Large missiles are in three categories, as follows:
ICBM—Intercontinental Ballistic Missile, range: 1,500-5,500 miles;
IRBM—Intermediate Range Ballistic Missile, range: 450-1,500 miles;
MRBM—Mid-Range Ballistic Missile, range: 200-750 miles.

well as their specific strength in many areas, puts them in a position of clear advantage. As a consequence, they now have the initiative and they continue to outmaneuver us, diplomatically and strategically. It is a sobering consideration. However, our resources are many and our spirit, if far from soaring, is at least willing. We are entirely able to do something about the situation if we have the will to do so. But first of all we must be honest with ourselves in appraising our weaknesses and our strengths vis-à-vis those of the USSR.

There is, for example, the "missile lag." Just what is the "missile lag"? And what is its significance?

The "missile lag" describes a period, and it is one that we are now entering, in which our own offensive and defensive missile capabilities will so lag behind those of the Soviets as to place us in a position of great peril. This may be understood by examining the situation between the two countries as it pertains to manned bombers, Intercontinental Ballistic Missiles, and antimissile missiles.

For quite a few years the manned bomber has been the basis of our retaliatory policy. We have assumed that it has also been the main striking weapon of the Soviets. Now, however, the manned bomber is facing early obsolescence. It will become obsolete as soon as surface-to-air missiles carrying nuclear warheads are on site in numbers. It is important that we realize this is the determinant of the manned bomber's date of obsolescence—when effective nuclear surface-to-air missiles can be employed against it, not when either side has ICBMs to replace it. The ICBM is the consequence of manned bomber obsolescence, not the cause.

Surface-to-air missiles carrying high explosive warheads that can far outperform any manned bomber have been in existence for some time and they have spelled the inevitable doom of the manned bomber. Our first surface-to-air Nike Hercules, carrying an efficient nuclear warhead, is on site now. These will be extremely effective against any Soviet bombers and, combined

4

with the Hawk low-altitude missile, will cause manned bombers to diminish rapidly in their effectiveness, to the point, in fact, of total uselessness.

About the Soviet surface-to-air missiles much less is known. Surface-to-air missiles were displayed in the Fortieth Anniversary Parade in Moscow on November 7, 1957. They were of good size, mobile, and capable of carrying a nuclear warhead. There is no doubt that the Russians have them in operational numbers. As for an opinion on their effectiveness, in an interview with Mr. Reston of the *New York Times,* which appeared in that newspaper early in October of 1957, Mr. Khrushchev had this to say: "Bombers lack both height and speed for modern combat and are vulnerable to attack by rockets." And in the same newspaper, on November 16, he was reported as saying: "In spite of what American officials say, bombers are useless compared to rockets. How many bombers can get through and actually deliver hydrogen bombs?" He was later credited with the remark that bombers belong in a museum.

Now, if this was rather sanguine of Mr. Khrushchev, it is understandable. He has had to carry forward his scheming designs under the ever-present shadow of the United States Strategic Air Command. His relish at being in a position to predict its early deterioration is understandable, although perhaps overly enthusiastic. Nevertheless, most scientists would agree that the end of the manned bomber is now clearly in sight. Obviously, a policy based upon massive retaliation by manned bombers will require early revision. Either the policy will have to be revised or we will have to step up missile production so as to have, at an early date, an arsenal of combat-ready, mobile, intermediate and long-range missile systems.

Let us examine, through the limited evidence that has been made available to the public, where we stand in the ICBM race. Testifying before the Johnson Committee in November of 1957, Dr. Edward Teller, in reply to a question whether or not the Russians had an intercontinental ballistic missile, stated: "Well,

I certainly do not know, I cannot say with complete certainty, but I would like to say this: that they have said that they have the weapon. There is every reason to believe that they have it at least in the state where they have constructed it and tested it."

Testifying before the same committee a month later, Dr. Wernher von Braun, upon being queried on whether or not the Russians could put a "hydrogen warhead on the city of Washington," stated: "I would think so. Yes, sir."

And on January 23, 1958, General Dwight Beach of the Army testified that the Soviets could have an ICBM capability in July of 1958, although a very limited one.

Little has been released of a factual nature on the U.S. ICBM program, although it is a matter of general knowledge that it will be several years before we have an ICBM capability of any significance. This suggests that we are now entering a missile-lag period in which the Soviets will have a steadily increasing ICBM striking capability that we will be unable to match for several years, thus making missile "retaliation" as such, by us, rather meaningless—meaningless except for such shorter-range missiles as IRBMs that we may be able to deploy and maintain on foreign soil or in foreign waters. These will also seriously lag the Soviet capability in the same ranges.

The Soviets now have shorter-range missiles (seven hundred mile and twelve hundred mile) and their threat at the time of the Suez crisis was not an idle boast. Appearing on "Capitol Cloakroom," a CBS radio broadcast, on December 10, 1956, the Honorable C. Douglas Dillon, then the U.S. Ambassador to France, made quite clear that in his opinion it was the Soviet threat that upset British-French plans to go through with the Suez operation. If this is true, then it was missile diplomacy at its best, and we shall be exposed to more of it as we get farther into the period of "missile lag."

There is another significant factor in this missile equation: the anti-ICBM missile, or the antimissile missile. Testifying before the House Armed Services Committee on January 22, 1958, Major General John P. Daley of the Army stated:

To summarize my remarks on the Nike-Zeus [the Army's anti-ICBM missile], the Zeus development is on high priority and we believe that a significant capability could be gotten against ballistic missiles by 1962 *if* deployment is accelerated.

Thus we will not have a missile to use in defense against a Soviet attacking missile for a number of years either.

This is a situation that we should be frank to recognize, and we should realize that this imbalance, for its duration, will be in the favor of the Soviets. How long will it last? For at least three, and more likely for five years, depending entirely upon the effort we are willing to make to reduce it. The Soviets have already announced their intention of increasing their present margin of lead over us. We are in for a hard pull and no sugar-coated reassurances of our superiority will help us. Only hard work and courage will help. Of interest is a British view of this situation as recently described in *The New Statesman:* "The Gaither Report has revealed that, irrespective of any efforts which America may now make, the Soviet preponderance in advanced weapons has reached such an absolute stage that America's national survival will depend, until 1961 at least, on 'Russian benevolence.'"

Benevolence has never been conspicuous among the traits of the Communists; it is as rare as Khrushchev's shrimp's whistle. Instead of benevolence we may expect repeated urgings to accept invitations to summit conferences. These will be accompanied by proposals that the West disband NATO, SEATO, and the Baghdad Pact, and by allegations that such alliances threaten the peace-loving workers of the Soviet Union. There will be proposals that we not arm Germany with modern arms, that all nuclear weapons tests be brought to a stop, and that we join the Soviets in the search for new ways to peace. While these things are happening the Russians will make every effort to widen the margin of advantage that they enjoy in the missile-space race. If we decline to attend a summit conference we may expect Russian proposals to other Western powers to attend without us in the cause of lasting peace. Within the councils of the West there will be increasing talk of the need for some form of disengagement. This will be accompanied by frantic diplomatic efforts to find a formula that would provide us with the security that the military-power imbalance denies us. As disillusionment and discontent grow among our allies they will become increasingly critical of us. At home, in the United States, there will be talk of withdrawal, reducing foreign aid, and a marked trend toward isolationism. Our position will become very difficult indeed, as it aways does when a nation leads from weakness. I am not saying that these things *will* happen but they certainly *may* happen unless we wake up and do something about the missile lag.

The "missile lag" so far described pertains to the United States itself. Let us briefly look at the situation overseas, where there are many vital installations, two field armies, and extensive Air Force and Navy deployments. The Soviets, by their admission, have had a mid-range missile, on the order of 400-750 miles, in their inventory since 1956. On November 7, 1957, they paraded a missile through Red Square that was capable of firing hundreds of miles. Its exact range is uncertain but there is no doubt that it is of far greater range than any ballistic missile the Western Allies now have deployed, for instance, the Corporal, with a range of seventy-five miles. Thus, they are in a position today to give immediate tactical missile support to their forces operating in the Middle East and in Europe. And under the protection of their own surface-to-air missiles they can continue this support without fear of decisively harmful retaliation by manned aircraft.

The development of a missile with a range of five hundred miles was undertaken by the United States Army in 1951. Approval granted to the Department of the Army to go ahead with it at that time was later withdrawn by the Department of Defense. By a memorandum of November 26, 1956, the Army was limited to a range of two hundred miles in its tactical surface-to-surface missiles. There have been no restrictions placed on the characteristics of the missiles of the Navy, Marine Corps or Air Force. Only the Army so far has expressed a need for a mid-range surface-to-surface missile. Nothing was done to correct this situation until early 1958, when the Army's program was again authorized. Such missiles should become operational in quantity in the early sixties.

The problem of defense against mid-range missiles and the longer-range IRBM (fifteen hundred miles) is far more difficult than that of defense against an ICBM. This is due to a number of factors, principally the very quick identification and reaction time required in the defensive system. There has been a program to develop such an antimissile for several years but it has not been given sufficient money and we will be well into the 1960's before it is available for deployment. Thus the "missile lag" at home is matched by a "missile lag" overseas and for the first time in our history we have field armies deployed overseas confronted with weapons against which they can neither retaliate nor defend themselves.

The one bright spot in this otherwise somewhat gloomy picture is the 1959 availability of Jupiter and Thor in some quantity, and the availability of the Navy submarine-launched Polaris several years later. The deployment overseas of Jupiter and Thor should begin in 1958. It will be several years, however, before they are available in adequate numbers and are of adequate reliability. In addition, we must realize that they are the Model Ts of the missile age and we must find ways and means of improving their mobility and reliability. Particular attention must be given to their mobility—they should be entirely mobile. Tactically, Maginot-Line-like missile-launching facilities offer little promise of dealing effectively with the highly mobile Soviet missiles that they will be matched against. There is an alarming tendency to think of the operational employment of missiles in terms of static facilities such as airfields, and blockhouses and bunkers reminiscent of the Maginot Line. Unless we intend to make the same mistake the Germans made with the first V-2 launching sites, we had better plan on mobile missile systems now. They must be mobile to be effective.

There is also a disturbing tendency to become so preoccupied with missiles as to overlook the mobile ground handling equipment, and target acquisition and reconnaissance drones so essential to missile warfare. The latter problem is far from being solved. The assumption is made by many that missiles merely replace bombers and fighter bombers, and that target information will still be obtained through the use of manned reconnaissance aircraft. This simply is not so. If manned bombers cannot live within the range of enemy missiles, manned reconnaissance craft cannot live there either.

We have an impressive unsolved technical task ahead of us if we are going to have combat-worthy missiles systems. A strange exchange took place at one of the weekly press conferences of the President in Washington on May 8, 1957. Martin J. Arrowsmith of the Associated Press asked the question, "Why should not the Army extend its ballistic missile program to ranges of 1,500 miles, to meet the requirements for tactical missile support . . . ?" The answer was given, "Now, just why or when or what reasons they assign any particular missile, any particular type to one service, is not always readily apparent, but I would say this, just from a knowledge of the Army: Why would the Army want a 1,500-mile missile itself, because the first requisite of using that kind of weapon is that you have very good observations to find out whether it is doing the job you thought it was. The only way that you can find that out would be with an Air Force that could penetrate at least 1,500 miles into the enemy territory, and that puts you right square into the Air Force business."

The question referred to "tactical missile support," and the operational concept for such support is to deploy the missiles far to the rear, perhaps a thousand miles or more, depending upon the terrain and the depth of the enemy army's tactical missiles. In any case observation must be provided by an unmanned reconnaissance vehicle; for a short-range missile it will be a recoverable drone and for an ICBM it will be, in time, a satellite. Development of both of these is lagging behind the missile program and there is a real probability that when our IRBMs are deployed there will be no reconnaissance systems to support them for some time. One thing is certain, manned reconnaissance aircraft will not be able to fly against the Soviet surface-to-air missile displayed on November 7, 1957.

An analysis of the foregoing, I believe, begins to explain the reason for the widespread concern in political-scientific-military circles for our immediate security. As expressed by Marshal of the RAF, Sir John Slessor: "We should be in mortal danger if Russia were to get ahead of us in the means of defense against the manned bomber, for instance, or in the development of the really long-range guided missile that will replace it."[2] We *are* in mortal danger and the "missile lag" does portend trouble—trouble of a perilous nature. Under a canopy of fear thrown up by a growing awareness of the Soviet margin of advantage we will be subject to steadily increasing pressures. In the pattern that Lenin described so well, the pressures will be economic and political, and military force will be used only when necessary, but when necessary it will be applied "ruthlessly." Lenin liked to use the word "ruthless," both in describing international military policy and in dealing with internal political policy within the Communist party itself. Whether in a limited action or general war there will be no hesitancy, no moral scruples—force will be applied ruthlessly. The pattern that we have recently seen of the Communists supplying arms to the Algerian Nationalists will be repeated in other areas. Arms support, followed by economic, technical, and political penetration, is the harbinger of armed intervention—if armed intervention proves really neces-

[2] *The Great Deterrent,* Sir John Slessor.

11

sary. Regardless of the means required, the goal will be sought, always with due care to avoid giving us an issue worthy of a Washington-Moscow missile exchange.

A much discussed topic today is limited war and much of it, I fear, is wishful thinking. For a limited-war concept is only valid within an impressive over-all capability to wage general war. No opponent will ever accommodate us to the extent of allowing us to fight a limited war merely because that is what we want to fight, and, more significantly, because that is all that we are capable of fighting. Actually, a nation dare not risk a limited undertaking without possessing the obvious capability of fighting a general war. And to the extent that we have the latter capability we may indulge ourselves in the former. This applies to both the U.S. and the USSR.

Much of our talk about limited war is retroactive in nature. Ten years too late we have come to realize that we should have had a limited war capability at the time of Korea—which we lacked. It was assumed by many that a limited capability was but a small part of a general-war capability, and that if we could fight a general war we could certainly fight a limited war. Deputy Secretary of Defense Quarles has said that "if we have the strength required for global war we could certainly meet any threat of lesser magnitude." This is not true, for limited war in its own way is a highly specialized form of combat, more specialized than general global war. It is as though one were to compare skillful surgery to a killing blow. The first requires special instruments applied with restraint, quickly and accurately, the latter a bludgeon with only one object, complete destruction. To assume that SAC can deal effectively with every type of limited action is the same as to assume that since a tank battalion can be used to control extensive land areas, one tank can be used to catch a pickpocket or car thief. To win limited war requires special weapons, equipment and techniques. These may be useful, and probably would be, in general war but the contrary is not true; the Strategic Air Command would be of limited value in limited war.

Immediately following Hiroshima and for a number of years thereafter our nuclear weapons program was well ahead of that of the Soviets. But this advantage is now disappearing, both in weapons and in their associated delivery systems. The *New York Times* on April 13, 1958, in reporting a talk given by H. Rowan Gaither[3] at the California Institute of Technology, reported him as saying, "The relative strength of the United States in comparison with the Soviet Union and Red China is ebbing." And while our strength is ebbing our obligations are increasing. Since Korea we have made numerous treaty arrangements, NATO and SEATO for example, that imply a responsibility to come to the aid of our allies in case of trouble. The skimpy forces that we do have are scattered world-wide—in the front lines. We have no geographically placed reserves of the type that could deal with limited conflagrations to back up Korea, Southeast Asia, the Middle East or Europe. So far the talk about a fire brigade is just that—talk.

Until our position improves, limited wars, if we were to be favored with them, would result in limited defeats—limited defeats that we would rationalize at the time but that would ultimately lead to general defeat, or to general war. Thus, by failing to provide adequately for something less than general war, by failing to provide for limited wars, we invite general wars, and such a war is one that no one will win. This is the great danger of the "missile lag."

The "missile lag" can be overcome by an all-out effort on our part, and it will take an all-out effort. So far there is insufficient evidence that we do, in fact, intend to go all out. There has been a tremendous amount of propaganda from the services and from industry about what they are doing, but this reflects more a change in our national public-relations policy on release of missile information than it does substantive progress

[3] H. Rowan Gaither is Chairman of the Security Resources Panel of President Eisenhower's Science Advisory Committee.

in our missile programs. And, of course, beyond the missiles themselves is the problem of space and space exploration.

Perhaps the most serious setback, both psychologically and technically, that we have suffered since World War II, came from the launching of Sputnik I. And even now there is evidently considerable public misunderstanding about what actually happened. As well informed an individual as Admiral Rickover stated in the *U.S. News and World Report* of March 21, 1958, that we couldn't get up anything as heavy as the Russians did and that while we had the same basic knowledge as they had we didn't know how to exploit it. This simply isn't true, as the record will show. Our failure was in the decision-making processes in the Department of Defense, specifically a bad decision by the Secretary of Defense and an Assistant Secretary of Defense.

Scientists in the United States knew as early as 1954 that they could launch a satellite, and proposals to launch one were prepared at that time. The Department of the Army urged, in the spring of 1955, that it be permitted to go ahead with a satellite program. At about the same time the Department of the Army also sought authority to undertake an IRBM program. It is obvious now that if the Jupiter program had been started then instead of in the fall of that year, and if it had been given adequate money support, we would now have Jupiters deployed overseas in operational numbers and we would have a militarily useful reconnaissance satellite in space. By "militarily useful" is meant a satellite that can conduct a photographic survey of any portion of the earth. Such a satellite, when available, will be invaluable to an international body, such as the United Nations, in maintaining peace.

However, the decision was made to go ahead with the Vanguard. Vanguard was an excellent scientific program that had a marginal opportunity to meet its deadline—launch a twenty-pound satellite before the end of the calendar year 1958. It was based upon a complete new missile development program.

The Army's proposal, on the other hand, was to use proven components then being developed in the Redstone program. In a memorandum to the Secretary of Defense on August 15, 1955, it was pointed out to the Department of Defense that we very likely would have difficulty with the proposed Vanguard program and that the damage to the United States would be serious if the Soviets launched before we did. Frequently thereafter, the Department of the Army sought permission to launch a satellite.

As part of the Jupiter program the Army developed a missile known as the Jupiter C. The Army was confident that we could orbit a satellite and it proposed to the Department of Defense that we be allowed to do so. This was refused, and finally, on May 15, 1956, I received a directive containing in its concluding remarks the statement: "The Redstone and Jupiter missiles will *not* be used to launch a satellite." This was addressed to me personally and the tenor of finality should have put an end to our pleas. It did not, however, and our concern only grew with each passing week. In the first place, the Jupiter C proved to be as successful as we had anticipated and on September 20, 1956, it fired a small nose cone that achieved an altitude of 684 miles before plunging back into the atmosphere at a range of 3,355 miles. On August 8, 1957 it fired a nose cone that was successfully recovered after achieving an altitude of 248 miles. (This was the nose cone shown on television during the "chins-up" talks following Sputnik I.)

While these things were happening the Soviet programs were also moving ahead at a fast pace. We were following these programs carefully and their successful launching of a twelve-hundred-mile missile in June, 1957, made it quite apparent that they had reached outer space and thus that their prospects of launching a successful satellite during the calendar year 1957 were very good. They had done exceptionally well in achieving a range of twelve hundred miles so soon. If they were to launch a satellite in calendar year 1957 and we did not launch one of our own for at least another year, the psychological and technological defeat could be disastrous. How disastrous it would be difficult to predict, but there was a high probability that a satellite could serve useful military purposes. It could possibly carry out photography of military value, do mapping and geodosy as part of an ICBM system. To those of us associated closely with the research program, we were facing a technological Pearl Harbor.

So far, Congress had been given no information on the situation and every request of the Army for authority to launch a satellite had been denied by the Department of Defense. I thought occasionally of the young man who first, on December 7, 1941, saw the incoming Japanese aircraft on his radarscope and, upon bringing it to the attention of his superior officer, was told to "forget about it." Should he then have bypassed his superior and taken the matter at once to someone else who might understand the seriousness of the situation? Obviously the country would have been better off if he had, and many lives would have been spared and, no doubt, the war won sooner.

I searched my soul for an answer to the problem and decided that the best thing in the national interest would be to examine the possibilities of developing a satellite that would be able to intercept a Soviet satellite. Thus, at least, we would be in a position to deny Soviet intrusion of the Free World air space if, for any reason, it became necessary. We did not want to seek Department of Defense money for such a program, since it would very likely be disapproved. I therefore asked my Deputy to go to the Army's Redstone Arsenal at Huntsville, Alabama, and talk to General Medaris and Dr. von Braun about the feasibility of a satellite interceptor. He did so on June 21, 1957, and reported that they would undertake a study of a satellite interceptor at once. On August 26, 1957, Mr. Khrushchev announced to the world:

A super-long-distance intercontinental multi-stage ballistic missile was launched a few days ago. The tests of the rocket were successful.

They fully confirmed the correctness of the calculations and the selected design.

The missile flew at a very high, unprecedented altitude. Covering a huge distance in a brief time, the missile landed in the target area. The results obtained show that it is possible to direct missiles into any part of the world.[4]

This information was soon confirmed by other intelligence and it was clear that the Soviets were on the threshold of launching their satellite. The information was studied carefully and, at a meeting of the Army Scientific Advisory Panel on September 12, 1957, I told them that in my opinion, the Soviets would launch their satellite within thirty days.

On October 4 I had lunch with Dr. von Braun and Dr. Schilling at the Redstone Arsenal, at which time we agreed that, based upon all available intelligence, the Soviet launching was imminent. We discussed the situation at some length and we agreed that if a launching took place, two steps had to be taken, as matters of highest national urgency: the development of a satellite to intercept the satellite, and the development of a large, militarily useful satellite.

That evening a number of scientists, businessmen and military people were gathered together for dinner in the Officers' Mess at the Arsenal, when the announcement of the Soviet satellite launching was received. I felt crushed and wanted to take a long walk to think the situation over alone. The last thing that I wanted to do was to attend a dinner party. But it was not the time to be antisocial.

After all of our efforts to launch first we had been beaten into space. And, more important, we had no idea what the satellite carried. Even now, we realize that we may never know.

I turned to the president of one of our large business corporations who was present and told him how disturbed I was, and he replied: "Oh, it's nothing at all, nothing at all. It doesn't

---

[4] Excerpt from text of Soviet statement, *New York Times*, August 27, 1957.

amount to a thing." That disturbed me almost as much as the satellite launching itself, but I didn't realize until the next day that this opinion was shared by many. The reaction varied from Secretary Wilson's "a neat scientific trick" to others' "a silly bauble," "a hunk of iron," and Madame Cafritz' observation as reported in the Washington *Post* on October 7, 1957: "The satellite is very appropriate for Russia to have because she has so many of them."

Fortunately, there were some who realized at once the importance of it. Senator Henry M. Jackson, in the *New York Times* of October 6, 1957, described the Soviet launching as "a devastating blow to the prestige of the United States." In the following month, Dr. Edward Teller, testifying before the Johnson Preparedness Subcommittee, said:

> It has great military significance because, among other things, it shows that the Russians are far along, very far along, in rocket development. But it has also some intrinsic military significance. In addition, it has all kinds of scientific developments, because it allows us to find out a great number of things about outer space, looking back on earth, some of the properties on our own globe. It has great significance in both these directions.

Others testifying before Congress stated that it was the most significant military event of our time, which is exactly what it was.

Before leaving the satellite, I would like to comment on the cost aspects of it. For there are those who will say, "Well, we simply couldn't afford everything, and it would have been wasteful to put money into another satellite program." The facts are that Jupiter C, as was well known, is part of another program and its satellite launchings have cost but a few million dollars. The first cost estimates of Vanguard were in the vicinity of twenty million dollars. Both of these together cost but a small part of another program that was being carried on at the same time. That was the Navaho, an unmanned bomber, which was promptly discontinued by Secretary McElroy shortly after he took office. The Navaho had cost seven hundred million dollars before being canceled. The big question is why in the name of heaven was money being spent on such a scale and in such a wasteful manner while we were denying ourselves a satellite. Was it caused by industrial pressure, service interest, or simply poor decision-making in the Department of Defense? Of one thing we may be sure, our failure to launch a satellite first was not due to lack of money in the Department of Defense budget.

Now we can foresee that by the end of the Decade of Decision, 1965, manned space flight will be here. We will then be ready to undertake manned exploration of the planetary system. The earth will have shrunk, in a military sense, to a rather small tactical theater. It will be entirely possible to launch weapons from any point on the earth to impact at any other point on the earth, exactly as in past combat it has been possible in a tactical engagement to engage directly any opponent with the weapons at hand.

In World War II, for example, a tactical theater was usually thought of as a continent, or a major segment of a continent. By 1965 missiles and satellites will have shrunk the world to such small size that the earth itself will be a tactical theater. We will truly live a hair-triggered existence in a "balance of terror." Everyone will be faced with the threat of immediate death and destruction, if means of guaranteeing peace are not found. Surely this is a grim and forbidding prospect and it is one from which we dare not shrink if we are to survive—not only the Western world but the Soviet world as well.

The challenge with which we are faced is tremendous and the implications of it far-reaching. The very nature of strategy will change, leaving the realm of physical combat and going into full-scale psychological warfare, and leaving the earth's environment and going into space. War, which we have thought of in three dimensions, has now acquired a fourth dimension: strategy. Modern strategy is the fourth dimension of warfare.

Our organizational structure to deal with these problems needs radical changing, both in the Department of Defense and in the Joint Chiefs of Staff. The Armed Forces themselves, and the missions they may be expected to perform, will, of necessity, change radically. And by 1965 they will be entirely overlapping in their capabilities. The old definition of functions based upon land, sea and air will be far outdated. There will be risks and sacrifices inherent in almost any solutions found to these problems, but they must be solved and the beneficial results to be gained are well worth the extraordinary effort required to solve them. And the fundamental and essential ingredient in our thinking and planning absolutely must be moral courage.

Finally, whether we like it or not, the burden of leadership has been thrust upon us. And any failures will not be our failures alone; they will be the failures of free men everywhere. Leadership and power are inseparable, and the power available today surpasses man's imagination. We must learn to live with that power, and to cause it to serve us and not become slaves to it. This should be the essence of our leadership.

> On us the burden falls to lead the nations
> Out of this frightful wilderness of steel;
> On us depends the course of that which is
> To come hereafter—whether freedom was
> A stolen dream from Heaven, or is the truth
> On which to found the future of mankind.[5]

[5] From *My Country* by Russell W. Davenport, published by Simon and Schuster, Inc.

2

As the Twig Is Bent

To each of us there comes a time in our lives when we think about our childhood. We attribute a meaning to it, and we think of the effect that it has had upon our attitudes and our later life. To me the occasion was the Battle of Sicily. As a paratrooper I was isolated with a small group of troopers behind the enemy lines. It gave me time to think, and it gave me much to think about.

Combat, especially prolonged combat, is a time for introspection, perhaps too much at times. Memories go back to one's childhood, to the pleasant days of boyhood when the fields and green hills beckoned and each day brought new things to be seen, to be heard, and to be tried. Sooner or later one asks oneself, "What in the world am I doing here?" It is a good question and one for which all of the wisdom of mankind has, so far, been unable to provide an answer. A more simple question would be about one's attitude toward combat. For this is first formed in the conditions of boyhood and it is given final stamp in the impressionable school years of the late teens.

I remembered when I was a small boy in the coal regions of Pennsylvania.

"Be kitchin with the treacle, Shamus," my mother said. For we were a poor family—perhaps not exactly poor, but certainly not far from it. And syrup was not too often on the table—when it was, it was molasses.

I was born on March 22, 1907, in Brooklyn, New York. My family lived on Deane Street, and I was born in a hospital several blocks away on the same street. Both of my parents were Irish immigrants and both died before I reached the age of two. Through the intercession of the Church, I was adopted by an Irish family, the Gavins, again both from the Ould Sod.

Martin Gavin, my foster father, was kind and generous, and a God-fearing man. He heard his first radio broadcast from a small crystal set that I was making one day. He listened with disbelief for a moment and said, " 'Tis the work of the devil." He was a hard-working miner and he was well liked throughout the town. He had no faults of which I was aware, he drank moderately except on Saint Patrick's Day. It was well understood and accepted that he was expected to hang on a real rip-snorter on Saint Patrick's Day. The strongest language that I ever heard him use was "The curse of Cromwell on you," and it was some years before I found out what that meant.

My foster mother, Mary Gavin, was typically Irish, given all too frequently to invoking the intercession of the entire Holy Family and all of the Saints while she lambasted me for some not too minor misdemeanor. It always struck me as an incongruous combination of prayer and violence.

"Holy Mary, Mother of God, where have you been, Shamus?"

"Oh, out."

"May the Lord have mercy on our souls, out where?"

"Oh, nowhere."

"Glory be to God, nowhere he says." Wham, and a resounding blow would descend on my anatomy, any part of it, usually the part nearest to her.

But it was fortunate that I was adopted by the Gavins, for I grew up amidst a clan of Irishmen that had all of the supercharged attributes of that fine race. Years later, reading James Farrell, John O'Hara and Edwin O'Connor, I was impressed with how intact the mores and habits of the Irish are, especially when one realizes that they come from a very small place and that they

22

are scattered to the four corners of the earth. The Gavins were characteristic. They and their relatives were settled in two small villages on the edge of Mount Carmel, Pennsylvania, Dooleysville and Connorsville. As a group they were idealistic, emotional, took their patriotism for granted, held strong views about most things and expected other people to do the same. They never hesitated to express their views, and it was assumed that one would fight for them if need be. There was a clan of them, all related, and the first came over in the late 1800's: the Delaneys, Harvertys, McDonalds, Kulicks and Hennesys. They didn't talk much about the latter, because the Hennesy men had been stemwinders in the Molly McGuire movement in the coal regions at the turn of the century and one ended up in potter's field via the gallows. Like all Irish, they were religious and hard workers, especially the young men. One of my earliest memories is of being impressed with the need to work and to contribute to the support of the family. Education was not considered important.

As soon as I was big enough to carry papers and find my way around town, I got a job delivering a Philadelphia morning paper, the *North American*. By the time I was in the fifth grade and reached the age of eleven, I had both morning and evening routes and I was the local agent for three out-of-town papers. By thirteen I had cornered two Sunday routes and had a couple of boys working for me. I suppose that I was well on the way to becoming an entrepreneur, but it was a rough life. You had to fight for the best corner on which to sell and be ready at any time to fight for your papers and routes. One incident bearing on this has always lingered in my memory.

Most of us were willing to live and let live, and we tried to get along in friendly competition. Occasionally a fight would break out, but they were really not welcomed by either side. A friend of mine who was also a competitor—we sold rival papers at the door of the main hotel in town—was having trouble with one of the bigger toughs in town. The big guy was giving him a hard time and was about to take some of his route customers away from him. One cold winter evening, not long after dark, my friend and I were standing near the hotel door, trying to sell our papers and talking about the things boys talk about. He was telling me about the pushing around that this guy was giving him, when up the street he came. He would have gone on by; it was dark and he hadn't noticed us. Suddenly my friend, who was considerably smaller in size, dropped his papers, ran into the middle of the street, and started swinging on the tough. In seconds, the bully took off on the run. I was amazed, and the memory of the incident still lingers with me after many years. The smaller man physically was in the right, but more than that he had the moral courage to stand up for what he believed when he knew a fight was inevitable. By having the courage of his convictions and acting in the right as he saw the right, he won, although the odds were clearly against him.

But life was not all work. There was school, and I loved school, for there I had a chance to read books, and I somehow could not get enough books. I went through the Horatio Alger series, *Pluck and Luck, Work and Win, The Tin Box,* etc., Tom Swift, the Rover Boys. But the real windfall came when I found an entire bookcase full of books in the back rooms of the First Presbyterian Church.

I was taken to the church by a boy friend, and as I looked at the bookcase, I hesitated for a moment, torn between intellectual hunger and religious restraint. I had been brought up as a strict Catholic and I knew very well that God would strike me dead for going into a Protestant church, or at least, the parish priest would find out about it and then I would really catch it. It was bad enough to enter a Protestant church, but to read a Protestant book was going entirely too far. But it took only a few minutes to decide that my curiosity had to be satisfied. The books were very good, and just what I wanted—boys' books, and they had nothing to do with religion.

Religion was something to be reckoned with in Mount Carmel in the 1910's. There were a half-dozen Catholic churches, representing the different national groups, the Italians, the Poles, the Lithuanians, etc. The Irish went to the Church of Our Lady on Market Street. There was a parochial school on the grounds that I attended four of my grade school years. There was Mass every morning before school, prayers said kneeling on the classroom floor before morning and afternoon classes, and High Mass on Sunday. In the meantime, you were cautioned to beware of the temptations of the devil. But the flesh was weak and temptation was sometimes irresistible.

One such irresistible temptation was *The Perils of Pauline*, showing for five cents every Saturday afternoon at the Arcade Theater. Once you were caught in the coils of sin with the beautiful heroine, Pearl White, you'd had it. Because she invariably ended up just about to be cut atwain by the lumber camp buzz saw, with the villain at the switch, and then it was "to be continued next week." You couldn't resist going back the following Saturday. Besides, you were given a free pass for the Monday afternoon show, that you could see after school. In between, the wages of sin were exacted from our anatomies on Monday morning by the parish priest. He would arrive shortly after classes began, give us a lecture on the horrors of hell that awaited those who lied, and then ask all who had gone to the movies Saturday afternoon to raise their hands. The unfortunates who admitted their guilt then went to the front of the room to be punished before the class. This took the form of holding out your hand while the priest whacked you across the palm with a ruler. It hurt, I can testify to that, but the embarrassment hurt almost more. It didn't take long to find out that God wouldn't strike you dead for not holding up your hand and, in retrospect, I realize that was a very effective way of teaching boys not to tell the truth. Aside from that, the school was very good, and exacting in its scholastic standards—no basket weaving. The teachers were Catholic nuns and a more dedicated, friendly, hard-working group I have never known in my life.

School came to an end with the first warm days of summer.

Then came the time to pick coal for the coming winter. All of the boys in my part of town would start picking coal as soon as school was out and this was continued until the family coal shed was filled to the roof. Coal picking consisted of going to the nearest culm bank or strippings and digging and separating the coal from the rock, slate and debris. The coal was then loaded into burlap potato sacks and carried back to the coal shed. One full sack of good clean coal was a good morning's work for a boy, so that it took almost the entire summer to fill a coal shed. The boys and the old men picked coal while the able-bodied men worked in the mines—when they weren't on strike.

There were a lot of old men, or so it seemed to me. I remember seeing them rocking on the front porches. The Civil War veterans as often as not wore a part of their uniform, perhaps a hat or a blue vest. The Spanish-American veterans were much younger and more active. So active that when the First World War became imminent in the spring of '17—I was just turned ten at the time— one of the Spanish-American War veterans named Gable turned out all of the prospective candidates for military service for close order drill. Every evening he would put a group about as big as an oversized squad through the intricacies of "Right Foot, Left Foot" in the street intersection near my home. All of us kids would hang around, enviously dreaming of the glories of war and of coming home as bemedaled heroes. We felt sorry for ourselves that we were so young.

People, it seems to me, were far more patriotic in those days. I remember every thirtieth of May. All of the veterans would gather in mid-town and then walk in a long column to the cemeteries. Each would carry a small American flag on his shoulder, and upon arrival at the cemetery, he would place it upon the grave of a departed comrade. We boys would run and walk alongside of the column. We had a great deal of respect for the veterans, and we were convinced that the finest thing that could happen to us would be some day to get a chance to serve our country in either the Army or the Navy, if ever a war should come. This was taught in school, too, and we learned at an early age that these liberties that Americans enjoy were not easily won. They cost lives, flesh and blood consumed in the holocaust of war. And war is never easy. War is bitter and war is costly.

I loved to walk over the hills around Mount Carmel. I had an insatiable curiosity about what was across the next mountain, so much so that it was almost my undoing at times.

There were few of the means of traveling that there are now, and we boys went everywhere on foot. Several hours of walking across a mountain or two could be real adventure. I shall never forget when I walked to the west over two mountains, and across a deep forested valley known as Brush Valley. As I came over the second mountain, a vista opened before me the like of which I had never imagined. Beautiful checkered patches of color of the rolling Pennsylvania Dutch farm country lay at my feet. It was too late in the day to go on so I had to return home. The next Sunday I skipped going to Mass and got an early start. I continued down into the farm country until I came to a group of young men loafing about a country store. They even seemed to speak another kind of language; it was Dutch, Pennsylvania Dutch. They gave me directions that took me home by another route, which was equally fascinating.

It was an all-day trip. I couldn't wait until the following Sunday, to try the opposite direction. I had much the same experience, and after a couple of hours' walk came to beautiful farming country—clean and entirely unlike the coal towns. I continued to explore that valley, going quite far, several miles down it. I made some friends in a small town with a quaint name—Helfenstein. But the excursions and meanderings had to come to an end, just as the summer also had to come to an end. It was time to go back to school.

Eighth grade stands out in my memory as the year when I first learned about the Civil War. I devoured everything about it that I could lay my hands on. My schoolteacher, a Miss Roberts, put an outline of the war on the blackboard and I bought a second-

hand typewriter and typed a copy of it. She later bought the outline from me for twenty-five cents. In the meantime, I was reading
everything about the war that I could find, particularly biographies.

I couldn't understand how a general could control that many
men—thousands! I remembered how difficult it was to handle a
half-dozen on a hike. To control in battle one hundred thousand,
as Grant and Sherman did, was pure magic. Magic, I decided,
that was taught at a place called West Point. I had just read a
biography of General Pershing, who had gone to West Point, and
I thought how wonderful that would be. The trouble was that he
had finished school and become a teacher before going to West
Point, so he must have been very smart. And my prospects were
not very good. My family had decided that eighth grade was
enough education for anyone; after that it was time to get out
and work.

I had already given up my newspaper jobs, and I was working
in a barbershop. It paid better. Every day after school I would
work in the barbershop until seven in the evening. Saturday the
hours were from eight in the morning until eleven at night. We
were supposed to either keep busy or look busy, and not sit down.
By eleven my legs felt like one long toothache. Between rubbing
lather in the miners' whiskers and doing general clean-up work, I
stood around and absorbed the wisdom of my elders. And the
wisdom emanating from the miners was something for a boy to
remember. Among other things, it convinced me that I didn't want
to become a miner. I was sure of this. But the problem of an education was weighing heavily on my heart and mind. By then, to
the best of my knowledge, I had read every book in town that
I could get my hands on, and they only whetted my appetite for
more.

I finished eighth grade in June of 1922 and immediately got a
full-time job. I worked as a clerk in a shoe store and the pay was
very good for those times—$12.50 a week! About then auto-
mobiles were becoming popular and filling stations were mush-

rooming up throughout the coal regions. I got a job managing one for the Jewel Oil Company. On the side I acquired the agency for Gargoyle Mobiloil Products, so I was doing quite well. But I still was terribly restless and concerned about a future. An education seemed to be the first essential and how to get one was the problem. My classmates from grammar school were now well along in high school and we had drifted apart.

I finally took another, better-paying job with a filling station, and then decided that that was enough. I was merely going from one job to a better one, but the fundamental for real advancement was lacking: a good education. Without that I could never get anywhere, but how to get it was the problem. Certainly it was not to be had in Mount Carmel. I had saved a few dollars, so I decided to go to the biggest place of all—New York City.

I left Mount Carmel on March 22, 1924, my seventeenth birthday. As soon as I arrived in New York, I began to look for work. There were a number of employment agencies around mid-town and I checked all of them. But they wanted mostly handymen and laborers. Obviously, no one was going to hire me to send me to school. This was unmistakably clear. No one but one—the Armed Forces.

I met and talked to an Army recruiting sergeant down in Battery Park. The only thing that he seemed to be interested in was whether or not I had what he called venereal disease. I wasn't sure what it was, but I assured him that I didn't have it. I had heard the miners talk about it in the barbershop, but I knew that I wouldn't know it if I saw it. Then, with this technical hurdle passed, he asked my age. This was more difficult. I had been seventeen four days before and the minimum enlistment age was eighteen. Eighteen with parental consent and twenty-one without. Obviously I didn't qualify as a prospective soldier under either count. I wasn't about to ask my parents for consent. I knew very well what the answer would be. He didn't seem disturbed. With a resourcefulness not uncommon to Army recruiting sergeants in those days, he suggested that he might be able to provide parents for me who would look with favor upon my joining the Army. I said that it sounded like a good idea, let's try it. Off we went to the Whitehall Building, a few blocks away, where, to my surprise, I joined about a half-dozen boys in identical straits. The sergeant then took the group of us to Broome Street. We entered what appeared to be a lawyer's office. A few questions were asked and upon learning that I was a waif, alone in this world, he signed a paper that said I was eighteen and that he was my foster father or guardian, and that furthermore he consented to my enlistment in the United States Army. He did the same for all of us. I do not know what his fee was for this service to the United States but at the moment I was grateful.

The recruiting sergeant had been describing the educational opportunities offered to "bright and deserving young men, to earn while you learn," and I just couldn't wait to get in. I held up my right hand in the Whitehall Building on April 1, 1924. The name of the officer who swore me in was on his desk and I have always remembered it because it was the name of a Civil War general, Captain Buckner. He was the first captain of the United States Army, in uniform too, that I had ever seen and I was impressed. I repeated the oath after him with an enthusiasm that must have surprised him. I soon found out that the recruiting sergeant's sales talk assayed high in exaggeration. But I liked the Army from the beginning and it did give me educational opportunity. But I sure had to work for what I got.

I went to Panama, where I joined an artillery battery defending the Atlantic entrance of the Canal. I was assigned to a 155-mm. gun crew and my education began under a fine old Irish sergeant, a Sergeant McCarthy. He was a slave driver and as hard as nails, but he took good care of his soldiers. I learned a lot from him. Our first sergeant was an Indian, over six feet and hefty. He stood for no nonsense, but he took excellent care of his troops and I learned to like and respect him. When he found out that I could read and write with some facility he made me battery clerk. I then learned of a vacancy for a noncommissioned officer who knew semaphore. I studied semaphore and was made corporal in about six months, rather young for a corporal in those days, but I was learning and getting along well.

Panama offered little then in the way of diversion for a soldier. As I recall, the pay after deductions were made was $18.75 a month. I sent $10.00 home, so that did not leave much for the tailor, cobbler and laundry. Fortunately, there was a post library. I found it about a month after arriving and it provided an un-ending source of interesting books. I soon came across Dodge's *Great Captains*. I was fascinated with them and devoured the biographies of Alexander, Hannibal and Napoleon. I was always a bit concerned lest the soldiers in the battery find me reading such things. It was not for a private to dream of being a great captain, nor to dream of being a high-ranking troop commander either.

But I still aspired to West Point, and dreamed of going there. The more I read, the more I became aware of the contributions made by West Point graduates to our nation's history. If one were to be a soldier, that was the place to go. But such a possibility seemed far beyond attainment in the summer of 1924. It did to me, anyway, but evidently not to my first sergeant, "Chief" Williams.

Entering the orderly room after first sergeant's call one day, he sounded off.

"Well, Gavin, I just saw a memorandum up at Post Head-quarters announcing appointments for West Point next year. You go up and take a look at it."

"Okay, Sergeant, I will, but I am not ready to tackle that yet. I ought to study another year or so."

"Well, those West Pointers *are* smart bastards. They must make them study a lot when they go there and it must be hard to get in, but you can't lose for trying. Take a look at it."

"Okay," I said, "I will."

I went up to Headquarters and got the memorandum. It offered an opportunity for any enlisted man who could pass the physical examinations to go to a prep school and take the West Point entrance examinations that were to be given on March 1, 1925. It was then mid-August, 1924, and the school was to be started on September first. I applied, passed the physical, and ended up at Corozal, Canal Zone, with a dozen other aspirants, on September first. Among them was Frank Merrill, later of Merrill's Marauders fame. He was a staff sergeant in the Engineers and he impressed me tremendously. Among other things, he could use a slide rule, and I had never seen one before. Besides, he had taken the entrance examinations the year before and had passed except for an eye deficiency that could now be waived. We had a wonderful instructor, First Lieutenant Percy Black of the Chemical Corps. He was a gentleman, he was obviously intelligent, and he was very patient. And believe me, he needed the latter quality in abundance.

We soon settled into a work routine. Lieutenant Black arrived every morning at eight o'clock and spent four hours with us. One hour each was spent on algebra, geometry, English and history. History began with Ancient, in a few weeks went through Medieval, and ended up in the spring with Modern. It was planned that we would finish our studies shortly after the first of the year and the remainder of the time until March first would be spent in taking old entrance examinations for practice.

Since we were clipping off thirty to forty pages a day, I had a terrible time keeping up. In fact, I didn't. I was soon so far behind that I had to make a basic decision. I had to decide whether to give up trying to keep up and to master each page before turning to the next (this especially applied to math), or simply to skim along on what I could absorb and stay with the class schedule. I decided that I had to do the former, learn each page before going to the next. It meant studying all afternoon and then usually until midnight. I was quite far behind when Christmas came, when most of the students took time off. I continued to work and by February, there appeared to be a chance of making it.

Throughout the entire time, Lieutenant Black worked patiently and diligently with us. Finally came the big day, March 1. We took a four-hour written examination on each subject. I did not think that I did very well. I remember one of the questions in English required us to write a short composition on the theme of one of Shakespeare's plays. We were given a choice of several. I couldn't for the life of me remember enough about any of them to try doing a composition, so I turned in a blank paper. Lieutenant Black refused to accept it. He probably violated his instructions in doing so, but he insisted that I go back and write something. I had remembered a bit about the plot of *The Merchant of Venice,* so I went back and did the requisite number of words. I have always been grateful to Lieutenant Black for his insistence. Somehow I felt that that was what enabled me to pass.

I was admitted as a cadet on July 1, 1925. The first semester was a nightmare of work. Math was the most difficult and they were pouring it on mercilessly. The only way that I could keep up with it was to get up at four or four-thirty in the morning and study in the basement latrines, where there was a light. I didn't do this any more than I had to, probably a couple of times a week, but it enabled me to keep up.

The first semester "Writs" were given the Plebe Class in December. If we failed those, we were then to take a final "Turn-Out" Writ to determine whether or not we would be turned out of the Academy; that is, dismissed. I passed all of my first "Writs" with a margin of safety and later I realized that that was the turning point. There were about 450 in the class, and my class standing was then around 385. The next semester came and I continued to move along without too great difficulty. History was one of the subjects the next year and I found myself in the first section in academic standing. So I could afford to quit studying history and concentrate on math and languages, which were both more difficult for me.

But academics were no longer a worry and by my First Class year my class standing was somewhere around 100. It averaged

33

out for the four years at 185, and there was no problem in going into the infantry, which was my choice.

The Military Academy at West Point can make a tremendous impression upon a young man. In the first place, from end to end it is a gigantic museum, containing the finest relics of American history. Many facts that few outsiders are aware of are brought to the attention of the cadets daily. They occupy the old cadet rooms once occupied by Grant, Lee, Sheridan, Jackson, Pershing, Patton and MacArthur. The old chapel containing the British colors taken in the Revolution, even the rocky hills that were etched by proud patriots who wanted all who would ever pass by to note their contribution to the Republic, the present-day chapel, the statues, and the forts and redoubts of the surrounding hills, all burn into the young mind and heart one thing: Patriotism! Not the transient, sunshine-patriot variety, but something on the order of the old immutable truths of all time: men had fought and died for this country and were proud to do it and no greater privilege could come to a man than the opportunity to do likewise if ever our democracy were to be challenged again.

"May we find a soldier's resting place beneath a soldier's blow"[1] asks simply that a soldier be granted the challenge of combat and if death be his lot, then he asks not to be moved, for that is as far as a man can go, physically, intellectually.

Cadets are taught to be honest in all things and there is a resoluteness about their honesty that grips a man to the marrow. Once a matter is resolved into right or wrong, then the right must be chosen, and always the harder right rather than the easier wrong. Even the Academy itself is a monument to this principle, as it stands on a granite mountain that alters the course of the mighty Hudson River on its way to the sea. So must her sons adhere to the right when the issue is drawn. May there never be compromise when our Country and our Honor is at stake.

Finally, cadets are taught to have a sense of duty, a sense of responsibility for their fellow man, for the troops charged to their

[1] "Benny Havens," a cadet song.

care. They become aware, most of them for the first time, of Aristotle's belief that a man's worth is not measured by his wealth, nor by his position in society, but by the amount of himself that he has given to his people.

Along with this, they are required to pursue their studies with zeal and industry. As a general rule, each cadet makes a personal recitation on at least one subject daily, sometimes several.

It is no wonder that I loved the place as I did. From the day I entered until I left, each minute there seemed to give me something. I left determined to repay her, my Spartan mother, for what she had given to me. I went forth to seek the challenge, to "move toward the sound of the guns," to go where danger was greatest, for there is where issues would be resolved and decisions made.

Needless to say, subsequent assignments were for a long time anticlimactic, but I was learning the profession of a soldier. I had learned the theory, and now I had to learn the practice.

My first assignment was to the flying school at Brooks Field, Texas. That was the first and worst letdown of my career as a soldier. I am not sure what they were doing at Brooks Field in 1929, nor am I sure that the authorities there were. The object seemed to be to keep graduated cadets from learning how to fly.

I was in a group of five that reported to a Lieutenant Rodgers, who confidently told us that he would probably eliminate all of us. He advised us as a parting precaution not to start spending our flying pay right away. I loved flying, as I do to this day, but love of flying wasn't enough. It was a lot of fun flying those open cockpit biplanes, but after a couple of weeks, I was told to report to a check pilot for probable elimination. He was busy, the weather was bad, and he didn't get to me for a couple of more weeks. By then I was so far behind the regular class that he was appalled. With a shake of his head and a "tch! tch!" I was sent on my way. As an afterthought he explained that I should not be concerned; that flying was not a science to be learned, but an art that you either had or didn't have a flair for. If you had it, as he put it, you were a birdman. If you didn't, you weren't. So, why worry? I didn't.

I applied for assignment to a post as far away as I could go— Camp Harry J. Jones near Douglas, Arizona, on the Arizona-Mexican border. Washington must have been so shocked by anyone applying for duty at that remote place that they approved it at once and I arrived just before Christmas in 1929.

The life of a lieutenant of infantry was rather prosaic thirty years ago. There was the annual routine; the marksmanship season, maneuvers, winter schools, spring training, civilian components and CMTC followed each other as night followed day. The Army was small and the public showed even smaller interest in it. After all, we had just ratified the Kellogg-Briand Peace Pact of 1928, outlawing war as an instrument of national policy. There was never going to be another war. If we were training for anything, it was for a war that would never come. I, at times, bemoaned our fate with my contemporaries. We, the unfortunate ones, who were destined to go through life without hearing a hostile shot. How wrong we were!

The drill days were rather short and there was an abundance of time for extracurricular activities. I should have spent more time on my books, but tennis, golf and riding offered too much competition. But I liked troop duty and I liked being with troops. The long night marches, the sudden skirmishes on maneuvers, were all teaching me the things I would have to draw upon if war came.

Fort Benning and the Infantry School followed Arizona, and next came the Artillery School and Fort Sill, Oklahoma. At Fort Sill I began once again to study, and I did a great deal of riding. For three years I rode on the hunts twice a week and, looking back later, I was to realize that the nearest thing to jumping out of an airplane is riding a reluctant horse over a difficult jump. Giving him the legs and going in with a bad spill in prospect seems to call for the same kind of mental decision as jumping

36

from a plane. They have in common a high degree of mixed apprehension and elation.

I was assigned to the Philippines in 1936 and there I joined a Philippine Scout regiment. The troops were all professionals and very good. They gave a splendid account of themselves on Bataan a few years later.

On the international scene war clouds were clearly in evidence. Mussolini was deeply involved in Ethiopia. Franco was fighting in Spain. And Hitler was chest-thumping in Germany.

Our maneuvers began to have more meaning, although our weapons and equipment were not much better than those used in the First World War. Several times we rehearsed the withdrawal to the Bataan Peninsula. We then maneuvered, falling back as we anticipated the World War II pattern of fighting on the peninsula. The situation was far from good. There were wide gaps in the center of the defenses, and obviously inadequate food and water for the thousands of soldiers and civilians that would crowd into the place.

The terrain was unusually rugged and I remember the problems of supply and night patrolling—for instance, the night that Lieutenant Bill Ryder got lost with the mule train and we ordered him to stay lost until we found him. Bill was in charge of the mules in our Philippine Scout regiment, and I was in charge of the trucks. We were both in Service Company. It was his job on Bataan to deliver rations and ammunition by pack train at night. Handling a string of pack mules at night on a dark jungle trail is a difficult job. Bill was good at it, but one night the mule column split and part of it, Bill's part, became lost. By the time he was able to phone in, the company commander was madder than hell.

"Ryder," he said, "I know you think you know where you are, but I know I know where you are. By God, you stay where you are until I find you. You stay lost until I get there."

Shortly after that, Ryder returned to the States, and not long afterward he volunteered to become a member of the first parachute platoon. We were to meet again, at night, over Sicily.

But the prospects on Bataan were grim at best. Inadequate food, inadequate water and insufficient troops with weapons that were already obsolete. Surely, I thought, there must be some Master Plan in Washington to take care of this situation. The American people were not just simply sitting idly by, accepting this as the inevitable and doing nothing about it.

Returning to the United States in the fall of '38, I joined the 3rd Infantry Division for my last extended troop duty until the war. I was with the 7th Infantry and it was gradually shifting to a war footing. The Division G-3 was Major Mark Clark and he was driving the division hard.

I was made a captain in 1939. My first sergeant turned out the company and he and the senior line sergeant pinned on the bars. We did not realize it, but those were the last days of the old regular outfits. The first sergeant was an exceptionally fine soldier, human and warm in his working relations with the troops. His name was Max Roth and I learned a great deal from him. He had been with the same outfit sixteen years, a length of time almost matched by a number of the other NCOs. We stayed together through the winter of 1939-40, during which time we made an amphibious landing in Monterey Bay and then went into camp on the present site of Fort Ord. Then, in the spring of 1940, I was ordered to West Point as an instructor in the Department of Tactics.

I had hoped for duty at West Point for some years, and so I was delighted with the assignment. It was an opportunity to discuss new tactical ideas and to study and learn through teaching. And although the members of the Department of Tactics spent much of their time looking after the personal disciplinary problems of the cadets, I was able, due to my position on the commandant's staff, to devote more than most to the problems of study and instruction.

Teaching tactics at the Military Academy in the winter of 1940-41 was a stimulating experience. The blitzkrieg was on every tongue, civilian as well as military. Then when we thought that we were beginning to understand that new form of lightning warfare, waged with thousands of armored vehicles, a new form appeared, vertical envelopment. One of the mysteries of the German defeat of France in the spring of '40 was the fall of the impregnable Fort Eben Emael. There were rumors of nerve gas, parachutists, gliders, and any or all in combination. Then, while the memories of the spring offensive of '40 were still fresh in our minds, the Germans struck through the mountainous Balkans with startling rapidity, and capped the campaign with the airborne invasion of Crete. The world was tremendously impressed and especially those of us at the Military Academy who were trying to acquire, understand and explain the lessons of this phenomenon. We were beginning to feel, too, that our country would not be able to avoid entering the war. The cadets were asking questions and expecting answers. I was fortunate to be able to participate in the search for the answers.

The blitzkrieg had been foreseen by many students of warfare so that it was not the surprise to them that it was to the public at large. Even so, it was impressive, and few foresaw the details of tank, assault gun, command vehicle, and similar hardware development that the Germans displayed in combat array when they overran Czechoslovakia. Even then, not many were aware of its full potential. It took the lightning destruction of the armed forces of France and Belgium in the spring of '40 to make clear that a quantum jump, technologically speaking, had been achieved by the Germans. We were impressing the cadets in teaching the blitzkrieg by sweeping red arrows off the old-fashioned maps—they were too small for this new kind of war—and airing our newly acquired knowledge in a knowing way; but the thought often crept into mind that this was not enough. For here was the generation that was going to fight this war, and they were likely to fight the very forces we were talking about so knowingly. It would not be enough to copy the Germans, and me-tooing them now would never provide a margin sufficient for victory. To win we needed ideas, we needed innovation, we needed to get a quantum jump on the Germans. But how? That was the question.

Of the many visionaries who had foreseen armored warfare, including Chaffee, Guderian, De Gaulle, and J. F. C. Fuller, Fuller was far and away my favorite. I had read his books avidly. He had described the evolution in warfare that would restore mobility to land battle. And he saw it with all of the attendant problems of communications, command and decision. But more important, he had fitted it into the pattern of history. And this was of the utmost importance, since far more important than "what" was happening was "why" it was happening.

This is the age-old problem of the military planner. Unlike his counterparts in other fields of human endeavor, his business is seldom put to a real test—the test of battle. There may be, and have been, twenty years between wars, and when the next one comes he must be ready. This despite the fact that he usually just barely survives extreme malnutrition—democracies are always proud of the millions they save in peace and they would rather not discuss the billions they waste in war. And since there is more fact than fancy in the saying, "Old soldiers' tales never win wars," the planner's only recourse is to the books.

I returned to Fuller and to the classics of military history and applied myself with more avidity than usual. There was so much to be learned, and there was so much going on even in the daily headlines, and the war was rushing toward us at an alarming pace.

Some things were becoming quite clear. The great technical revolution was in the complementary functions of mobility and communications. Fire power, the third essential function of a fighting man or war machine, had undergone no comparable change even though the numbers of automatic weapons had increased greatly. It was still a gunpowder war. But it was not a horse-and-wagon, nor voice-messenger-and-runner war. Mobility had in the past opened entirely new vistas and new opportunities of war and conquest. Alexander, Caesar and Genghis Khan had each in his time ravaged far and wide and destroyed any nation that opposed him, each through the exploitation of mobility unmatched by his opponents. Now we had a new form of mobility and not since our own Civil War had the planet seen military forces range over such extensive areas, always capable of fighting a battle of decision when challenged.

The very nature of tactics and strategy was also changing. Tactics has to do with the handling of men and their war resources in the immediate presence of an enemy, in battle. Strategy has to do with the management of affairs caused by the interrelationship of tactical engagements, or battles. In Napoleon's time, Europe was his theater of strategy, and battles such as Austerlitz, Ulm and Marengo were his tactical pieces. But the world was shrinking rapidly and by 1940 Europe was but one tactical theater in which the blitzkrieg was the impressive, incisive instrument of war developed by the Germans. And the blitzkrieg was effective because it was part of an air-ground team, in which the Luftwaffe played a significant part. With this shrinkage of space, caused essentially by the rapidly increasing range of air power, the very nature of tactics and strategy changed.

Tactics began to encompass larger and larger land areas, until an entire continent could be considered properly a tactical theater. Strategy then became the interrelationship of the wars on the different major land masses—the continents. Thus, one of our nation's early decisions in the realm of strategy was to make our initial main effort an offensive one in Europe and a defensive one in Asia. This change in the nature of strategy continued, with even greater intensity, after 1940. But in 1940 it was necessary first of all to understand this phenomenon and, within that framework of understanding, find the innovation in tactics that would lead us to success in battle. We needed innovation in strategy also, and this I will discuss later. At the moment, however, the problem in 1940 was not simply to understand the genesis and working of the blitzkrieg; far more important was an understanding of what lay beyond it, for in that area would be found the innovations essential to the defeat of the Germans. By running breathlessly after them from one technical advance to another we would probably never catch up, and almost certainly not get ahead. The immediate problem in 1940, therefore, was to find an answer to the questions: wherein lies innovation and what can we do about it?

There was a clue in the airborne invasion of Holland, the capture of Eben Emael, and the later decisive success in the airborne capture of Crete. For here was a new form of mobility, just in its infancy. What was its meaning and how would this be applied to the future?

I studied carefully all that I could find on the German operations. We were able to obtain some intelligence documents and they were most helpful. The Russians, as early as 1928, had shown us the possibilities of large airborne exercises and, in fact, General Billy Mitchell in World War I had proposed large-scale parachute operations as being feasible and, very likely, decisive. But up to Crete, airborne warfare had merely been the transportation of such units as were suitable to fly by airplane to the scene of combat. Thereafter, they parachuted and glided and, in general, made the best of things. Answers were needed to the questions of how one could optimize the relationship between this new form of striking power and conventional land power. What were proper objectives for its employment? What type of organization was needed to have forces so disposed about their takeoff areas as to be perfectly responsive to the needs of a commander? In what order would they be loaded, in what manner would they fly, and in what way would they be delivered so as to be instantly effective upon touching the ground? On analysis, the organizational communications and command problems were staggering. And most of our military people looked with great skepticism on any effort to solve them.

From study of the patterns of past wars, and the relative mobility of opposing forces and the tactics that appeared in them, it became clear that our own Civil War was more akin to World

War II than World War I. So I soon found myself once again turning to the Civil War for engagements comparable in balance and mobility to those of World War II. And they were certainly not difficult to find. The campaigns of "Stonewall" Jackson were particularly meaningful. For through discipline and training, and above all his rare qualities of leadership, he achieved a quantum jump in land mobility over anything in the Union Army. He demonstrated it time and again in the Shenandoah Valley, Chancellorsville, and the Second Manassas. The last affair, the Battle of the Second Manassas, was a classic in one particular respect. It was a model of the type of leadership and tactical judgment required to execute deep penetrations, the kind that went right to the vitals of an opponent and paralyzed every fiber of his being. It deserved further study, so in the fall of '40, I made several trips to the Second Manassas battle area and went over the ground carefully. Between visits I studied all that I could find on the affair in the Military Academy library and in the spring of '41, I wrote it up as an article and sent it off to the Army's *Infantry Journal*.

Speculation was still rampant about the "nerve gas" that caused the surrender of Eben Emael and there was much wonder about the paralysis caused by the deep German penetrations. I titled my article "Jackson Is in the Rear" and its purpose was to examine the problems of decision and leadership associated with a penetration of the Eben Emael type, airborne envelopment. And there were many problems. Among them, what should the initial objectives be? How much of the force should be committed to the penetration and how quickly should link-up occur? If the initial attack was successful, what next? All of these problems were solved in an exemplary manner in the Second Manassas.

It was a classic in mobile warfare for a number of reasons. In the first place Lee was far outnumbered. Next, he was apparently on the defensive and it was expected that he would remain so, thus surrendering the initiative to his opponent. Instead, he chose to attack and in doing so divided his forces in the face of a numerically superior opponent. Not only did he divide them, he sent one portion deep into the rear of his opponent's position thus placing both parts of his army in great jeopardy. But he knew his opponent, knew his own forces, and he had the moral courage to make the decision to attack. The division of Lee's army had to be made with careful calculation, for each part had to be capable of fighting independently against Pope's army until reinforced. And finally, the tactics employed had to be carefully planned to avoid disclosing the daring nature of his plan and thus enabling Pope to destroy each wing of the army separately. All of these things he accomplished in exemplary fashion.

The Second Battle of Manassas took place in late August of 1861. It began with Lee and Pope facing each other, deployed along the Rapahannock River, Lee with about 55,000 troops and Pope, reinforcing rapidly, expected to have double that strength momentarily. Pope had just come from successes in the West and was already famous for heading his dispatches with "Headquarters in the Saddle." The Confederates were quick to point out the shortcomings of a man who didn't know his headquarters from his hindquarters. But Pope, if nothing else, was confident, and tossing off the observation, "Let the lines of communications take care of themselves," he prepared to deal with the wily Lee. Pope's trouble began with Lee not giving him the chance. Lee struck swiftly in a deep envelopment, placing a large portion of his command under "Stonewall" Jackson astride Pope's communications, between Pope's army and Washington. It took superb decision-making and leadership on Jackson's part to get there and to survive and keep the tactical initiative in the midst of overwhelming odds. But survive he did, and as Pope began to disintegrate, Lee rapidly reinforced Jackson, thus completing the kill. Pope's forces were sent reeling back across the Potomac bridges and Lee for the first time invaded the North. I was to learn a few years later that the Second Manassas and the airborne operations of World War II had even more in common than I had anticipated, even to the extent of allowing a locomotive to escape and alert the defenders of the envelopment.

The more I studied the combat of World War II, the more I became convinced that the innovation we needed to perfect in order to achieve a margin of advantage in the war would be found in airborne operations. At that time, the spring of '41, our airborne forces were of the size of a battalion and by later standards were rather primitively equipped. There were some skeptics who said that we would never need units larger than platoons and those merely for raiding. But if history had any meaning, it was that this concept would grow. One could not be certain of the manner of its growth, but if the theory were correct, it was up to us to create the means.

I applied for airborne duty and parachute training in April of 1941. The superintendent disapproved my application with the following endorsement:

Hq., U.S.M.A., West Point, N. Y., May 1, 1941
To The Adjutant General, War Department, Washington, D. C.
    1. Disapproved.
    2. I can appreciate Captain Gavin's desire for assignment to duty with one of the parachute battalions. However, in order to replace him, it would be necessary to have an officer of equal ability ordered to this station, and inasmuch as he has been here less than a year, he is now approaching his maximum usefulness to the Corps of Cadets. Further, so far as I know, he is not peculiarly fitted for this type of duty. . . .

I was disappointed and deeply disturbed. I continued to fret over the problem in my mind and I decided that the solution was in the words, "it would be necessary to have an officer of equal ability ordered to this station." Upon the completion of work the following Friday night, I drove to Washington to see a friend in the office of personnel, in the Chief of Infantry's office. He was Major Bill Kean and he was most sympathetic and helpful. We decided that by locating the list of officers that the superintendent had desired for assignment the preceding year, and verifying their availability, I would be able to present him with a suitable replacement. It took several more trips and numerous conferences.

Both the superintendent and the commandant were most considerate and I was ordered to parachute duty in July.

I started training as a paratrooper on August 1, 1941. Colonel Bill Ryder was in charge of the school and doing a wonderful job. An entire new world opened to me. Problems of weapons, equipment, training and tactics all were begging for solution. I graduated from the parachute school in late August and was given command of a parachute company, C Company of the 503rd Parachute Infantry. Shortly thereafter, I was promoted to the grade of major and moved to Battalion Headquarters, and then to the top Parachute Headquarters in the Army, the Provisional Parachute Group, commanded by Brigadier General Bill Lee. I was given the job of S-3 and at once set to work writing the first manual for *The Employment of Airborne Forces*. On November 21, we staged the first big parachute jump in the history of our country, a battalion jump of the 502nd Parachute Battalion at Fort Bragg, North Carolina. I was senior umpire of the exercise and it was a revelation of the problems involved, both in airborne attack and in defense against airborne attack.

Assignment to the Staff School at Fort Leavenworth followed early in '42. We were in the war then and a high pitch of excitement, muted somewhat by the sober realization that we were personally destined for combat responsibilities, prevailed. Except for the airborne instruction, the courses were excellent and just what we needed, as we were soon to learn in battle itself. The airborne problem in the course consisted of a map exercise in which a parachute platoon jumped on the roof of the First National Bank in Kansas City. I got some wry looks from the faculty and snickers from the class when I asked about a possible use of a parachute division. It was pointed out that this was utterly impossible for many reasons. In the first place, there was no such thing in existence and the problems of equipment, training and control, both in the air and on the ground, had not even been considered. Finally, even if one had a parachute division, it would take twenty-five airfields to enable it to take off, and this was too

fantastic even to think about—anywhere in the world. Normandy
was then two years away.

My feelings were assuaged by a story that an instructor told
me of a truck-mobility exercise conducted by the students between World War I and World War II. It was based upon the
German invasion of France in World War I. As history now
shows, the enveloping right wing of the German Army failed to
carry out its role and thus the French left wing, and perhaps the
entire army, was saved from annihilation. Analyzing the campaign in the twenties, and on the assumption that the gasoline
engine was here to stay and would be used in numbers in war,
the students were given unlimited truck mobility to carry out the
German attack once again in a map exercise. After loading all of
the German troops in trucks and stringing them back on miles and
miles of roads, they reached the conclusion that, as the battle
was joined, the trucks were a disadvantage and the German Army
would have been better off without them. They actually slowed
the German attack down. So, the conclusion: foot mobility is
better than truck mobility. And now we were encountering the
same logic in opposing air mobility.

Whenever a new weapon, or a new tactical method, is introduced, it
is always looked upon with the gravest suspicion. That is one reason
why a study of the History of War is so important, since through it can
be seen over the ages the effect on war of such novelties. Such a study
shows that the human mind has been slow to grasp the possibilities of
the new arrival and to adopt the tactics which will put it to the best
use. In fact, as in the case of the tank, the new arrival has usually been
treated as an adjunct to, and clothed in the tactics of, the older arms.[2]

This touches upon one of the most serious problems that will
always confront the Republic, the toleration of new ideas and
intelligent criticism. For without these two ingredients in our
thinking, particularly our military thinking, we will not survive.
And now, as we attain maturity in the world family of nations, we
must provide leadership, and leadership needs ideas and must

[2] *The War on the Civil and Military Fronts*, General G. M. Lindsay.

be able to tolerate criticism. "If our treatment of the honest and skilled dissident is not to be liberal, then the army will be filled with more time-servers than in the past and will stagnate, to the great waste of the nation's treasure and, later, its life."[3] As expressed by Robert G. Ingersoll:

I tell you there is something splendid in a man who will not always obey. Why, if we had done as the kings had told us five hundred years ago, we should all have been slaves. If we had done as the priests told us, we should all have been idiots. If we had done as the doctors told us, we should have all been dead. We have been saved by disobedience.

Heady tonic for a soldier! Nevertheless, we should be ever mindful of the need for tolerance toward new ideas. And as technology becomes more dynamic, the more reason to be more tolerant, since new ideas will come at a faster rate. For success or failure in war, and our very survival, will then hang by a thin thread indeed.

But in 1942 we still had time in our favor and the war was far away, although getting closer by the minute. School ended in early April and I returned to Fort Bragg where General Bill Lee had the Airborne Command. We were growing. Fortunately, I was returned to the job of S-3 and thus I was able to start to work at once on an organization for an airborne division. New gliders were becoming available and these combined with parachutes seemed to offer some prospect of combat feasibility for a thirteen-thousand-man division. The basic decision was made not to copy the German Crete operation and use regular forces, merely providing them airlift, but to go all out on a new type of organization and new types of equipment. But the problems encountered were almost beyond belief. Parachute artillery, for example—how were we to get it from plane to firing position on the ground in a few minutes? The project was headed up by a dynamic driving young paratrooper, now a minister, Colonel Shinberger. By breaking the weapon into nine parts, each could be dropped by

[3] *The Pattern of War*, Lieutenant General Sir Francis Tucker.

parachute separately. But recovering them from the treetops, ditches, rooftops and wherever they happened to land sometimes took days, if all pieces could be found at all. Schinberger finally tied the parts together with a rope, six under the plane suspended in mid-air and the remaining three in the door—all tied together with the same rope. A Rube Goldberg rig that took a brave pilot to fly. But brave pilots were in abundance—the Troop Carrier pilots of the Air Corps never asked what we were up to, they merely asked what we wanted them to do, and they always came through. My admiration for them increased with each day of the war.

About my last act with General Lee was to go to Washington and help select the first division to be made airborne. It was the 82nd Infantry Division and from it was taken, Eve-like, the nucleus of the 101st. It was activated that fall. In the meantime, I had been assigned to the 505th Parachute Infantry, my first regimental command. I looked forward eagerly to solving the practical problems about which we had theorized so freely in the past year. We went into training at Fort Benning and then moved to Fort Bragg before leaving for Africa in April of 1943.

One of our most troublesome problems had been that of dealing with tanks. It was just so much nonsense to put a division of thirteen thousand men into combat with no ability to stop a tank; they would simply be mincemeat. Just before leaving Fort Benning, I wandered out to the weapons test range one day to look at some new rifle grenades that were supposed to be able to penetrate tank armor. While there, I noticed a blanket-covered table and my curiosity drew me to it.

One of the test officers saw me coming over and said, "You got to stay away from that, Colonel, it's a new secret weapon."

That really whetted my appetite. "What is it?" I asked.

"Well, we can't tell you," he said, "but it will punch a hole in any tank living. They call it a bazooka."

"I'd sure like to see it," I said. "I've got a combat regiment and we won't be around long, and we sure need an antitank weapon."

"Well," he said, "in that case, I'll let you feel it, but I am not allowed to show it to you."

I walked over and felt the blanket under his watchful surveillance. It felt like a piece of gas pipe about five feet long. But that didn't matter if it could do as he said, stop any tank living. For that was what we needed more than anything else; a good antitank weapon was essential to combat confidence at that stage of our training. We did not realize it at the time, but our first face-to-face meeting with German Tiger tanks of the Hermann Goering Division was not far away.

3

Combat Is a Crucible

The proof of research and development decisions is in combat. We win or lose depending upon the soundness and timeliness of our decisions. There once was a time when we could correct bad decisions as a war went along but no longer is this true. We may no longer depend upon someone else to take the first brunt of combat, and we will not have the time to correct bad technological decisions. Now we must be right the first time.

In dealing with these problems of national defense, one can only bring to bear the sum total of his personal experience and acquired knowledge. These, in my case, result from long exposure to the problems of national defense, both theoretical and practical. My attitude has been conditioned by my boyhood, my schooling, and my long service in the Army. I was fortunate in having to learn the habits of hard work and study while young. Many opportunities were given me from my entry into combat in July, 1943, until Berlin in 1945, to study and experiment with new tactical ideas, and I enjoyed more than my share of good fortune during that time. Combat is a crucible in which men and their ideas are confronted with the greatest of all challenges—challenges for which the stakes are high: the life or death of an individual, a group of individuals, or a nation. We, as individuals and as a nation, may be in that crucible again, unless Mr.

Khrushchev did not mean it when he said: "We will bury you."

I spent twenty years awaiting the opportunity of combat. They were years of study, of hard work, and of constant search for new tactical ideas. As they came to an end, and as combat neared, a veritable revolution took place in warfare. Both the blitzkrieg, which had been anticipated by a few, and vertical envelopment, which had been anticipated by almost none, characterized the new pattern of warfare. Vertical envelopment, being the newer, was the more appealing as an area for the development of new ideas and I eagerly sought service with that arm. Time was short, much had to be learned, and much had to be unlearned, and battle was upon us before we knew it.

Opportunity came on the night of July 9, 1943. I had been designated as the Commander of the 505th Parachute Combat Team. My command consisted of over three thousand para-troopers, including Infantry, Artillery, Engineers, Medics and Signal Corpsmen. Our mission was to jump on Sicily six hours ahead of the amphibious landing, seize key terrain features, in-cluding one airfield, and block the movement of German and Italian reserves toward the beaches.

To me the battle in prospect was the climax of a lifetime of study and preparation. If ideas and new tactical concepts were really the payoff, here was to be the proof. I looked forward to it eagerly, fully confident of the fighting ability of the troopers and sure of the success of the plan. To the troopers it represented their first opportunity to test their mettle against veterans. If training and work—"A pint of sweat will save a gallon of blood" —combined with the best weapons in the world could do it, they had it made. They were confident that they had the best weapons in the world; not only had they been told this frequently, but most of us believe this about most things American anyway.

Air-landing in Tunisia just one month before, on June 9, 1943, we had time to lose about twenty pounds of weight per man from the combined effects of training, poor rations, and the seasonal siroccos then scorching the African earth. The month's time also gave me opportunity to make a night reconnaissance of the drop zones on the island. An RAF pilot from Malta took me in and I saw for the first time the exact drop zones on which we were to land.

The fateful day of July 9, 1943 seemed to rush upon us, so busy were we with last-minute preparations, and almost before we realized it, we were gathered in small groups under the wings of our C-47s ready for loading and takeoff. Appearing from a distance every bit like Strasbourg geese, the airplanes were so loaded with parachute bundles suspended beneath them that they seemed to drag the ground. Because of security restrictions, it had not been possible to inform every trooper of our destination until just before takeoff. Then each was given a small slip of paper which read as follows:

SOLDIERS OF THE 505TH COMBAT TEAM

Tonight you embark upon a combat mission for which our people and the free people of the world have been waiting for two years.

You will spearhead the landing of an American Force upon the island of SICILY. Every preparation has been made to eliminate the element of chance. You have been given the means to do the job and you are backed by the largest assemblage of air power in the world's history.

The eyes of the world are upon you. The hopes and prayers of every American go with you.

Since it is our first fight at night you must use the countersign and avoid firing on each other. The bayonet is the night fighter's best weapon. Conserve your water and ammunition.

The term American Parachutist has become synonymous with courage of a high order. Let us carry the fight to the enemy and make the American Parachutist feared and respected through all his ranks. Attack violently. Destroy him wherever found.

I know you will do your job.

Good landing, good fight, and good luck.

/s/ James Gavin
COLONEL GAVIN

The plan was simple. Taking off from Tunisia in a long column of flights of nine aircraft, we were to fly via the island of Linosa to Malta. There we were to dog-leg to the left, coming in on

Sicily's southwestern shore. This was an important point—the island was to come into sight on the right side of the approaching aircraft. The orders were that every man would jump even though there might be some uncertainty in his mind as to his whereabouts. No one but the pilots and crews were to return to North Africa.

Individual equipment was given a final and solicitous check and loading began. The equipment consisted of a rifle or carbine, rations, water, knife, grenade, compass, and here and there a bazooka. The latter were most important since they were the only weapons that the troopers were carrying that would enable them to engage German armor on reasonable terms. The pilots were revving up their engines and we were ready to roll down the runway when an airman from the weather station ran up to the door of the plane yelling for me: "Colonel Gavin, is Colonel Gavin here?" "Here I am," I answered, and he yelled, "I was told to tell you that the wind is going to be thirty-five miles an hour, west to east." He added, "They thought that you would want to know."

Well, I did, but there was nothing that I could do about it. Training jumps had normally been canceled when the wind reached about fifteen miles an hour, in order that we might minimize injuries. Few of us had ever jumped over twenty-five miles an hour. But there was nothing that we could do about this now. Besides, there were many other hazards of greater danger than the thirty-five-mile-an-hour wind in prospect.

At about this time in my troubled thinking another individual staggered to the door of the plane with a huge barracks bag on his shoulder. He heaved it through the door onto the floor of the plane, saying as he did so:

"I was told to give this to you or your S-1."

I asked, "What in the hell is it?"

He replied: "They are prisoner-of-war tags. You are supposed to put one on every prisoner that you capture, and be sure to fill it out properly."

54

It was no time for argument, when we were within seconds of roaring down the runway and so I merely replied, "Okay."

About an hour after departure, the S-1 (Captain Ireland) threw them into the Mediterranean.

We were airborne as first darkness touched the land. The flight was uneventful until Linosa was due. It was not to be seen. Likewise Malta, which was to be well lighted to assist our navigators, could not be seen. Suddenly ships by the score became visible in the ocean below, all knifing their way toward Sicily. Obviously we were off course since our plan called for us to fly between the American fleet on the left and the British on the right. In fact, the Americans told us that we would probably be shot down if we overflew them. We continued on, finally dog-legging to the left on the basis of time calculation. Soon the flash of gunfire could be seen through the dust and haze caused by the preinvasion bombing, and finally the coast itself could be seen off to the right. Unfortunately many of the planes overflew the Malta dog-leg and the island first became visible on the left, thus causing confusion and widespread dispersion of the troopers.

We turned inland; the small arms fire increased; the green light over the jump door went on and out we went. The reception was mixed. Some of us met heavy fighting at once, others were unopposed for some time, but all were shaken up by the heavy landings on trees, buildings and rocky hillsides.

I managed to get together a small group and start across country, searching for the combat team objective. I had with me Captain Ireland, the combat team S-1, and Captain Vandervoort, the combat team S-3. The cross-country going was rough, but we pressed on. Soon we came face to face with our first enemy.

It happened about an hour after we had landed. I was moving ahead with about twenty troopers. I was leading and Vandervoort was alongside. I had been picking up troopers as I moved along through the shadows in the olive groves, over stone walls, darting across moonlit roads, moving in what I hoped was the direction of our objective. There had been occasional bursts of small-arms fire, sometimes quite close, but so far we had not seen an actual enemy. Suddenly there were foreign voices, then the sound of a man whistling some distance away. As he got closer it sounded like *"O Sole Mio."* I had my group stay down and I moved up to a stone wall that paralleled the road he was coming along. It was a lone man, walking down the middle of the road, hands in the pockets of his baggy uniform pants, and whistling. After twenty years of military service, I was about to meet The Enemy face to face. I stuck my head up over the stone wall. It seemed like way up, but it was about an inch, just enough to clear my carbine over the top of the wall.

I gave him my best Italian, *"Alto."* He stopped in his tracks. Vandervoot rushed through an opening in the wall with a .45 in one hand and a knife in the other.

"I'll take care of him," Van said. I wasn't sure what he meant, but I said, "No, let's get the hell out of the middle of the road. Let's get over into the shadows and maybe we can get some information out of him."

There was still some doubt whether we were in Sicily, Italy or the Balkans, although the odds strongly favored the first.

About a half-dozen of us surrounded him and I tried the few Italian words I knew.

"Dove Palermo?" No reply. He seemed too scared or too bewildered to answer.

"Dove Siracusa?"

I figured that if he would point in the general direction of either or both of these two cities, which were at opposite ends of the island, we could get our first rough fix on where we were. Since he acted as if he had never heard of either, for a moment it seemed that perhaps we were not even in Sicily. But he was obviously very scared. We had heard that the Germans had scared the wits out of the natives with their stories about the atrocities committed by American parachutists. They spread the news that we were criminals and long-term prisoners who had been given our freedom in exchange for becoming para-troopers. This was given credence by the practice in many parachute units of having all of the men shave their heads clean. After the Battle of Sicily was over, the Sicilians pointed this out to us as being one of the things that convinced them that the Germans were right.

But to get back to Giuseppe, or whatever his name was. I hadn't been able to get anything out of him—neither his name, where he was from, nor where he thought we were. I reluctantly decided that we would have to take him along. Now Vandervoort had taken an intelligence course and knew how to handle a prisoner in a situation like this. The idea was to take the belt out of the prisoner's trousers and to cut the buttons off his fly so that he would have to hold up his trousers when he walked.

Van put his .45 in its holster, pressed his knife against the Italian's chest, saying as he did so: "I'll take care of the bastard."

The Italian was muttering, "*Mamma mia, mamma mia,*" over and over again. His concern was understandable. The moonlight was shining on the knife blade and it looked as though it were a foot long. He took off his belt and dropped it. Then Van went into Phase Two of the operation and reached for his fly, with one hand, bringing the knife down with the other.

A scream went up that could be heard all of the way to Rome. The atrocities of the paratroopers and the stories that he had heard about Ethiopia must have flashed through his mind; he was being castrated. He screamed louder, grabbing the knife blade with his right hand. The blood ran down his hand as we fell in a kicking, yelling, fighting mass. We were on the edge of a gully and we rolled partly down it. It was pitch-black and out of the tumbling mass he got away. I do not know how he did it, but one second he was with us and the next he was gone. I was madder than hell. I asked Vandervoort, "What in the hell did you think you were doing?"

Vandervoort didn't answer. I decided that we had better get

going. By now we had probably alerted any enemy for miles around.

We marched and crawled into the night. Although some men were wounded and suffering from jump injuries, they drove themselves toward the cascading flame and white phosphorus of bursting shells that could be seen far away on the distant horizon. The sight of shell bursts was reassuring, since it meant that we were in Sicily. That is where the battle was to be fought. And we were "moving toward the sound of the guns," one of the first battle axioms that I had learned as a cadet at West Point.

But human flesh could do only so much, and the night was demanding. By count at daylight, there were but six of us. I approached two farmhouses, but at each the natives were terrified and would hardly talk. I continued on in a direction that I figured would take us toward our objective. Suddenly, as we came over the crest of some high ground, there was a burst of small-arms fire.

We hit the ground. There was a sickening thud of near misses kicking dirt into my face. I reacted instinctively as I had been taught in the infiltration course by hugging closely to the ground. In no time I realized that I would not continue to live doing that; I had to shoot back. I started firing with my carbine and it jammed. I looked to Vandervoort about six feet to my left and he was having the same trouble. In front, about fifty yards away, an officer stood looking through low-hanging branches of an olive tree. He was wearing leather puttees and reddish-brown breeches, both plainly visible beneath the branches. Ireland gave him the first squirt of his tommy gun and he went down like a rag doll. I began to make my carbine work single shot. The leading trooper, who had gone down at the first fusillade, writhed and rolled over. He appeared to be dead, practically in the enemy position. Their fire increased and there was a loud explosion like a small mortar shell. I decided that there was at least a platoon of enemy and our best prospects were to try to work around it. I yelled to Vandervoort,

Ireland and the troopers to start moving back while I covered. It worked.

We had had a close call and nothing to show for it, and our prospects were not very bright. I continued to move cross-country in a direction that would take me around the area where we had the fire fight. We could hear intense firing from time to time and we were never sure when we would walk into another fire fight, nor were we sure of the manner in which we would get into the fight since we couldn't tell friend from foe. Then there was the problem of enemy armor. We were in trouble and virtually helpless against enemy armor. I decided to look for a place where tanks would be unlikely to travel and where we could get good cover to hole up until dark. I wanted to survive until dark, and then to strike across country again to the combat team objective. It was the high ground east and north of Gela, and there, with the help of God, I hoped to find troopers, and an enemy to fight. For that is what I had come three thousand miles and thirty-six years of my life for—the moral and physical challenge of battle.

By midmorning we came to the place. It was crisscrossed by several irrigation ditches. Along one of them there was a thicket of underbrush. The ditch was cut out of the side of a gently sloping hill and from its edge there was a good view for about a half of a mile across cultivated land. The ditch I picked was almost dry, although the others had a lot of water in them. It did not appear to be the place where a tank would travel by choice. And this was important. I took stock of the situation and it wasn't good. Among us we had two carbines that jammed, one tommy gun, a pistol and an M-1. We were holed up like hunted animals. Tired, wounded, hungry, but too sick at heart to eat, we apprehensively scanned the countryside for any sign of friend or foe. Occasional bursts of rifle and machine-gun fire could be heard in the distance.

"A hell of a place for a regimental commander," I said to Vandervoort, and he nodded his head in assent.

I remembered almost bursting with pride when General Ridgway, just two months before, took me aside one evening and told me that I was to command the parachute assault forces going into Sicily. It was a lifetime ambition about to be realized. And now my "command" consisted of four shaken troopers holed up in a muddy ditch.

A fusillade of shots rang out.

The firing was intense. It was far off to the right, perhaps over a mile away. Should I look into it? I couldn't afford to lose another man if I was to have enough strength to fight my way back through my own lines after dark.

"What do you think, Ireland?" I asked.

"Well, we've got two carbines that don't work. We have already lost one man. I have a bad leg. You have too. We have no idea where in the hell we are, except we believe that we're in Sicily. It doesn't make much sense for us to go wandering around looking for a fight and when we find it probably walk into the wrong side of it."

"Okay," I said, "but this is a hell of a place to be in and I don't like it. We will still figure on waiting until dark," I added.

It *was* a hell of a place. It was approaching noon and the hot July sun was burning down. Since early morning I had been aware of a big house about a half-mile away. It was three stories high with the bottom floor lost in trees and shrubbery, big for the Sicilian countryside. There were several windows that overlooked us and I kept watching for movement in them. Surely the house wouldn't be empty, but after several hours of watching not a sign of life was in evidence. Perhaps I should run a patrol over and look it over.

"Van, what do you think of that house? Have you been able to pick up any movement about it? Maybe we ought to go over and take a closer look."

"I don't know," he said. "I've been watching it too. If we break up into two groups, neither will be large enough to do much, and if we all go out there we may get pinned down and lose another one of us, and that we can't afford."

"I'm going to move down the ditch to get a better look at it," I said. I crouched over a bit and moved along the ditch to where I had a better view of the building. It had an ominous look about it and it appeared to be uninhabited. As I started back, my eye suddenly caught a sign of movement.

"A man," I whispered to a trooper posted as a guard on the edge of our group.

We both watched as he slowly made his way toward us. Apparently he was not aware of us. Or was he pretending, sent by the Germans to scout us out? Should I wait until he got closer and then kill him? We certainly wanted no prisoners. We were having a hard enough time taking care of ourselves. On the other hand, if I shot, the sound would give our location away. I decided that it would be best to let him keep coming in and then to jump him. Whether or not to kill him would depend on the situation then. In any event, we didn't intend to make the same mistake that we had made last night, when we let the Italian prisoner escape, and alert, I suppose, the entire damn countryside. But this was a different situation. It was broad daylight and we were not going to make the same mistake twice.

The man kept coming toward us in a wandering pattern, occasionally stopping to kick a stone or clod of dirt. About fifty yards away he stopped, seemed to look in our direction, and then turned and walked away. I doubted that he actually saw us and decided to let him get away. He crossed one hill, then another, until he was out of sight, over the hills and far away.

The Sicilian sun bore down. It was midafternoon, and since the lone man had disappeared over the horizon a couple of hours before, there had been no sign of activity. I had hoped that perhaps some troopers might wander by, or if we were near the coast that the amphibious assault forces would overrun us. No such luck. Occasional firing could be heard far away and sometimes an airplane would be seen high in the sky. But the Sicilian countryside was asleep in the middle of a hot July afternoon. I should have slept. I was dead-tired, but I was too worried to sleep. Where was the regiment of three thousand troopers? What had happened to our well-laid plans? Wasn't there something that one could do besides wait?

There was not. Nothing but to be patient and wait. Wait until dark. I was learning the hard way that the moral responsibilities of command weigh far more heavily on a man than the physical. And that moral courage is far more important and necessary than physical courage. Physical courage consists simply of one's pride making one do something that is manifestly dangerous. Moral courage comes from the soul. It can only come from confidence and belief in what one is doing. If I had any, it had to come from my upbringing and from what I had learned as a cadet at West Point.

Ah, West Point. How much simpler battles seemed when fought in the textbooks in the West Academic Building. But the instructors had not misled me. Besides, I had been an instructor in tactics myself. We had talked knowingly of "the fog of war," and the confusion and utter despair that would characterize some of the hours of greatest decision. This I had to remember. I must remember. I must remember West Point, and the days when I first aspired to go there. I must remember and I did remember.

We had landed in Africa early in May, '43, trained for a month, and then started moving toward our takeoff airfields for the Sicilian invasion. By then I was entirely confident that our operation would be successful. We had acquired many new techniques to accomplish reorganization and control after landing and a number of new items of equipment. Well trained, the troops were eager and absolutely sure of themselves when they left for their departure airfields—of such substance is valor born.

Now, twenty-four hours later, I surveyed the results of the

first day's fighting. As well as I could tell, it had been an absolute shambles. The regiment was scattered like chaff in the wind, and then possibly destroyed. I did not know. Could it be that the critics were right—that airborne combat was just so much nonsense?

The Sicilian sun was now low in the sky and soon we would be able to move out. Water was a first need; it was almost gone. For food we had a few cartons of K-rations and some concentrated things in an "escape kit." An escape kit was a small plastic box, about six inches square and an inch through. It contained the essentials for escape and survival behind enemy lines. In mine was a silk map of Sicily and it was the only map of Sicily that I had. The practice in those days was to take no unnecessary papers or maps, and certainly, under no circumstances, a marked map. We had memorized thoroughly the terrain around our objective and we had been confident that the Air Corps would drop us near the objective. So, why carry a small-scale map?

The escape kit also contained malt tablets, which were very tasty, and pills to keep one from going to sleep. It also contained a rubber-covered piece of a steel saw about five inches long, and a very good small compass about the size of a quarter. The saw was included so that in the event of imminent capture it could be concealed in one's bottom, later to be withdrawn and provide the means of escape. Looking the gear over, one of the troopers made the observation that there appeared to be clear advantages in being a girl in a situation like this. It did seem so.

But it was nearing time to move. It was getting dark and it must have been about nine o'clock.

It had been a hard day—in a way, one of the hardest days of my life. I ran over in my mind the things that concerned me most. First, there was the inadequacy of our weapons. It is nothing short of homicidal to send American young men into combat with weapons not up to the job that confronts them.

We needed a more reliable, faster-firing hand weapon than the carbine. And above all, we needed a tank killer for the individual soldier; otherwise, it would be better to have him stay at home and not go into combat. Inadequately equipped, he is a liability to everyone. Next, training had to be more realistic, so tough and exacting that combat would be a welcome relief. And while I was not back with my own troopers yet, I felt that I had probably been spared an untimely end by being able to live through this day. If I did survive, I decided that I would never forget the simple fundamentals that I had learned as a cadet—that I would live by them. And that, if allowed to live, I would take the best possible care of any troops charged to me. And "taking care of them" meant making them into the best fighting organizations possible, that they might survive and win in battle. George Patton's last words to us before we left Africa came home with meaning: "No dumb bastard ever won a war by going out and dying for his country. He won it by making some other dumb bastard die for his country."

I turned to Vandervoort.

"Okay, Van, move out. You be the point, just five or ten yards, depending on how black it gets. Stop after going through any ditches or bad obstacles to be sure that we are all through. If we hit a fight, I'm going to try to slide around it, so don't start any shooting unless you have to.

"Ireland, you follow me and stay close with that tommy gun. If I need you, I'll need you right away. You two troopers follow on the flanks, one on each side and not too far out; be sure that you can see me at all times. Okay, let's go."

And we went. Into the Sicilian night, heading for what we hoped was Gela, somewhere to the west. It was a relief to be moving instead of sitting and worrying. Sitting and worrying had been the hardest of all and I had done a lot of it.

After about an hour, we were challenged by a small group of wounded and injured under command of a Lieutenant Kronheim. We traded morphine Syrettes for their M-1 rifles and ammunition and continued to the west. About two-thirty, we were challenged by a machine gun post of the 45th Division and, at last, we had re-entered our own lines. We continued on looking for the 45th Division CP, engaged some of our own tanks with small-arms fire to their dismay—no one hurt—and kept going. Shortly after daylight, I joined up with about two hundred of the 3rd Battalion of of the 505th and we were back in business. We advanced at once toward Gela and by midmorning tangled with the German Herman Goering Division.

This action has been described in some detail in *Airborne Warfare*[1] and I will only touch upon those aspects of it bearing on the problem of weapons in support of innovations in tactics. In airborne ground combat, the big problem was antitank weapons. Meeting the Hermann Goering head on gave us a good opportunity to test our judgment in weapons development, for the Tiger tank with which it was equipped was the most formidable tank roaming the battlefield, not only in 1943 but throughout the war.

The leading unit, an engineer platoon of the 307th Engineers commanded by Lieutenant Ben L. Wechsler, a first-class fighting man, moved toward Gela. He had with him one bazooka with three rockets and one machine gun, in addition to the usual small arms. I joined him and we started up the road. At once the platoon met a blast of small-arms fire. The Germans were astride the road on a ridge to the front. The platoon bored in and drove them off. When we got to the top, we were pinned down by intense small-arms fire that was soon joined by mortar fire. The grand effect sounded as though thousands of bees were playing crack the whip; leaves and branches were falling all over the ridge, and occasionally someone would get hit. We brought up the remainder of the troops and continued to bore in. In no time those wounded, many of them seriously, were working back, all with the same story. The bazooka rockets were bouncing off the tanks and the tanks were then chewing the troopers to pieces. The next day we actually buried some troopers with pieces of bazooka ground into

[1] Combat Forces Press.

them by tank tracks. We captured one tank by grenading the crew when they came out to talk things over a bit too close to a trooper, a Lieutenant Swingler. The tank had four bazooka hits on it, none of which penetrated. We were fortunate that our infantry was far superior to the German infantry, for that saved the day.

The German force was the left column of the Hermann Goering Division attacking the Gela beaches, consisting of:

> Panzer Grenadier Regiment 1 (2 Battalions)
> 1 light Artillery Battalion
> 1 Tiger Tank Company

In the midst of the fighting, the German Division G-3 went forward to see the situation firsthand and he reported that "The leader of the combat command, Commander of the 1st Panzer Grenadier Regiment, lay with his adjutant under heavy hostile fire and could scarcely lift his head. He lay there an hour already and could not lead." The division commander relieved him of his command that night.

As the day came to an end I gathered all of the troopers that I could get my hands on for one last counterattack. The thought of Shiloh ran through my mind, how a battle was won by simply refusing to give up the battlefield. And I recalled the number of times in a meeting engagement when both sides withdrew after heavy losses on the mistaken assumption that they had lost the fight. Well, we would give it one last go. The Navy was helping with fire support, a company of Sherman tanks joined us, and just before dusk we jumped off. We caught the Germans in the start of a withdrawal, overran a company of 120-mm. mortars in position, some tanks and trucks, and captured quite a few prisoners. Best of all we recovered many of our wounded who were scattered about the area of the day's fighting. Darkness came quickly and as we organized for the night we could see the entire sky off toward the beaches aflame with ack-ack. It went on for some time and it was by far the most spectacular display of its type that we had ever seen. As we were admiring it, out of the din of the firing a steady drone of oncoming airplanes could be heard. We all grabbed for our rifles and got ready to join in the fun. Within seconds the planes emerged from the holocaust and we recognized their silhouettes in formation; they were our own Troop Carrier planes! Some of them were burning and troopers were beginning to jump from them, some landing on us and some on the Germans. Fortunately the group that I was with recognized them and did not fire on them but went to work trying to help those that they could reach. It had been a tragic mistake that has never been fully explained. Notice of the planned jump had gone out from the higher headquarters but it evidently failed to get down to the gun crews. Besides, the Germans had a bombing run over the fleet just before our planes arrived, and the very night that we were reinforcing by parachute, the Germans were doing the same thing with their 1st Parachute Division in the vicinity of Catania, far to the east. Our losses were twenty-three planes shot down and dozens damaged in varying degrees.

By daylight the next day some semblance of a command was being restored to the troops who had been through the previous day's fighting. The Germans had withdrawn and I pressed patrols toward Gela. We got through the following morning shortly after daylight.

I followed one of the patrols in a jeep, red-eyed and tired and carrying an M-1 rifle. There was no sign of the enemy except the dead and a burning tank. I made my way to the 1st Division's command post and there I met General Ridgway. Together we went on to Gela a few miles away. We came to the outlying buildings of the town on the edge of a cliff overlooking the sea. There, with his pistols on his hips, stood General Patton. He greeted me warmly and with a friendly touch of profanity. It was good to see him.

We went into a nearby farmhouse, where Colonel Bill Darby of the Rangers joined us. I was glad to see Bill. I had remembered hearing him describe how he planned to scale the cliffs and capture Gela before we went in. It had sounded crazy to me. I now learned that when he heard what we had planned for the parachutists he thought we were crazy too. Each to his own.

We assembled the division at Gela and went on to the west. The heaviest fighting for us was over.

The Battle of Sicily came to an end in late August of 1943. We knew that we had had a rough time of it and some hard fighting but we were less certain about what we had accomplished. It was with some satisfaction therefore that we read a German evaluation of the action after the war had come to an end. General Karl Student, who commanded the German airborne assault on Crete, upon being interrogated in a British prisoner-of-war camp in October, 1945, said:

The Allied airborne operation in Sicily was decisive despite widely scattered drops which must be expected in a night landing. It is my opinion that if it had not been for the Allied airborne forces blocking the Herman Goering Armored Division from reaching the beachhead, that division would have driven the initial seaborne forces back into the sea. I attribute the entire success of the Allied Sicilian operation to the delaying of the German reserves until sufficient forces had been landed by sea to resist the counterattacks by our defending forces.

The development of airborne doctrine and following it through from concept to combat had been a fascinating experience. It also had been a sobering one. Many of the ideas of the laboratory and classroom were found inadequate in the holocaust of battle. Vision, tempered by the caution that comes from practical experience, is extremely important in research. And equally important is the courage to make early decisions leading to advanced weapons systems in the future. Tardy decision-making is a luxury we can no longer afford.

In their postwar account of the Sicilian fighting, the Germans reported their first capture of a bazooka. They sent it back to Germany, tested it, found its defects and corrected them, and went into production on an improved model. When we landed in Normandy less than a year later, we were met with a large bazooka, about 3.5 inches in diameter. We were still equipped with the small 2.36-inch size. As a matter of fact, our infantry was still equipped with the 2.36-inch bazooka seven years later, in July of 1950, when it was attacked by Russian T-34 tanks manned by the North Koreans. They reported then, once again, that the rockets were bouncing off the tanks. We had had a big bazooka in development for some years. General Ridgway, who was an Army Deputy Chief of Staff in the summer of 1950, had production stepped up at once and new bazookas and ammunition were flown directly from the factory doors to the combat area. They contributed as much as any single factor to the survival of the 8th Army. But the laggardness in the decision-making and processes of research and development that caused that situation to occur seems to be almost inherent in our military programs, and I refer to the programs of all of the services. There are numerous examples of weapons, or their systems' components, being delayed or disapproved because the individuals who have funding control do not, or simply will not, understand the need of the fighting man in the field.

Before leaving the Mediterranean, we were to jump into Salerno. In the few weeks' respite that followed Salerno, we sought to correct the troubles that plagued us the night of the Sicilian landings. A small experimental group was established at Comiso Airfield in Sicily. It was under the control of Colonel John Norton of the Army and Colonel Joe Crouch of the Air Corps. Work was started at once on improving the accuracy of delivery of paratroopers. In a few weeks they submitted recommendations that we adopted, techniques which are still being used today. Pathfinder teams, consisting of carefully selected, well-trained battle veterans, were organized to jump into combat well ahead of the main landings. They were to carry navigational aids to assist the Troop Carrier pilots. About this time the Air Corps brought over the first airborne radar that we had seen. I took a number of flights over the Mediterranean to observe its work and was delighted with the prospect of improved navigation that it offered our pilots.

The problem of antitank weapons was more difficult. The only effective ones in existence were quite heavy, so heavy that they had to be taken into combat by glider. Since all of our combat operations were necessarily carried out under cover of darkness, we had to develop night-landing techniques for glider pilots. Drawing upon reports of night-landing exercises back in the United States, we established an experimental unit in Sicily. After several weeks of work, we staged a demonstration of our system. Senior airborne and troop carrier officers were flown in from Africa and Italy to see it. Tragically—and I did not realize it was happening at the time—substitute pilots were used the night of the demonstration and we succeeded in demonstrating the utter impossibility of attempting such a thing at night. Gliders were scattered all over the nearby Sicilian hills and farmhouses, most of them badly damaged, but fortunately few pilots were hurt.

While these things were going on, we gave much attention to new methods of control immediately following landing, new types of orders, simpler ways of reorganizing, all for the purpose of readying ourselves for the inevitable next jump wherever it would be. It was to be in Normandy six months later.

4

Normandy to Berlin

> "What miscarries shall be the general's fault, though he perform to the utmost of the man."—CORIOLANUS
>
> "If the German people despair, they will deserve no better than they get. If they despair, I will not be sorry for them if God lets them down."
> —ADOLF HITLER (1943)

Normandy was to be the first full-scale test of the airborne idea. Three airborne divisions, thirteen hundred airplanes, and over three thousand gliders were available for the assault. For the first time we began to pay close attention to the enemy's countermeasures, for by now he had fought against several airborne attacks, and he surely must have been developing new means of defense against us. I was fortunate to participate in the planning of the Normandy assault in the role of Senior Airborne Adviser to the Supreme Commander. I arrived in London in November, 1943, and went to work with the COSSAC[1] staff. Several years later, in *Airborne Warfare*, I described the problems of the forthcoming battle as we saw them then.

Airborne operations . . . are, for the opposing commanders and staffs, keen contests of wits and ingenuity. The possible area of operations is

[1] Chief of Staff, Supreme Allied Command.

vast and normally encompasses many thousands of square miles. The airborne targets and take-off airfields may be separated by hundreds of miles yet be within a few minutes' or a few hours' striking time.

The commander who intends to attack marshals his troop-carrier aircraft and shifts his airborne troops with as much attention to a cover plan for deceit as to the actual assault plan itself.

On the other side, defensive troops are hidden and exposed, and moved and countermoved. Anti-airborne obstacles are prepared to destroy the attackers; worthless but sinister facsimiles are prepared to scare them off. Good landing areas are totally neutralized by passive anti-airborne defensive measures, while others, equally as good or better, are left untouched to lure the assaulting airborne troops into organized and defended traps where they can be destroyed by well concealed weapons.

Thus in such situations there are two conditions that make airborne combat, in its broader aspects, markedly different from other types of fighting. First, the defender can prepare active and passive measures against an attack with comparative immunity from detection. Second, an airborne assault, once it is under way, is beyond immediate relief, alteration of direction, or even succor. The battle, when finally joined, is the payoff.

We were constantly preoccupied with three things, the plan, the enemy and our resources. The control of the latter was out of our hands and we had to depend upon the means shipped to us from the United States and from the Mediterranean.

Discussions of the proposed plan brought to light for the first time an unprecedented situation, and yet one common to the development of a new idea. We now began to meet with such enthusiasm for airborne operations, and from sources heretofore quite skeptical, that we had to caution them of the risks present in that type of combat. I remember talking to a senior officer, who, upon hearing one of the plans described, said to me: "Why man, it's like sending Michelangelo to paint a barn. Why jump so near the beaches? Make a deep penetration—hell, go all the way to Paris."

A staff team from the Pentagon actually did come over with a proposal that we make the airborne landings in the Orléans Gap, not far from Paris. What in the world they thought we would use against the Panzer Divisions goodness knows. But it is an interesting phenomenon that I have observed frequently, that those most reluctant to accept a new idea are often the first to yell "laggard" after the idea has been proven. As one writer has expressed it, "When it appears that the new idea is finding favour with the authorities and that adherence is likely to acquire merit, converts quickly appear; and they, like converts to a new religion, forgetting their former derision and opposition, soon become more fanatical than those who evolved the idea."[2]

The plans proposed to us ranged from jumping small teams of parachutists on all of the coastal weapons to penetrations a hundred miles deep. We finally settled upon a simple but effective plan of using the British division on the extreme left to capture crossings over the River Orne, and using the American divisions to (a) seize the causeways from the beaches inland and (b) block the movement of German reinforcements toward the beaches.

Knowing how close we had come to disaster in Sicily, and realizing that I was going to jump into Normandy, I probably had stronger feelings about the forthcoming battle than most of the staff in London. I studied the enemy with meticulous care and pored over air photographs. He gave us much to think about. Hardly had our final plans been drafted when countermeasures began to appear in the photographs. *Rommelspargel* (Rommel's asparagus) began to spring up overnight in many of the proposed landing areas. These were poles about six to twelve inches in diameter and eight to twelve feet long. They were sunk a foot or two into the ground and stood about seventy-five to one hundred feet apart. Soon improvements began to show up; the poles were being wired together, then mines seemed to be affixed to the wires. Machine-gun emplacements began to appear around some of the proposed drop zones, and fields of fire were cleared. Much of the photography gave us accurate locations of German headquarters and scattered ammunition and gasoline dumps.

Concurrently, intense training was conducted and we received

[2] *The War on the Civil and Military Fronts,* General G. M. Lindsay.

two new parachute regiments directly from the United States. They were enthusiastic and their junior officers were overflowing with energy and drive. How to condition them mentally and physically for the shock that lay ahead was the problem. American young men are so removed from battle experience that they think of combat in terms of athletic competitions, and thus in terms of sportsmanship. It almost takes the sight of a friend being killed by an enemy weapon for them to realize that it could happen to them. Physical stamina and personal bravery were present in abundance, but the cold, calculating stealth of the killer had to be given them. And the officers had to learn the clear-headedness and moral courage to make decisions under great stress; one took for granted their physical courage.

In training, profiting from my Sicilian experience, I resorted to a technique that I have often used since. All maneuvers in which decisions were required were preceded by a long grueling physical test, usually an overnight march of about eighteen to twenty miles with full combat equipment. Then when the men expected a rest, they were presented with difficult combat situations. After an all-day maneuver, when they were tired and hungry, a night march was ordered. After a couple of hours of marching, at about midnight, they would be ordered to halt and go into a dispersed bivouac, in anticipation of a night's rest. After about an hour of sleep, which was just enough to cause them to lose their sense of orientation to events and environment, unit commanders were suddenly awakened and given a new set of orders requiring immediate movement. They marched until daylight, when a new situation was given to them, usually a final attack order. In the meantime a daylight inspection was made of their bivouac to check whether or not they had lost equipment, etc. It was exacting training, but it gave me an opportunity to get to know a lot about them and for them to learn much about themselves. During such exercises we used enemy uniforms, weapons and live ammunition quite freely. Even so, rarely could the training be exacting enough to compare to the shock of battle itself, and the paratrooper unfortunately meets the shock head on in seconds, rather than via the gradual approach to battle on foot, as so often is the situation with our other troops.

As spring came to England and our training intensified we began to hear of something new—V-weapons. A conference was called of the senior commanders in London and they were given as much information as was available. It wasn't very much. We knew that the enemy had a new, long-range, supersonic rocket with a big high-explosive warhead that could be used against the area where our troops were billeted. At least we understood that it could, but the measures we were taking had, of necessity, to be passive. We made plans to disperse our troops in trenches if a bombardment of rockets occurred.

Actually, the British had been following the German rocket program for some time. Major Duncan Sandys was Chairman of the Flying Bomb Counter Measures Committee, and in the spring of 1943 he began to urge that additional photo reconnaissance be made of Peenemunde, the German missile development center. His efforts were rewarded and on the eighteenth of June, 1943, photography showed long slender objects in an emplacement that he deduced to be a very long-range rocket. He had some difficulty convincing the RAF but finally, after much discussion, that summer the first air attack on Peenemunde took place. The Germans then moved their test firings to Poland. Here the Polish Underground began to co-operate with the British. The first V-2 was fired in January of '44. The Poles reported to the British how it destroyed several cottages at a distance of nearly two hundred miles from the town of Blizna. Not all of the V-2s were completely successful and many of them detonated at distances not much more than fifty to sixty miles from the launching site. Although the Germans attempted to recover the fragments, the Polish Underground collected many of them. As a British officer personally concerned with the problem described the situation:

. . . from time to time essential parts such as turbocompressors, fuel reservoirs, rudder chains and electrical equipment were captured. Later the "scatter" became less, not more than 10 miles. This was very helpful to the Germans and equally unhelpful to the Poles, who might quite reasonably have, at this point, given up the unequal struggle. But their patience, skill and courage had its reward. One of the rockets dropped on the bank of the River Bug and did not explode. This was near the village of Sarmaki where some of the "Underground" were active. These men reached the spot in time to roll the weapon into the water and by various common-sense devices, such as watering large numbers of cattle upstream of the V-2, made the water so muddy that the German search-parties failed in their intention. That night the Poles fished the weapon out of the water and in great stealth dismantled it and removed the vital parts. Later it was flown to England by a DC-3 that made a night rendezvous with the Polish underground.[3]

In the meantime, the Germans began their spasmodic V-1 (a subsonic winged bomb) launchings against England. They preceded their effort by an elaborate construction program and by December of 1943 approximately a hundred launching sites were in advance stage of construction. On December 20 the Allied Air Forces launched an all-out attack on the sites and by April of '44 almost all of them were badly damaged or completely destroyed. The Germans then devised a mobile system, readily transportable and difficult to detect. Although we did not know it at the time, they were having a heated internal dispute between their scientists, airmen and soldiers. Dr. von Braun recounted the story in his testimony before a committee of the United States Senate on December 17, 1957:

MR. WEISL: Dr. von Braun, will you please tell the committee what lessons were learned from the operation of the V-2? I am now speaking of mobility, guidance, and such other lessons as were learned that are now applicable to the manufacture and use of missiles.

DR. VON BRAUN: Sir, when it was decided to put the V-2 into military operation, it was still full of bugs, as we used to say in the rocket field. It was a brandnew weapon, a brandnew technology. Particularly, the engineers and scientists at Peenemunde, for whom I was speaking at the time as the technical director, we were of the opinion that a fixed base concept was the only feasible solution at that time to put this weapon quickly into operation. So we insisted more or less laboratory

[3] Air Chief Marshal Sir Philip Joubert in his excellent book, *Rocket*.

type fashion. The missiles would only be wheeled out to the launching site a few minutes prior to the launching.

The military at the time told us continuously that it was a hopeless undertaking to build and to operate such concrete pens, such fixed installations, in view of the unchallenged Allied air superiority in that area.

So the military insisted on mobility, while I myself along with my technical associates, were utterly skeptical that the V-2 was sufficiently advanced for mobile development.

Finally a compromise was reached. A few of these pens were actually built while we also continued pursuing the mobile concept.

The net result was that all the pens were completely destroyed before they were ever put in operation, and that not a single V-2 missile was ever lost at a mobile launching site—and this despite the fact there was a 30-to-1 air superiority by the United States Air Force, along, of course, with the Royal Air Force, in that area.

MR. WEISL: In other words, the Royal Air Force and the American Air Force destroyed the static launching platforms, but most of the mobile platforms were saved?

DR. VON BRAUN: All of them.

MR. WEISL: All of them were saved?

DR. VON BRAUN: Yes. A number of V-2's were lost during transportation on the roads and on railway trains, but there is not a single case on record where a V-2 was destroyed in a mobile launching site, and I believe with the V-1 missile they had exactly the same experience.

MR. WEISL: From your experience in supervising the work on the Redstone missile and the Jupiter missile, you agree with General Gavin, I take it, that they are mobile?

DR. VON BRAUN: Yes.

MR. WEISL: And mobility should be the fundamental purpose in the use of those weapons?

DR. VON BRAUN: Yes, sir. I am convinced of this. In the Redstone missile we have achieved complete mobility, not movability, but mobility, true mobility. With the Jupiter missile, such mobility can even easier be attained than with the Redstone, because the empty weight of the missile is less. The Jupiter is shorter and lighter than the Redstone. [Range of the Redstone is 200 miles, the Jupiter 1500 miles.][4]

[4] Inquiry into Satellite and Missile Programs. Hearings before the Preparedness Investigating Subcommittee of the Committee on Armed Services, United States Senate, 85th Congress.

Training in preparation for Normandy continued and a final full-scale rehearsal was staged in May of 1944. It was conducted at night under approximately the conditions we anticipated on D-Day. The takeoff was normal, we got most of the division into the air and then found that we could not get it down. Fog and bad weather closed in on us, the drop zones could not be located, and close troop carrier formations could not be flown. A few drops were made but most of the troops had to be air-landed at airdromes scattered over England. The few unit jumps that were made, combined with the many months of intense training behind us, were considered adequate for the job ahead and no additional rehearsals were attempted.

We continued to follow the German defensive preparations and to our surprise, in late May, a German division was moved into the very area into which we were to land. These combined with the pattern of *Rommelspargel* caused many of us to suspect that the Germans knew of our exact plans. Plans were changed and we moved the drop zones several miles to the east. Recalling the German propaganda effort that was so successful prior to our landing in Sicily, I went to see the Chief of Psychological Warfare in General Eisenhower's headquarters and urged that he print and drop a leaflet to the French to counter the German effort. After some explanation, he convinced me that it could boomerang. The Germans could duplicate it and use it against us by merely changing some of the wording, so the idea was dropped.

By early June all was ready, as ready as we could make it. The anticipated V-weapons did not attack the troop areas, the troops were trained, they were bivouacked around the airfields, ammunition, orders and maps were issued, and we were ready for takeoff. I continued to worry about tanks, but we were taking along twelve antitank guns in gliders that were going to attempt to land with us at night. They would help.

June 5-6 was a good night for an operation and while there appeared to be some apprehension about the high winds, to those of us who had been in Sicily, it was of little concern. Take-

78

offs were normal, and until we entered a dense fog bank soon after we crossed the Coast of France, all went well. I was flying in the lead plane, as commander of a task force of three parachute regiments, and looking back it was a most reassuring sight. At that moment, as so often happens in combat, everything seemed to go wrong. Within seconds everything changed and there wasn't an airplane to be seen. From the moment we crossed the Coast of France we had twelve minutes in which to make the jump decision; after that deadline we would have crossed the whole Cherbourg Peninsula and have been over the ocean again. At eight minutes, the fog began to dissipate, the flak and small-arms fire thickened, the green light went on, and with one last precious look at the layout of the land below, we went out. What followed, although a bedlam in many respects, was far better than Sicily and by daylight I had about 125 troopers under my control. I managed to regain control of additional units, get close to our first objective, and at the end of the first day's fighting, General Matt Ridgway joined me at a railroad overpass about five miles west of the town of Ste.-Mère-Église.

"Jim," he said, "how are things going?"

"All right, I guess," I said. "We have had very heavy fighting and I have lost a couple of battalion commanders as well as quite a few troopers. We have not been able to get our first objective [a bridge over the Merderet River], but we are holding our own. Tanks at the bridge site are giving us a difficult time."

"Well," he said, "I have heard rumors that the amphibious landings did not come in on account of weather. We may have a hard time of it."

We discussed this a bit further and decided, as far as possible, to keep it from the troops and to make the best of things.

Fortunately, the amphibious landing did come in on schedule, with the heavy equipment that we so badly needed. Soon we attacked across the Merderet River overrunning the German positions. We captured our first big bazooka. It was exactly like ours except that it appeared to be about twice the size. I also found boxes of rocket-like objects with the name *"Faustpetrone"* lettered upon them. I had no idea what they were and could not imagine how they might be used. They appeared to be oversized German potato-masher grenades. Later I was to learn that they were a new form of rocket, built on a German application of the principle of our bazooka ammunition. In a few months, we captured a more advanced type labeled, *"Panzerfaust."* Translated it means "armored fist." It consisted of a warhead about six inches in diameter fired with a small rocket charge from a small tube. The warhead remained, like an onion on the end of a stem, outside the tube. Later, in combat in Holland, the German directions were translated into English and distributed to our troops. We captured as many *Panzerfausts* as we possibly could and carried them with us. Though considerably shorter in range than the bazookas, they were the parachutist's best antitank weapons and we were grateful to the Germans for having developed them. Soon we found them useful in close infantry combat as well. Colonel Reuben Tucker's 504th Parachute Infantry captured a truckload that they kept with them until the end of the war.

After thirty-three days of fighting in Normandy, the division was relieved. There is no doubt now that the three airborne divisions had contributed decisively to the success of the operation, but it had been costly. Of the 11,770 troops of the 82nd Airborne Division committed to the battle, only 6,545 were returned with us to England. Officer casualties were particularly high, especially in the infantry regiments, ranging from 52 per cent in the lowest to 63 per cent in the highest. But the airborne attack had succeeded and the opportunities were now beginning to appear unlimited, provided we could get adequate airlift and further improve our methods.

As soon as we returned to England we sent back to the United States for technical assistance in solving the assembly and reorganization problems immediately following landing. The request went to the office of Dr. Vannevar Bush and he sent over Dr. Charles E. Waring. Dr. Waring worked closely with us for the remainder of the war developing infrared assembly lights, scanners and equipment to make possible their use with path-finder teams. At the same time, we studied the interrogation reports of over a thousand German officers and enlisted men with whom we had been in contact immediately following the landing. Our purpose was to find out what they knew about our airborne operations, what measures they had taken to defend against them and their plans for defense in the future. There is no doubt that they had done an excellent job of preparing their troops for the airborne attack, even though we defeated them. An excellent booklet, *What Every Soldier Should Know about Airborne Troops,* had been printed and distributed. Numerous training exercises had been conducted on a realistic basis. The troops had been impressed with the "no quarter given" type fighting that they might expect from the parachutists and they were prepared for it. All in all, it appeared that our next airborne assault would meet stiffer opposition unless the Wehrmacht was disintegrating. This, however, it appeared to be doing.

"End the war in forty-four," was the hope. It seemed possible of attainment. By late August the Germans were reeling back into Germany and there appeared to be nothing in prospect that would save them except possibly our own mistakes. We planned one airborne jump in Tournai, Belgium, and then had to cancel it at the last moment because the Germans were falling back too rapidly. We then planned the Eindhoven-Nijmegen-Arnhem jump. It was known as Operation "Market-Garden."

Operation "Market-Garden" was intended to break the back of German resistance and bring the war to an end in '44. If it succeeded, Montgomery's Second Army would reach the North Sea, thus cutting off major German formations and placing us in a position to strike into the heart of Germany. As Montgomery expressed it, "My own view was that one powerful, full-blooded thrust across the Rhine and into the Heart of Germany, backed by the whole of the resources of the Allied Armies, would be likely to achieve decisive results." Actually, there was a basic conflict in strategy. Montgomery believed in defending along most of the front using a single main thrust to make a decisive penetration to the heart of Germany, in the north. General Eisenhower was more inclined to a broad-front approach and General Patton wanted to make a single all-out effort in his area in the south. The decision made was a compromise. Based on a conversation of General Eisenhower on September 5, 1944, the Chief of Military History reports:

> The Supreme Commander, while giving priority to Montgomery's advance to the northeast, thought it important to get "Patton moving again so that we may be fully prepared to carry out the original conception for the final stages of the campaign." As he saw it at the time, the logical move was to take advantage of all existing lines of communications in the advance toward Germany and to bring the southern wing of the OVERLORD forces on the Rhine at Koblenz. At the same time, airborne forces would be used to seize crossings over the Rhine thus placing the Allies in a position to thrust deep into the Ruhr and threaten Berlin. . . . None of Eisenhower's executives liked the compromise but their complaints were not so loud at the moment as they became in later months, and years, when each felt that he had been deprived of victory in consequence of that decision. Patton called it "the most momentous error of the war."[5]

Somehow the decision was made to give Montgomery the ball, but to keep Patton happy, he was allowed to carry one too but with not as much support as Montgomery. Patton didn't like it. General Bradley says that Patton came to his headquarters "bellowing like a bull," roaring, "To hell with Hodges and Monty. We'll win your goddam war if you'll keep the Third Army going."

The operation was carried out on September 17, 1944. The British First Parachute Division landed at Arnhem, the 82nd Airborne Division about twenty miles south at Nijmegen, and the 101st Airborne Division was farther south at Eindhoven. The 101st was the first to link up. The fighting was quite heavy. The British Guards Division linked up with the 82nd on the morning of September 19. On the twenty-first the big bridge at Nijmegen was

[5] "How The Allies Let Victory Slip in 1944," Captain Liddell Hart, *Marine Corps Gazette*, July, 1957.

in our hands and the British armor was advancing toward Arnhem. By then, the Germans had cut our long tenuous route extending back into Belgium at several places. Tragically, both an American and a British officer, contrary to the standing orders of both airborne divisions, carried with them copies of the complete battle orders and these soon fell into German hands. I am inclined to believe that without this information, even though Field Marshal Montgomery lacked adequate strength, the objective of the operation would have been realized. The North Sea would have been reached and the scene set for ending the war in the fall of 1944. Reacting promptly, however, with the information of our own plans in their hands, the Germans strongly attacked across the long road up to the airhead. Soon the momentum of the entire attack was brought to a halt. With an additional corps of three divisions on land, or a single additional airborne division in the airhead, Field Marshal Montgomery could have accomplished his objective. As it was, for lack of adequate airlift only part of each of the divisions was flown in the first day, and bad weather detained the remainder of the lift for a critical period of time. Thus greater airlift could also very likely have contributed decisively to the success of the operation.

To those of us in the battle the lack of divisional combat strength and lack of airlift was obvious. Both Montgomery and Patton were apparently making a main effort, in the north and in the south, but neither had adequate strength and neither was successful. Somehow, the decision behind this attack stuck in my mind in a very bothersome way, for it epitomizes the problem of generalship in a democracy.

Generalship in a democracy is rife with compromise. It should be of concern to our military students and our combat leaders of tomorrow. By mid-'44, most of our military decisions were being made on the basis of absolute certainty not to fail; ultimate success appeared inevitable and could wait. This attitude seemed to permeate the lowest of commands, and venturesome, skillful tactical schemes were rare indeed. Methodical phase-line-by-phase-line attacks were preferred. The thought often occurred to me that a "Stonewall" Jackson would have been given short shrift as a tactical commander. He probably would have been relieved for falling back or giving up ground. I am not unmindful of the spectacular achievements of General Patton. We need more General Pattons. I would feel better about future military relations with the Soviet Union and its satellites if we had more like him. But innovations in applied tactics, and in combat behavior and leadership, are as rare as innovations in concepts and research.

But winter came and still no peace. On December 17, 1944, I was the acting commander of the VIII Corps and I was with the 82nd Airborne Division at Sissone, France. That evening I received an alert of a move to the front where the Germans were doing unexpectedly well. After getting the 82nd and 101st Airborne Divisions in motion, I left for Spa, Belgium, to report to the commanding general of the U.S. First Army. He was General Hodges and I met him in his office at about ten in the morning. His chief of staff, General Bill Kean, was there as well as the Army G-3, General Thorson. The enemy situation was vague, to say the least, and the corps that I commanded was on the way by truck toward Bastogne, an obviously important road center in Belgium. The problem was what to do with the corps. It was the last uncommitted Allied reserve. General Kean ran his finger over the map and suggested Bastogne for one division and Werbemont for the other. General Hodges approved. Since the 82nd was leading I ordered it to continue on to Werbemont and after making a reconnaissance of that locality, I went on to Bastogne. The VIII Corps had its headquarters in a school in Bastogne and there was considerable confusion and much doubt about the situation. The VIII Corps was pulling back and they did not have much information to offer. Just before dusk the commanding general of the 101st arrived, Brigadier General Anthony McAuliffe, and I gave him what information I had. I then gave him his orders to organize and defend the locality. His orders were clear, he was to stay there unless told otherwise. His gallant defense with a great division, the 101st Airborne, is now history. Immediately after issuing him his orders, I went north to join the 82nd and in about twenty-four hours General Ridgway arrived to reassume command of the corps. Then followed one of the bitterest periods of fighting of the war.

The first signs of spring were in the air when we reached the Roer River. Spring was most welcome. It had been a cold and costly winter. Our casualties had been heavy and the fighting at times very difficult. With the coming of spring came rumors of a spring offensive. The hardened veterans no longer talked about ending the war, then or later, and if there had been a favorite slogan, it would have been, "Stay alive in Forty-five." I remember a remark made by a senior British officer in a meeting that I attended. He and most of his troops were veterans of the desert fighting and, at the time of our meeting, an attack that he had planned with great care was making absolutely no progress. Speaking wistfully of it he said, "Ah, if only I had one good green division."

The 82nd Airborne Division was withdrawn and preparations were made for another airborne operation. It was to be a jump on Berlin. This was to be the kill, and while a bit apprehensive about our prospects in another daylight jump, we knew that this would be the last, in Europe anyway. Maps were issued, orders prepared and all of the details carefully checked. It was to be a three-division effort, two American and one British. The American sector, as it turned out, was approximately the same sector that we were to occupy after the war ended. It was the southwestern portion of the city, including Tempelhof Airdrome.

Once again I went back to studying all available intelligence with care. I read the RAF and Air Corps daily digests as well as the Army reports. The antiaircraft gun deployments around our approach routes to the city appeared to be less impressive than they had been in Holland, near Nijmegen. Our estimate was that we could take care of them. There was something else, however, that began to show up in the pilot interrogation reports that bothered me. I remember reading of it first in an RAF postflight interrogation report. It was a story about what appeared to be a rocket or missile. One of the digests contained a picture of the flaming, corkscrew-like path of one of them in flight. Some of the pilots reported that it appeared to home on the plane and if they attempted evasive action it seemed to change course and follow them. There was much speculation but unfortunately very little factual information except a few pilot reports. If it were a homing missile, its use in numbers would be disastrous to us. My hope therefore was that it was still in development and would not be available in numbers before our proposed Berlin operation. But our concern was soon brought to an end by the cancellation of the Berlin jump. We returned to ground combat.

We were placed in a sector along the Rhine River near Cologne. It was a quiet area except for Colonel Tucker's 504th Parachute Infantry, which made a river crossing and did some very heavy fighting near the small town of Hitdorf. In late April we were on the move again, this time to the Elbe River far to the north, in the area of the British Second Army. Soon we were to meet the Russian forces then storming across northern Germany. I shall always remember the meeting of our forces for a number of reasons. The 82nd Airborne Division was under the command of the British Second Army. The Army Commander was General Sir Miles Dempsey, a brilliant and at the same time quietly efficient, modest type of British officer, who to my mind was one of the great soldiers of the war. The 82nd Airborne Division was strung back in trucks over the roads to Cologne for almost a couple of hundred miles. The head of the column was just below Hamburg near the town of Bleckede on the Elbe River. Directly to the north about sixty miles away was the Baltic Sea. I had made an early reconnaissance of the Elbe River line and it appeared that the German build-up on the far side was heavier than usual. The river was very wide and running swiftly in spring flood. I had about two battalions of infantry up and the remainder would arrive during the night. The prudent thing would have been to wait twenty-four hours at least before attempting the crossing.

General Dempsey and General Ridgway came to my CP to talk about the situation. I had fought in General Dempsey's army in Holland for over six weeks and I had great respect for his judgment and ability. He asked: "Jim, when do you think you can cross? I would like to get established on the far bank as quickly as possible."

"I have some engineers and light assault boats up as well as about two battalions of infantry," I said. "I am not sure what is on the far side, but the high dikes along the river seem to be well organized for defense and I have seen quite a few German troops digging in. I would like to get a chance to bring up more troops and delay for about twenty-four hours on the crossing. The river, as you know, is very wide and running very swiftly and it will not be an easy one."

"I know," he said, "but this I must tell you. It is of the utmost importance that we get to the Baltic Sea as quickly as possible. We must keep the Russians out of Denmark. I will give you a battalion of Buffaloes. [Buffaloes are amphibious track-laying vehicles that are lightly armored and well suited to river crossings.] I will back you with everything we have, but the crossing must be made as quickly as possible."

I discussed it briefly with General Ridgway and he assured me of the support of elements of the U.S. 8th Infantry Division, which was also building up nearby for the prospective crossing. At the time, it was a moment of education for me. In the United States Army we are brought up to abhor the contamination of military battles with political objectives. I had heard and read of the British military sensitivity to the political aspects of their fighting but this was the first time that I had encountered it personally. I was impressed and I realize in retrospect that I certainly should have been, for the British point of view was absolutely

right. To have stood idly by and naïvely allowed the Soviet occupation of Denmark would have been tragic in its postwar
implications.

I agreed to make the crossing during the night. The first assault
boats and Buffaloes hit the water about four-thirty A.M., an hour
before daylight. I crossed with the assault and the opposition was
light. We dug out at bayonet point the Germans who had covered
up for the night. There were two unusual aspects of the operation:
German artillery came down in greater volume than I had experienced in the entire war. It literally shook the earth and the
surrounding buildings, and all that one could do was to hug as
closely as possible the ground or a protecting wall. Next, the
Germans for the first time used an influence mine that was
difficult to deal with. Although we didn't realize what it was at
the time, it turned out to be a sea mine with an explosive charge
powerful enough to throw a jeep high into the air killing everyone aboard. It did not go off when first run over like other mines.
It detonated as preset, depending upon the specific number of
vehicles that had gone by. We finally learned how to locate and
how to take care of them. The 82nd Airborne and 8th Infantry
reached the Baltic, swung to the south and in twenty-four hours
met the Russians.

I made my way by jeep, with a couple of well-armed troopers
and a Russian-speaking American sergeant, through the Soviet
troops. They were looting and destroying everything in sight. As
we went through the square of a small German town, Grabow,
they had a huge hogshead of wine that they had knocked open
and they were helping themselves with buckets, helmets, etc. As
we approached the Russian division commander's headquarters,
a big truck loaded with Soviet soldiers yelling and waving their
firearms, came careening down the road toward us. To my disbelief, about fifty yards from us it began to climb the high grass
bank beside the road skidding and turning over, spilling soldiers
across the road and pinning some beneath the truck. Those who
could got up laughing and gesticulating, seemingly paying no

attention to those under the truck. I felt like giving a hand, but they were all too drunk and excited to understand, and our uniforms were unfamiliar to them, so I went on to a German house a short distance away where the Russian division commander was found.

Our meeting was rather friendly and a bit reserved. We went to the dining room of the house where I laid out a map on the table to show him the location of my forces. He seemed reluctant to tell me where his were. Having just come through them, I had a pretty good idea anyway. Furthermore, I already had reports from two of my regimental commanders giving me a detailed description of the location of the Soviet troops and their behavior. I proceeded to tell him the location of his leading elements and he seemed to thaw out a bit. The ubiquitous political commissar hung over his shoulder listening to every word. A fleeting impression crossed my mind of what the meeting in Poland between the Germans and the Russians a few years before must have been like. Perhaps this very general had taken part in one of those meetings —at least he had heard about them—and he knew that they had turned and fought each other to the death very soon thereafter. Moreover, I understood his stiffness, for it was obvious that he didn't understand Americans or what was on our minds.

We tentatively agreed on two lines on which our forces would be deployed allowing for a kilometer of "no man's land" between them. I say tentatively because he obviously had no authority to make any sort of agreement, even though something had to be done about the situation. I had been sent forward with complete freedom to make decisions and do what was reasonable. He was under such rigid control from higher up that he apparently could make no decisions. This situation characterized my relations with the Soviets from then on. Even the simple matter of exchanging decorations for enlisted men and junior officers apparently had to be referred far to the rear for decision. The inflexibility inherent in such a system must be very difficult for a military commander to live with and to fight effectively under.

The presence of the commissar was typical. In the weeks that followed, our relations with the Soviet military forces warmed up considerably. We had many friendly dinners and visits with each other's forces. They gave me a ride in their T-34 tank and showed me some very fine-looking troops and antitank equipment. We in turn put on a small parachute jump. I had a professional civilian jumper, Dan Bost, who delayed his parachute opening until a hundred feet or so above the ground. The Soviet general witnessing the event was so overcome that he rushed over and kissed him, taking off one of his own medals and pinning it on Bost's breast. Always there was the omnipresent commissar and it was evident that when he could be kept at a distance, say, a room or so away, the Soviet officers were much more relaxed and free in their behavior and seemed to enjoy themselves more. As he approached, the knowing look quickly went around. In a week or so the word came down. Stalin said the party was over. We were being returned to the pre-World War II category of enemies of the proletariat.

The meeting with the Russians was one of the most interesting events of the war. I was very much interested in their lack of large airborne formations and the fact that they had conducted no large-scale airborne operations. Since ours was a parachute division, we attracted quite a few visitors of parachute background. I discussed airborne operations with the Russians at considerable length. There is no doubt whatsoever about why they had never conducted large-scale airborne operations—it came out quite clearly in our discussions. They had never solved the organizational and equipment problems for units of a size larger than a battalion. Those were partisan battalions equipped with small arms only. They had had an early start in individual parachute training, and in the late twenties displayed large-scale airborne drops. When the war came, they dissipated their airborne resources rapidly in the delaying, partisan warfare that stopped the Germans. After that, they never could assemble the nucleus of an airborne effort. They had many individual jumpers, and those that I met were enthusiastic about parachute jumping, but they were completely at a loss as to what to do to develop some sense of organization and efficiency of combat-unit performance out of their resources. They were quite frank on these points and obviously very much interested in what we had been able to accomplish. Since World War II, their airborne capabilities have vastly improved and they now have several airborne divisions.

My discussions with the Russian airborne officers brought home once again the fundamental problems of introducing and developing new operational concepts. Early decisions are needed. It takes courage to make them because, for the few who will support a new concept, there will be hundreds who will point out why it cannot possibly work. Furthermore, the concept is but the beginning. To be combat-worthy requires the fullest support of our scientists and our industry and all services playing their part. Thus may we bring innovations to useful combat application— innovations without which we can never survive as a free people.

5

The Decade of Dilemma:
1945-1955

A. THE LESSONS OF WORLD WAR II

The atomic bomb overshadowed all military thinking during the period 1945 to 1955. Especially was this true early in the decade. Hiroshima was fresh in our minds, the Soviets had no atomic bomb and no immediate prospect of getting one, and a revolution in military technology suddenly was being thrust upon us. To some extent, military thinking seemed to be paralyzed by the bomb, and the lessons of World War II were ignored or quickly forgotten. The prevailing attitude seemed to be that after Hiroshima, it was a time to "throw the books out the window." Military texts had to be rewritten. Little that we had learned in World War II, it was said, would have meaningful application in the future. Any historian could have told us that this was nonsense, for there was much to learn from World War II, much of it of immediate value in dealing with our national defense problems, which were soon to become critical.

We were fortunate in World War II. We were provided with a shield of time, space and, to a degree, circumstance, that protected us as we readied ourselves. The Atlantic and then the Pacific Ocean provided a physical barrier not easy to cross. In Europe our allies took the brunt of the first blow, recoiled under

severe punishment, and finally held. The British fought valiantly
at home, on the seas, and in North Africa. Despite this, when war
reached us we were not ready, neither the Army nor the Navy
nor the nation as a whole. This is not to say that we did not respond energetically and completely, for the record shows clearly
that we did; but we were not ready, and never again can we afford
not to be.

Our nation has always been slow to arouse itself from the
idyls of peace. The avoidance of foreign entanglements has been
the keystone of policy and it has been with reluctance that we
have sent our sons to fight on foreign soil. The problem of political
leadership, therefore, can be a most difficult one, as the political
careers of Woodrow Wilson and Franklin D. Roosevelt will show.
As late as the presidential campaign of 1940, Mr. Roosevelt was
holding forth to the electorate a promise of nonparticipation in
foreign war—"Your sons are not going to be sent to any foreign
wars," and "You can nail any talk about sending armies to Europe
as a deliberate untruth." Even Congress, always a barometer of
grass-roots attitudes, had difficulty in passing the Selective Service Act. It did so by one vote late in the summer of 1941. World
War I should have taught us that millions of men cannot spring to
arms overnight, and that the American tradition of the frontiers-
man leaving his plow, grabbing his musket and going off to war
has long been outdated.

Our military establishment had a few years in which to observe
the workings of the newest war machines in Europe. They could
have been years in which to train and acquire weapons and vehicles for this new form of war. Despite this, much of our equipment was obsolete when the war began. In land warfare, our
tanks, in terms of armor, gunpower and range, were outperformed
from the beginning to the end of the war. Our antitank weapons
and our heavy machine guns were inferior, quantitatively and
qualitatively.

Our one unique contribution to land warfare was the jeep,
which was unmatched in military utility in any army of the

world. In a class with the jeep was the C-47 airplane, which was the true workhorse of the war, and if available in sufficient numbers, could have brought it to an end in the fall of 1944. Despite its build-up, the B-17 never performed up to its design concepts. In naval warfare, our torpedo was seriously deficient, a situation we were unable to correct until 1943.

Perhaps our outstanding resource was our manpower, particularly its quality. The American GI was mechanically inclined and mechanically capable, and this was the last great war of the machine age. The attitude of the American GI—his adaptability and resilience in adversity—was, in my opinion, one of the great factors contributing to our victories.

In the prewar period we followed closely the growing French military establishment, and we had great confidence in it. It was rated as the greatest army of all time, and its Maginot Line was believed by many to be impregnable. Our press was flooded with favorable pictures and articles during the "phony" war, the period between the attack on Poland in 1939 and the invasion of France in 1940. I remember a picture in *Life* Magazine showing a sloppy-looking French soldier doing guard duty sitting in a chair, being interrogated by a brigadier equally unkempt. The caption pointed out that this was clear evidence of the democratic character of the French Army. We were soon to realize that instead it was clear evidence of a lack of the fundamentals of discipline, a lack which was to prove its undoing when it faced the Wehrmacht onslaught months later.

Contrary to popular opinion, the Germans did not have greater manpower nor did they have more tanks, nor was the French Army taken by surprise. The French had a military establishment that stopped thinking with the end of World War I, that assumed that the pattern of war would not change and that the great battles of France in the past would be repeated in the future. The Maginot Line was a monument to this state of mind. I discussed this in Strasbourg in 1953 with a French officer who had just written an article, "Were We Betrayed by the Concrete?" He demonstrated that they were not, and of course they were not. They were betrayed by their own thinking. As expressed in the Paris magazine *Match* in 1950:

> It is painful to some Frenchmen to recognize that they were beaten primarily by the power of brains. They would prefer to ascribe their national disaster of 10 years ago to a superior physical strength. They confess readily that France was undermined by a bad political system and they are almost glad to refer to the seeds of treason artfully planted by nazism into French soil. But to admit that stupidity was the reason for defeat, that the famed brightness of the French mind was obliterated, that the French military "elite" was unable to understand the changing form of warfare and to conceive accordingly a new doctrine of war, deeply hurts the national pride.
>
> Before 1940, in the French military academies, it was a rule and almost a rite to invoke in any circumstance the "lessons of the war"— meaning, of course, the 1914-18 war, which was looked upon as if it had been the only one in history. All the French military system, including the really ridiculous Maginot Line, was drawn up according to that alleged teaching. That blind obedience to the past led the French army directly to disaster. Nothing is more dangerous to a nation than a previous victory.[1]

One of the truly great contributions to the Allied victory in World War II was made by scientists—our own and those of our allies. Unprecedented in its magnitude and scope, the scientific contribution weighed heavily in our favor. Radar is the first thing that comes to mind. Developed by the British and significantly improved by our Army and Navy, particularly the Navy, it gave us a tremendous advantage in combat. The antisubmarine warfare challenge was one of the greatest ever to confront the nation. It was a nip and tuck scientific battle from the beginning, with the Allied scientists finally gaining the upper hand. Rockets, the proximity-influence fuse, new types of landing craft, improved communications, all were a part of the scientific contribution, as

[1] "Why France Fell—Last-War Thinking," Washington *Post,* Monday, June 12, 1950.

was the atomic bomb itself. The role that science can play, and in fact must play if the Free World is to survive, is one of the great lessons of World War II.

Finally, which service contributed most toward winning the war? None, in my opinion. The combined contributions of all were sufficient unto victory, and it would be impossible to say that one did more than another. It was, however, a war in which a concept developed between wars was to be put to a test; that is, whether or not air power, as an independent entity, could achieve decisive results.

Arriving at an unimpassioned, objective answer to this question has been very difficult. This is true for several reasons. First, the genesis of the idea was in the theory that, "Nothing that has happened in the history of warfare can affect aerial action." This thesis was used as a basis for propounding the theory that only offensive air power would be decisive. In the final analysis, nothing else would matter.

> . . . aerial warfare admits no defense, only offense. We must there-fore resign ourselves to the offensives the enemy inflicts upon us, while striving to put all of our resources to work to inflict even heavier ones upon him.[2]

Further, the nation that developed the greatest air offensive would win, and very likely win in a matter of hours. As an American spokesman for this point of view, Major Al Williams, was quoted in *Time* of October 23, 1939:

> If the issues between England and France on one side, and Germany on the other, are destined to be settled by force, the decision, win or lose, will be reached in a matter of 72 hours—in short via a *true* air war.

Like small boys hurling imprecations at each other over the back fence, Herman Goering came back in *Time* of April 1, 1940:

> At one order, Hell would be turned loose on the enemy! With one quick blow destruction of the enemy would be complete!

[2] *The Command of the Air,* by Giulio Douhet.

Earlier, in 1939, Goering said, "We tingle with eagerness to show our invincibleness in action." But his enthusiasm began to chill somewhat by 1941. Then for the first time a heretical note became apparent when he spoke of defense:

> As Reich Minister for Air, I have convinced myself personally of the measures taken to protect the Ruhr against Air attack. In the future, I will look after every battery, for we will NOT expose the RUHR to a single bomb dropped by enemy aircraft.[3]

By World War II the Royal Air Force had already established itself as an independent military organization, and as we entered the war, the U.S. Army Air Corps was given a marginal degree of independence, a promissory note of full independence that would follow the war. In a way, this independence was tied to the soundness of the Douhet theory, for if Douhet were not valid and if the airman did not have a degree of operational independence and a decision-making capability in his own medium, what reason was there for a separate air force? The proponents of a separate air arm sought, therefore, from the mid-thirties to prove the validity of the Douhet philosophy. The opponents were few and passive. Much of the judgment on the contribution made by air power was far from objective. Yet if there ever was a time when we needed objectivity and an understanding of the most useful combat function of the airplane, 1945 was the time; for that was the year of the birth of the atomic bomb.

The advent of the atomic bomb appeared to fully validate the Douhet school of thought. Here was a weapon to bring about offensive air strikes that were utterly devastating, and without comparison in human history. The advocates of Douhet pointed to the Strategic Air Command and its combat record as irrefutable evidence of the superiority of the Douhet concept. Actually, if we were to plot a line reflecting, by its rise and fall, the effectiveness of the Douhet concept, we would find that it was at the peak of its validity when first propounded, in the 1920's. At that time,

[3] *Time,* July 28, 1941.

there was no defense in prospect against manned aircraft attack resolutely delivered. Gradually, however, the primitive defenses improved. Interceptors and antiaircraft artillery made heavy bomber strikes more and more costly. The Luftwaffe was the first to learn that there is more to air power than an all-out bombing offensive. The British had foreseen the value of the interceptor, and so the world's greatest manned aircraft battle, the Battle of Britain, was decided in their favor. When the German Panzer Divisions reached the English Channel, all that stood between them and the decision in land battle that they sought was the defensive power of the Royal Air Force.

Schweinfurt was another test case. The Schweinfurt factories produced ball bearings, vital to the continued German war effort. We made two great bombing attacks on Schweinfurt in the fall of 1943. Reported an observer:

... [We] met what was in fact (though it was never so announced) one of the major defeats of the war.

Many theories had to be abandoned. Even with the Flying Fortresses (the B-17) and the almost equally powerful B-24 Liberator the losses had proved prohibitive. . . .

. . . in the grim conclusion of the U.S. Strategic Bombing Survey "there is no evidence that the attacks on the ball bearing industry had any measurable effect on essential war production."[4]

As the war came to an end, the U.S. Strategic Bombing Survey was appointed to move in the wake of the advancing armies and assess the results of our bombing effort. The findings were reported in over two hundred detailed reports. They were never, in my opinion, given the recognition that they deserved. One of the most interesting aspects of our bombing effort was that German production increased in the same ratio as our bombing effort until late in 1944—until "well after the ground armies were ashore to make good the job at which the airplanes had been unsuccessful."[5]

The foregoing is not to say that air power did not make a contribution to victory. Quite the contrary, air power was the most

[4] *Arms and Men,* Walter Millis.
[5] *Ibid.*

significant entity of our war power in World War II. Without it, we never could have established ourselves on the Normandy Peninsula, and we might not have established ourselves in southern Europe. But air power was most effective as a component of our over-all war power, not as an independent entity:

> This dumping of enormous quantities of high explosive directly upon civilian homes, factories, power and communications facilities, and upon the cowering people who lived in or manned them, was perhaps the most striking feature of the Second War; it produced ruins more vast and somber than those of antiquity, of a kind which civilized man had never expected to see again. But if it was the machine's most gruesome and dramatic contribution to warfare, it was by no means militarily the most significant. The combination of the tank and the tactical airplane continued to dominate most theaters down to the end."[6]

One additional factor worthy of note has been the loss of attacking aircraft from ground fires. Loss to surface fire as a percentage of all operational aircraft losses has gone up steadily, reaching its peak in Korea. With the advent of the surface-to-air nuclear missile, it will continue to rise and unquestionably will make prohibitive the use of manned aircraft against missiles. The atomic bomb of 1945, therefore, did not lie on the rising curve of manned combat aircraft effectiveness, for it represented a new order of fire power, and—as we were soon to learn in the missile era—defensive as well as offensive fire power. Douhet had become obsolete almost before the ink was dry on his book in 1923.

The true lesson of the airplane in World War II is that, like other forms of mobility in the past, air mobility is most useful when employed to move man and his means of waging war to the area of decision, and there to continue to work closely with him. As we reached the fall of 1944, hundreds of bomber aircraft were idle for lack of targets and still the German forces fought on. At the same time, our own forces were stopped for lack of logistical support, while every air transport and fighter bomber that could be flown was committed to battle.

[6] *Ibid.*

One immediate consequence of our failure to understand the lessons of World War II was the separation of our air force and land force at the very time that they should have been becoming more closely associated. Only the Marine Corps retained an integrated land-air team. The Army and Air Force separation proved very costly, as we learned in Korea. Now, belatedly, we are searching for a solution, through reorganization, to the problems and fratricidal bickerings that have followed in the wake of that separation.

The very nature of the media, the land, sea and air, in which the separate services sought to operate with independence denied them that independence. They were then, and were later to become even more, mutually interdependent. Air power and land power, like air power and sea power, are inseparable. They are part of each other.

But our Armed Forces had little time to ponder the lessons of World War II, so many were the problems that were thrust upon them in its wake. They realized that they had not been as ready as they should have been when the war came. There was general satisfaction, however, with the way in which science and industry had teamed up with the military. A number of new combat concepts had been born and brought to full fruition as a direct result of this close teamwork. Among them were airborne operations, large-scale amphibious operations, strategic air operations, and our far-reaching carrier task force operations. All were brought from prewar maneuver concepts to full-blown combat techniques. And the success of all of them was directly attributable to the contributions of science and the tremendous capacity of our American industry.

We were confronted at once at war's end with the atomic bomb and the concept of associating this with an independent air arm. Few people were well informed on nuclear matters. The Smythe report, although a good technical paper, was not a book for general consumption. Some of the first books to appear caused considerable misunderstanding and little was written on the character of nuclear weapons of the future decade. Even the titles had a ring of alarm; for example, *No Place to Hide* and *The Absolute Weapon*. Out of this lack of awareness of the public of the real meaning of nuclear weapons grew a conviction, and it was fostered by industrial and service support, that the most effective employment of nuclear weapons would be in the same combination of plane and bomb that destroyed Hiroshima. And we found ourselves, at the outset of 1946, committed to two clearly divergent courses of military preparation for the future. We were going to build up our nuclear striking forces on one hand, while we cut back our "conventional" forces on the other.

Even today, little over ten years later, much that was then written has a hysterical ring:

We now have enough improved atomic weapons to immobilize the Russian nation. . . . a staggering proportion of the inhabitants of Russia's key cities—millions of persons—can be killed or maimed in the first raid. . . . this terrible retaliation will surely come if Russia attacks the United States or another of the free nations. . . .[7]

Later, turning to the problem of "conventional" forces, this author says: "Choosing to fight Russia with divisions is like choosing to fight a lion with a bowie knife." Less than two years later, the Russians were to choose the weapons, not we. The initiative was theirs. It still is.

The real problem was caused by a dwindling budget and the same writer got to the heart of the problem several months later:

We cannot afford a choice of arms by buying all kinds of weapons. We cannot maintain in readiness the world's largest army, the world's largest navy and the world's largest air force. We cannot spend much more than 18 billions a year on our military establishment and remain economically healthy.[8]

Less than a year and a half later, we were in the Korean War, and our annual budget in that war reached more than fifty billion

[7] "The Facts Which Must Prevent War," William Bradford Huie, *The Reader's Digest*, December, 1948.
[8] *Ibid.*

101

dollars. In the same article, the author finally proposed a formula that would "assure our allies and the Kremlin that we intend to maintain a constant, well-advertised, undisputed, five-year advantage over Russia in air-atomic weapons." Six months later, the Soviets fired their first nuclear device. It was five years ahead of our estimates. Still, we believed in the efficacy of the concept, and as we continued to build up our nuclear striking power, we cut back on our other forces. So mesmerized were we by the overwhelming strength at our disposal that we began to think of it in absolute terms. It would be sufficient unto itself. Writing in February of 1949, Major Alexander de Seversky gave it the ultimate support:

> Today the air has become the primary medium of global power. An air force capable of commanding the skies can enforce its will on everything below. . . .
> The current program of defense through balanced forces operating from a chain of bases means only one thing; the perpetuation of the methods of the last war.[9]

Somehow it escaped him entirely that he was perpetuating the methods of the last war in insisting on the manned nuclear bomber, of Hiroshima vintage, as an exclusively unique and absolute weapons system instead of searching for the innovations that would in the future allow us to live with nuclear weapons and win a nuclear war, after the Soviets acquired a nuclear capability. And our scientists assured us that they would acquire a nuclear capability.

At the time, in the years immediately following the war, it seemed to many that the real air-power lesson of World War II was in air mobility. Yet our capability in this field was diminishing rapidly, as our bomber strength increased. Having studied the lessons of World War II and having related these to the growing Soviet intransigence and our own international commitments, it seemed to me that air transportation would be as important as or perhaps more important than bombers. This is not to say that we

[9] "Peace Through Air Power," *The Reader's Digest*, February, 1949.

would not need both, for we would, but we could not afford to eliminate either. Yet this is what our growing bomber capability tended to do. I wrote an article on the subject in late 1948 and submitted it to the Department of Defense for clearance. It was returned with "a nonconcurrence in its publication and a number of specific items to which the Air Force objects." Some of these follow:

We will need large strategic aircraft, bigger and of different types than those now being used in "Vittles" [Berlin airlift] in order to move our war power to economical striking range of the enemy. . . .

Failing to realize this, and putting all of our dollars in one airplane will invite disaster. . . .

When man develops the means to move his war power entirely through the air with no loss of its striking effectiveness, he will begin to realize the full potential of air power. . . .

. . . would our leaders, in any future war, use the bomb against the people of countries that are and have been our friends but that now, unfortunately, are occupied by the forces of the USSR and her satellites? . . .

The strategic bomber is the ballista to be employed on a global scale. The ballista was but a small part of war power and so is the big bomber. In addition to bombers and fighters, we need transports, as many types as there are missions to perform. . . .

Lured by the fascination and glamour of the big bombers to the state where we neglect the remainder, and by far the most important part of air power, is to invite disaster. And that is just what we are doing today.

Included in the material objected to for publication were verbatim extracts from the United States Strategic Bombing Report:

From examination of the records and personalities in the ball-bearing industry, the user industries and the testimony of war production officials, there is no evidence that the attacks on the ball-bearing industry had any measurable effect on the essential war production. . . .

Aircraft acceptances were higher in March, the month after the heaviest attack, than they were in January, the month before. They continued to rise.

When we refuse even to allow another point of view to be expressed we are in trouble, and trouble became apparent sooner than we expected. In the meantime, we continued to build up our strategic bombing effort at the expense of our other forces. The B-50 followed the B-29, and it in turn was followed by the B-36. The latter were recently thrown away as being of no further value, either for combat or for scrap.

Returning to the lessons of World War II, in administration and personnel handling there was also much for the Army and Navy to learn. The expansion from the peacetime establishment had been unprecedented. The Army, for example, had increased from a quarter of a million to over eight million men. It had mobilized and trained sixty-nine infantry divisions, twenty armored divisions and five airborne divisions, with the thousands of service and support units needed to back them up. Sir Winston Churchill spoke glowingly of the effort when he visited the Pentagon in 1946:

I greatly admired the manner in which the American Army was formed. I think it was a prodigy of organization, of improvisation. There have been many occasions when a powerful state has wished to raise great armies, and with money and time, and discipline and loyalty that can be accomplished. Nevertheless the rate at which the small American Army of only a few hundred thousand men, not long before the war, created the mighty force of millions of soldiers, is a wonder of military history. . . . I saw the creation of this mighty force—this mighty Army—victorious in every theater against the enemy in so short a time and from such a very small parent stock. This is an achievement which the soldiers of every other country will always study with admiration and envy.[10]

This great expansion was possible only because of the excellent National Guard and the organized Reserves. And to my mind, one of the truly great contributions of the prewar system was the ROTC. An army is not one mite better than its leaders, and without the ROTC we would never have had the leaders that we needed so badly. I have known thousands of young ROTC officers in battle and out, and I consider that the nation owes them a

[10] *Military Heritage of America*, Colonel R. E. Dupuy and Colonel T. N. Dupuy.

great debt of gratitude. It does not take a long memory to recall the troubles the ROTC had in continuing the support of its program between the wars. Frequently the object of campus puns, it was not appreciated until war came; but when war did come, the ROTC came through. In addition to the ROTC, both the Army and the Navy had an extensive service school system that contributed directly to the capability of the services to grow rapidly.

When the war came to an end, the services were faced with a problem perhaps more serious than that at the beginning. The Navy shrank from a strength of three and one-third million men in 1945 to less than a million in 1946. Ships had to be decommissioned and mothballed, bases and facilities closed down and stocks disposed of all over the world. The Army, from a strength of eight and one-quarter million in 1945, was reduced to less than two million in 1946.

The system of demobilizing the Army, known as the "point system," deserves a word. It was based upon allowing an individual to leave the service when he acquired sufficient points, which in turn were based upon length of service, days of combat, decorations, etc. From a scientific point of view, it appeared to be sound and the troopers expressed a preference for it. However, it came close to destroying the military establishment. The system was put into operation at a time when the administrative burden was the greatest ever known in the history of the United States Army. At first, when only the few very high-point men left, the impact was not seriously felt. Soon, however, it began to cut into the very muscle and bone of the organization. I should add, at this point, that the buck had been passed down to the field and unit commanders, who were informed that they could retain an individual otherwise eligible to leave if he was considered essential to the functioning of his organization. It takes little imagination to see how that worked.

When Private Jones's number came up, he wanted to go and no one could justify to him his "essentiality." He had been receiving dozens of letters from home about the return of the other heroes of the neighborhood, many of whom had presumably joined the service after he had, and his family just didn't understand why he didn't come back. Was it that he really didn't want to? You couldn't tell them that he was essential to the war effort now that the war was over; they knew better than that. Soon the telegrams and letters began to come from members of Congress and, surprisingly, letters came down the command chain from higher headquarters asking for an explanation as to why Private Jones was essential. The very headquarters that conceived the system and authorized exceptions now demanded to know why they were being made. Troop commanders quickly learned that there was but one thing to do—when a man's number came up, out he went. He went whether he was ready to go or not. It was the only sensible thing to do. In the meantime, organizations were rapidly being deprived of their key officers and noncommissioned officers, cooks, clerks, mechanics, and even medical personnel. Thousands of soldiers were in paper organizations awaiting return to the United States, with no officers that they knew in charge of them and with officers who did not know what they were in charge of. We were not demobilizing the Army, we were absolutely destroying it, and the Communists encouraged it. It was an experience without precedent for the regulars who were to stay, and frequently it taxed their abilities beyond any of the demands of the combat that they had just been through.

At about this time, the Doolittle Board began to look into the abuses of the so-called "caste" system. A Board of General Officers was appointed by the Department of the Army to travel about, and inquire into the low morale of the Army. A committee of outstanding jurists was appointed in Washington to look into the manual of courts martial to rid it of the abuses that, presumably, had been perpetuated during the war. Looking back, I am amazed that any army existed at all at the end of that period. From the viewpoint of the lower unit troop commanders, it was the most shocking and wrong thing that we have ever done in the history of our army—to demobilize it in such an irresponsible manner.

Little wonder that there were so many abuses, boards and investigations. Little wonder that there was hardly any army left.

B. THE GROWING IMPORTANCE OF AIR MOBILITY

It would seem, from all of the foregoing, that there could not have been much attention given to the lessons of the war. Nevertheless, there was considerable. The outstanding lesson to those of us in the airborne business was the growing importance of air mobility. We saw the Germans, in the Mediterranean, accomplish with one air-transported division a combat task that would have taken half a dozen infantry divisions. This occurred when they poised the German First Parachute Division at Marseilles at the time that we threatened to land in Sicily. Not knowing whether the landing would take place in Italy, Sardinia, Sicily or Corsica, and not having adequate reserves for all of those localities, they gave air mobility to the one division that they did have, and it was a very fine division indeed. We, too, had used air mobility to fly a division back and forth from Africa to Sicily and then to commit it to Salerno to tip the scales of battle in our favor. We had used air mobility to fly a division from England to the continent at the time of the Battle of the Bulge. We had used air mobility to resupply Bastogne and to supply General Patton's fast-moving 3rd Army. In fact, I have no doubt whatsoever that with half again as much air mobility we could have won the war in 1944 and occupied Berlin first.

Finding the means, and developing the techniques, to achieve efficient air mobility was the big challenge in the wake of World War II. It meant more than merely acquiring additional aircraft. It meant completely redesigning and streamlining the equipment of the airborne division, as well as re-equipping the Troop Carrier units of our Air Force.

Some of these lessons were summarized in *Airborne Warfare,* published in 1947; among them were the following:

American ingenuity and industry have met every requirement of our armed forces in the past. That it will in the future there is no doubt.

We have barely begun, however, to solve the problems of airborne transport and equipment. . . .

Organizations created to fight the last war better are not going to win the next.

What was Pearl Harbor in 1941, followed in six months by an amphibious effort at Midway, will, in the future, be a missile barrage followed in six minutes or six hours by an airborne attack. To even begin to cope with such a tactical situation, adequate, trained, and properly equipped troop-carrier and airborne forces must be available.

Never again may troops concentrate as they have in the past. For example, a build-up such as that for the Normandy assault would suffer a most disastrous scorching if caught under an atomic bombing or missile attack. Never again may troops and ships congest a beach as they did. . . . Not if they are to survive the counterattack of missiles certain to be directed against them.

We are at a critical point in the evolution of military science. We are in a competition, a competition in which the winner will emerge from the present crisis with the best means and methods of fully using the space about our planet.

Airborne troops are our best national security and the world's most promising hope for international security.

The knowledge of the existence of a well trained airborne army, capable of moving anywhere on the globe on short notice, available to an international security body such as the United Nations, is our best guarantee of lasting peace.[11]

Air mobility in 1947 began to take new form. The workhorse of World War II had been the DC-3. It either delivered troops by parachute or it landed, requiring about three to four thousand feet of runway. Replacement of this airplane began immediately afterward with the "Flying Boxcar," the C-82. This airplane was designed to meet a requirement of carrying ten tons of cargo one thousand miles and return. The rear of the plane was so designed that the entire cargo could be delivered by parachute in one piece, provided large enough parachutes could be developed— and they were. Beyond the Flying Boxcar, other air transports were in prospect, some of considerably greater range and more global than local in their performance.

The performance of the DC-3 was augmented in World War II

[11] *Airborne Warfare*, James M. Gavin, published by the *Infantry Journal*.

by towing gliders behind it. These were of tubular construction, covered with fabric or, in the case of the British gliders, with plywood. They proved highly inflammable in heavy flak. I flew as an observer in the airborne operation that crossed the Rhine in March of 1945, and I was appalled by the sight of gliders and planes going down in flames. I remember at one time counting twenty-three, all burning like torches and falling rapidly.

After the war, we sought to develop an all-metal glider. Two gliders were produced and their cost convinced us that adding small engines would be a worth-while investment. Thus was born the STOL idea, the "short takeoff and landing" aircraft. It was officially called an assault plane, and it was intended to replace the glider and thus reinforce a parachute assault by air-landing heavy cargo and supplies in the battle area. It appeared, therefore, to have tremendous potential. A third form of air mobility had its genesis in this early postwar period, the VTOL, "vertical takeoff and landing." Thirteen Bell helicopters were assigned to the 82nd Airborne Division for evaluation and tests in 1946. We did not know what to do with them at first and considered them for possible replacements for the L-4, or artillery spotting planes used so extensively in World War II. We put quite a bit of time into them and it soon became apparent that we had in our hands an air vehicle of great versatility. Additional types were in prospect, and we urged their procurement as a matter of priority.

Efforts to obtain both new types of air vehicles ran into difficulty at once. In the first place, they were so radically new that there was little interest in them in the newly established Air Force. In the second place, with the establishment of the Air Force, the Army had agreed to procure all of its air vehicles through the new service; thus the Air Force assumed the responsibility of judging the air-worthiness of the Army's expressed requirements. And there was almost as much reluctance to go into these new forms of air mobility in the Army as there was in the Air Force. Most of our senior Army officers had experience in combat with other than air mobile units and they looked with considerable skepticism on the enthusiasm of these zealots who were insisting, sometimes with considerable exaggeration, that everything in the Army had to fly. As anyone knew who had fought extensive Panzer formations, much more was needed to win a land battle than parachute and glider troops. But there was no doubt that our reserves had to be air-transportable. It was a frustrating experience, trying to sell the idea of air mobility and its rapidly expanding field of tactical application.

Both the helicopter and the assault plane seemed to have intriguing possibilities. I talked about them at our service schools and on our boards and urged their procurement in numbers. In 1948 I was appointed president of the Army's Airborne Panel, which was charged with evaluating our present situation and proposing solutions to the problems of the future. But we were soon to learn that all of the studies, panels and boards were of no avail if we could not convince our colleagues in the Air Force of the soundness of our air ideas. A good segment of the Air Force, particularly those who had been with Troop Carriers during the war, thought as we did, but they were rapidly being subordinated to the Big Bomber generals. And while it is easy to accuse the Big Bomber people of poor judgment, it would not be fair to do so, because they too were working within the tight framework of a limited budget. Many of them in decision-making positions were intellectually convinced that we could afford but one thing—more and bigger bombers matched to a nuclear retaliatory power. On the other hand, many of them sensed the sterility of such a program, feeling that we needed greater versatility if we were to cope with the Soviets; and they realized that when ultimately the USSR matched our retaliatory power, we would be in a very dangerous position if we had no other capablity. We persisted, therefore, in trying to convince the Air Force of the soundness of our thinking, and of course this was necessary since they passed upon the air-worthiness of our air vehicle requirements.

In the case of the helicopter, I followed the project through the various echelons of the military establishment, finally discussing it personally with the Director of Requirements of the USAF. Our discussions were of a rather protracted nature, extending over the better part of a day on the trip that we took through the West Coast aircraft industries. He finally became exasperated with my insistence and said, "I am the Director of Requirements and I will determine what is needed and what is not. The helicopter is aerodynamically unsound. It is like lifting oneself by one's boot straps. It is no good as an air vehicle and I am not going to procure any. No matter what the Army says, I know that it does not need any."

Thus the door was slammed in our faces as we sought to enter an entirely new, and absolutely essential, field of combat air mobility. Thanks to a last-minute crash program, and the programs of the Department of the Navy and the Marine Corps, we were able to save thousands of lives by helicopter in Korea. But more than that, the helicopter could have given us a great mobility advantage over the North Koreans and Chinese Communist forces in Korea if we had been allowed to develop its great potential. Now we are "discovering" the tactical wonders of sky cavalry, ten years too late.

The history of the assault plane was equally depressing. Michael Stroukoff of the Chase Aircraft Company developed the first useful assault plane, the C-122, which soon grew up to be the C-123. It met all specifications and far outperformed any competitor in the field. Takeoff and landings of eight-ton combat payloads out of pastures and cultivated fields on a few hundred feet were accomplished with little difficulty. Despite repeated requests from the Department of the Army, and ultimately from the Chief of Staff and Secretary of the Army himself, assault transport procurement was delayed year after year. Actually, none were ever procured in the original configuration. A much more sophisticated airplane called an assault plane was finally procured as a replacement for the Flying Boxcar long after the

Korean War. Thus another field of air mobility remained un-exploited as we continued to drift toward a war on the Asiatic mainland, with a primitively equipped Asiatic army.

C. THE ROLE OF NUCLEAR WEAPONS

Fission in 1946 posed the greatest challenge to our military planners that we had ever known. So great was it, in fact, that military thinking seemed, at the outset, to be paralyzed by its magnitude. I know of no one, for the first few years following the war, who questioned that its military use would be exclusively in bombs. The first atomic bomb was of such size that the B-29 that carried it had to be especially modified for the purpose. Such being the case, our earliest nuclear thinking in the Army was in terms of how to defend against use of the bomb on us, and how to team up with nuclear bombers in the offense.

It seemed possible to match nuclear bomber attack with a parachute assault, provided we offered no nuclear targets to the enemy while staging the operation. The first standard operation procedures to accomplish this were tried in the 82nd Airborne Division in 1947. We simply drew a five-mile circle around our takeoff airfields. Troops were restrained from entering the area of the circle until minutes before takeoff; thus they were kept dispersed and concentrated only at the moment of loading. Little thought was given to tactical use by the Soviets of nuclear weapons in a surface-to-surface role since they did not have such weapons and it was unlikely that they would for quite a few years.

However, the results of the Bikini tests in 1947 began to suggest new fields of possible tactical application. Certainly the results of those tests made clear that the large amphibious operations such as the Normandy operation would never again be possible against an enemy equipped with nuclear weapons—just as nuclear weapons could have been used effectively against the Normandy defenses. Thus the pattern of future attacks seemed to be emerging as a combined airborne-nuclear assault, using tactical weapons. This concept found little receptivity in the Air Force, however, which was discouraging since the Air Force would have to provide both the airlift and the air-delivered weapons. In fact, it would be fair to say that it encountered something close to actual hostility, because it diverted part of the small stockpile of fission material to tactical rather than strategic uses. And at the time—the latter half of the forties—an increasing segment of military and public thinking was becoming committed to nuclear strategic retaliation as an exclusively valid policy.

"Urban" bombing was accepted as a sound and proper strategy in most military and civilian circles. This profoundly disturbed me, for obviously the strategy would only remain valid so long as the Soviets were not in a position to deliver nuclear strikes against our own urban areas. When the day did come that they could, and it was inevitable that it would, then the proper target for our nuclear striking forces would have to be the sources of Soviet nuclear strength, that is, their long-range striking air power. Further, to devote all of our nuclear striking power to urban areas, even though we did so because we considered them to be the indices of industrial production and thus determinants of a war-making capability, would have overlooked the impressive and combat-ready array of Soviet "conventional forces" deployed ready to strike. I often asked the obvious question: What were we to do if cities in Western Europe were overrun? Destroy them, too? And if Western Europe or other areas friendly to us were to be occupied by the Soviets and slowly consumed into the Soviet system in the pattern of Estonia and Latvia, were we to destroy all those areas with nuclear weapons? These were questions that made one very unpopular for the asking, and questions that were never answered.

I became increasingly interested in these problems. It was with great pleasure, therefore, that I received orders to the Weapons Systems Evaluation Group in March of 1949. The Director of WSEG, Dr. Philip Morse, assigned me the project of studying the possible tactical employment of nuclear weapons. I devoted the entire summer of 1949 to reading everything on the subject that I could get my hands on and visiting our laboratories and talking to our scientists. By summer's end, nuclear weapons became more understandable to me and I drafted a paper on the subject. I had become convinced that nuclear weapons had a tremendous field for tactical application, in fact, in the long run, probably the most promising field of all. One of the recommendations in the study was that we should reconsider our then current national policy of allocating all fissionable material to strategic use. This recommendation was very unpopular with my Air Force colleagues and, for the study to be accepted, had to be stricken from it. It made little difference since the study was stamped "Top Secret" and promptly buried in the archives. Fortunately, the publication the following year of the government's unclassified *The Effects of Nuclear Weapons* released much of the information.

In September of 1949, the White House announced the firing of the first Soviet nuclear device. This development was profoundly disturbing to many of our scientists, who had assumed that we had at least five more years of grace. Now the Soviets were in a position to undertake a pattern of nuclear diplomacy as they were to do later in missile diplomacy.

I was called into conference in the fall of 1949 to consider the problem of whether or not to develop a thermonuclear weapon. The problem had been referred to WSEG. Our scientists had been discussing it for some time and their views ranged from, on one hand, "It would be like trying to light wet asbestos in a windstorm and thus it is not worth trying," to "It is feasible and we should go ahead with it as a matter of high priority." Dr. Oppenheimer was present at one of the conferences and he expressed a view in which I found myself in complete argreement. That is, that more important than trying to devise new ways and means of destroying a bigger portion of the human race, we should try to find ways and means of living with the powers we

114

had already created. This was quite fundamental, in that our manpower and nuclear resources were limited and by diverting them to a thermonuclear program, we would, to some extent, be taking away from the other weapons programs. If the urban bombing concept were to remain policy, and thermonuclear weapons were to be added to it, and if that concept were morally and militarily unsound in the beginning, it certainly would be more so with the H-bomb added. I believed that it was unsound and that Dr. Oppenheimer's views were valid. I went to the office of Major General Kenneth Nichols, who had been a deputy to General Groves in the Manhattan Project, and discussed the technical aspects of the program with him. He pointed out that the basic calculations for a thermonuclear weapon had been made sometime ago and that very likely they were now in the hands of the Soviets. Further, that this information was known to Dr. Fuchs and to Pontecorvo, both of whom had gone over to the USSR. He was convinced that the Soviets had a capability of developing a thermonuclear weapon. I had to conclude reluctantly, therefore, that if this were so and if we did not develop one, our position would be very bad indeed. Therefore, I decided that we had to undertake an H-bomb program as a matter of highest priority and I so recommended in WSEG.

In the meantime, however, an increasing number of people were talking about the possible tactical uses of nuclear weapons. An advance study group in the JCS headed by Brigadier General Don Zimmerman, USAF, had done particularly good work in this area. The scientists, too, were beginning to see the possibilities of much smaller sizes and smaller yields. The economics of the use of fissionable materials were being studied also. I recall a figure used by General Zimmerman that when we exceeded twenty-five B-29 bombers delivering high explosives instead of using one carrying an atomic bomb, we were making an uneconomical use of our resources.

Thus we approached the Korean crisis, grossly lacking air mobility and exclusively preoccupied with our newest form of fire power, nuclear fire power, packaged for strategic use. However, even though so packaged, it could have been used tactically. And when the Korean situation broke and the prospects of the defeat of the 8th Army were real and compelling, General Nichols and I went to the office of General Ridgway and urged that he recommend to the Chief of Staff that he in turn recommend to the President that we use nuclear weapons against the North Korean forces. It would have been militarily inexcusable to allow the 8th Army to be destroyed without even using the most powerful weapons in our arsenal. Yet, we almost did so! We had already made two combat bombing strikes of about 175 B-29s without decisive results. The situation in the summer of 1950 offered us a number of well worth-while tactical nuclear targets if we had had the moral courage to make the decision to use them. But this we did not have for reasons that have been the subject of much soul-searching ever since. Dr. Henry A. Kissinger's *Nuclear Weapons and Foreign Policy* treats the subject well. To a large segment of our military planners, Korea just simply should not have taken place. "It has been remarked more than once that had the Korean War not actually taken place, we could never have believed that it could have." And: "The assumption behind our military planning had been that our wars would be fought against a principal enemy and a major challenge, but that our forces-in-being need only be powerful enough to gain us the time to mobilize our industrial potential. This doctrine presupposed two related contingencies: that other powers would bear the initial brunt of aggression and that the threat would be unambiguous."[12]

D. GROWING SOVIET INTRANSIGENCE

In the meantime, while schisms were developing in the Pentagon with the attendant frustrations and delay of programs that should have been advanced, our State Department was dealing with a Soviet government that was becoming increasingly in-

[12] *Nuclear Weapons and Foreign Policy*, Dr. Henry A. Kissinger.

transigent. Many of us had felt that we could live with the Soviets without serious conflict in the postwar period; if there were to be differences, we believed that they could be dealt with through the machinery of the United Nations. This would, of course, have depended upon the continued good will of the Soviets. That they were of a different point of view was made apparent as early as 1945, when *Pravda* published a statement by Stalin, that first had been made to the American Labor Delegation visiting Moscow in September, 1927:

> . . . In the further progress of development of the international revolution, two world centres will be formed: The Socialist centre, attracting to itself all the countries gravitating towards Socialism, and the Capitalist centre, attracting to itself all the countries gravitating towards Capitalism. The fight between these two centres for the conquest of world economy will decide the fate of capitalism and communism throughout the whole world, for the final defeat of world capitalism means the victory of socialism in the arena of world economy. . . .

It was like a pirate running up the skull and crossbones pennant as a declaration of irrevocable intent before closing in the attack. But our leaders continued in their efforts to find a working arrangement with Stalin. From the beginning, they were baffled by the complete and continuing non-co-operation of the Soviet Union; and while the Soviet Union became increasingly difficult to deal with in international discussions, it pursued a course of relentless aggression. To be sure, the United Nations succeeded in forcing its withdrawal from Iran, but this was, now in retrospect, hardly a serious setback. It soon made manifest its intention to gobble entirely the small European nations it had occupied at the end of hostilities. Incidents such as the unwarranted shooting down of an American C-47 airplane by the Yugoslavs, then fully committed to Soviet policies, kept the problem before the public. It was becoming evident that the "hearts and flowers" period of the postwar honeymoon had come to an end.

For better or for worse, we had to face up to the fact that the teachings of Lenin were Soviet policy once again, and that according to this policy either we or the Soviets would survive, not both. "The existence of the Soviet Republic next to a number of imperialist states for a long time is unthinkable."[13] And while they prattled peace, they prepared for war and engaged in war. We called it cold war, but to the Soviets it was war, pure and simple, that they liked to describe, Orwell-like, as peace.

E. THE DEVELOPMENT OF A COLLECTIVE SECURITY PROGRAM

Since collective security was the basis of Free World planning, it soon became apparent to all the Western nations that they would have to look to their own future survival through coalition agreements. The Rio Treaty of 1947 brought together the majority of the nations of the Western Hemisphere. In the spring of 1948, five nations of Western Europe—Britain, France, Belgium, Luxemburg and the Netherlands—banded together to form a Western Union, agreeing to come to the aid of each other in the event of an armed attack in Europe. Great Britain, which had been giving support to the Greek government, found itself in difficulties and the United States agreed, upon the request of the Greek government, to come to their assistance. Turkey, likewise, was in need of assistance and thus was born the Truman Doctrine. But more was needed than military aid, for many nations of the Free World were still suffering severely from the economic effects of the war. And since low standards of living and attendant widespread discontent offer fertile fields for Communist exploitation, the United States considered ways and means of coming to the assistance of nations in need of such aid. The Marshall Plan was proposed and the United States firmly embarked upon a policy of containing Communism through economic assistance to countries in need. In furtherance of our goal of achieving collective security, President Truman in addressing Congress on March 17, 1948, proposed that the United States should match the deter-

[13] Lenin.

mination of the free countries of Europe by doing our part to help them. The following summer, Congress adopted a resolution reaffirming our policy as follows:

to achieve international peace and security through the United Nations so that armed force shall not be used except in common interest, and advise(d) the President that it was the intent of the Senate that the United States should associate itself with such regional and other collective arrangements as are based on continuous and effective self-help and mutual aid, and as affect its national security.

There followed the North Atlantic Treaty, the first peacetime European military alliance into which the United States has entered.

Thus our international commitments, with attendant military obligations, continued to grow. That they were absolutely necessary there is no doubt—our survival lies in the direction of collective security. By mid-1950 we were committed to defensive arrangements with fourteen NATO partners, and with twenty of our Latin-American neighbors under the provisions of the Rio Treaty. Our military assistance program continued to expand, ultimately involving bilateral defense agreements with forty-six different nations. The Anzus Treaty was signed in 1951 and the SEATO Treaty three years later. Separate mutual defense treaties were signed with the Philippines, Korea and the Republic of China, and a bilateral mutual security treaty with Japan. Thus the policy of achieving security through collective agreements has continued since World War II until the present.

From the viewpoint of the military planner these treaties are what they purport to be—commitments to do something, or to provide something, or both. The wording of the treaty determines the exact nature of the obligational burden that our nation assumes. In general, we agreed in most of the treaties to participate in the common defense in the event of aggression. This implies a capability on our part to do so, and this means military strength in being or in immediate prospect. Thus to a planner it would appear that as our obligations increased, our military strength to support those obligations should have increased also. The contrary was the case.

Our collective security program and our own military readiness programs were quite clearly divergent in the spring of 1950. The Army strength had been reduced from over eight million at the end of World War II to 593,000. The Navy had been reduced from over three million to 381,538, the Marine Corps from in excess of 474,000 to 74,000 and the Air Force from in excess of two million to slightly over 411,000. The Army stretched its strength on occupation duty from Japan to Berlin. Four divisions at reduced strength were in the Far East, and they had skeletonized and stored their heavy combat equipment. One division plus a constabulary force was in Europe.

We had increased our strength tremendously in one category— our nuclear retaliatory capacity. Unfortunately this had been accomplished at the expense of our other forces, a trend that had continued to preoccupy our senior Army and Navy leaders since the war. Cautioning against a tendency to overlook our other forms of military power of lesser magnitude, General Bradley testified before a committee of the 80th Congress in 1948, "Numerous intelligent and thinking people in many quarters have gained the impression that the atom bomb and other weapons of mass destruction have all but eliminated the need for an army in any war which may come." And more alarming than the exclusive reliance that we seemed to be placing in our nuclear bombs, was a by-product of the trend. It was the curtailment of the research and development programs of the so-called "conventional" forces. At a time when we should have been avid in our search for new means and new methods to match the dynamic shifting pattern of war we were, in fact, closing our minds. Never was the saying more true that a nation's greatest danger is in winning a past war, for nothing so stultifies military thinking as victory. We continued to adhere blindly to the ageless pattern of trying to do better the thing that we had done best in the last days of the last war. There is an initiative in military technology, as there is in military operations, and we frequently reassured ourselves that the initiative was ours. Sadly, we soon learned that we had it neither technologically nor operationally.

Spring of 1950 came to Washington with the cherry blossoms, the annual visitation of the DAR, and thousands of school children trooping the halls of Congress and ascending the Washington Monument. No ominous signs of trouble ahead disturbed the peaceful scene. The Armed Forces looked their best as they swung down Constitution Avenue. Reporting on the scene in the issue of May 29, 1950, *Time* stated:

> The Armed Forces Day parade in Washington, marching past Harry Truman and other dignitaries, perhaps marked the last time the three services would be roughly equal in strength and cost. From now on, the U.S. Navy and Air Force would expand, and the Army would likely get less, as the U. S. fitted its needs and skills into the common pool of Western Defense.

General satisfaction with our state of readiness was the feeling of the moment. A few weeks earlier the Secretary of Defense in defending his fat-cutting budget had made the comment, "Our defenses were in grand shape," and "are adequate to the needs of the hour." Thus in the traditional pattern of the Republic, we drifted to the brink of war, inadequately prepared psychologically and physically. This time the war's first blow was to fall on our own forces.

F. KOREA—AND LIMITED WAR

It fell on June 25, 1950, when the North Koreans struck across the 38th Parallel. Acting promptly, and making one of the most courageous and farsighted decisions in our national history, President Truman sought and obtained the support of the United Nations. At first it was hoped that our air and naval power would bring the aggression to a halt. Many, in fact, were confident that it would. I was a member of the Weapons Systems Evaluation

Group at the time, and the senior Air Force member, upon learning that General MacArthur had called for the use of ground troops, remarked: "The old man must be off his rocker. When the Fifth Air Force gets to work on them, there will not be a North Korean left in North Korea."

For the Army, trading its lives for time and space, it was a bitter and costly experience. Six reinforced North Korean People's Army divisions came driving across the 38th Parallel toward Seoul. They were spearheaded by one hundred Russian-built T-34 tanks and amply supported by Russian-provided planes. In three days, Seoul fell and the North Korean Army's momentum southward continued. General MacArthur scraped together two companies of infantry and a battery of artillery and some supporting weapons, including "six 2.36 bazooka teams (whose weapons, it was discovered, could not stop the T-34 tank)."[14] He had the force flown to Korea; it was all that our limited airlift could transport. Thus the great might of this industrial nation, five years after the defeat of the Axis powers, could do no better than to airlift two rifle companies and a battery of artillery to meet six aggressor divisions.

We paid for it dearly. It is easy to read now of the magnificent resistance, gaining precious time for us, but this does not excuse our lack of vision and lack of readiness. The impact of the Korean War reached every home and hamlet in America. Thousands of veterans of World War II were recalled as the war went on, fought on Communist terms, until 1953. Our casualties when it ended amounted to 142,154 and those of the United Nations forces, other than United States, to 17,190. Of the United States's casualties, in excess of 96 per cent were ground troops. Thus the "Bigger bang for a buck" and "We will use machines and save manpower" were brought to a paradoxical conclusion: our casualties were once again mostly in the ground forces who were not expected to have to do much of the fighting. But from a tech-

[14] *Military Heritage of America, op. cit.*

nological point of view, the real tragedy of Korea was that this great nation, with its scientific resources and tremendous industrial capacity, had to accept combat on the terms laid down by a rather primitive Asiatic army. Neither our imagination nor vision in the years since World War II had given us a combat capability that would provide the technical margin of advantage that we needed in land warfare to win decisively and quickly. That we could have gained this margin of advantage is clear now; that we didn't is the real tragedy of Korea.

There has probably been more critical comment, both oral and written, about Korea than of any war in our history. And it is understandable, for never have we suffered a tactical defeat of such magnitude as the defeat of the 8th Army at the hands of the Chinese in December of 1950. And rarely have our leaders shown such tactical brilliance as General MacArthur in planning and carrying out the Inchon operation. Furthermore the war developed profound arguments of policy that were without precedent in our political-military history.

The most hotly discussed point of all was whether or not, in seeking victory—and this General MacArthur properly defined as the object of war—General MacArthur should be allowed to expand the magnitude of the United Nations' effort. As he expressed it, "The general definition which for many decades has been accepted was that war was the ultimate process of politics; and that when all other political means failed, you then go to force; and when you do that, the balance of control . . . the main interest involved . . . is the control of the military. . . . I do unquestionably state that when men become locked in battle, there should be no artifice under the name of politics, which should decrease their chances of winning. . . ."[16] Victory was what he sought and victory was what he was to be denied, for in seeking it he would, as General Bradley argued, "tie down . . . our sea power and our air power . . . in an area that is not the critical strategic prize . . . this strategy would involve us in the wrong war, at the wrong place, at the wrong time, and with the wrong enemy."[15]

Somehow, the violence of the argument and the strong personalities involved tended to obscure the fundamental problem. It was not whether or not the war should have been allowed to expand as our commanders in the field sought victory. For there was little prospect of victory, once we were in it, short of total war, and this we did not want. And only total war could bring victory because we had neglected to develop and provide the technical means of winning anything but a total war, a total nuclear war. And Korea was not that kind of a war, nor were we willing to make it that kind of a war.

One frequently hears the expression in Washington, "We don't want another Korea." I do not know what the speakers mean by such a statement, nor am I sure that they do themselves. Referring to limited wars collectively, I once heard Secretary of Defense Charles E. Wilson say, "We can't afford to fight limited wars. We can only afford to fight a big war, and if there is one that is the kind it will be." If we cannot afford to fight limited wars then we cannot afford to survive, for that is the kind of a war we will be confronted with. That is the only kind that we can afford to fight. Certainly we don't want another Korea, not if it means exposing our forces to tactical defeat because of our preoccupation with a one-weapons-system strategy, nor because of self-imposed artificial restrictions upon the research and development programs of forces other than those associated with that one-weapons system. Nor do we want another Korea if it means our military thinking will be so preoccupied with past combat success that we lack the vision and energy to foresee the innovations that are essential to our combat success in the future.

Korea was a peripheral war and a limited war, a form of war to which we had given little thought. It would have been entirely possible between World War II and Korea to develop the tactical means to defeat the North Korean forces, and any force sent

[15] United States Senate, "Military Situation in the Far East."

to reinforce them, decisively and quickly, if we had invested sufficient of our national product in the undertaking. It was not an issue of embarking on a major war on the mainland of Asia and entering Manchuria and China. The issue was a limited one, limited in geographic area, in objectives and in the resources that the participating nations were willing to commit to the area. There is but one way to deal with such a war, and that is by having *superior* means at hand to respond to the aggression, swiftly and severely. That we obviously lacked.

G. INDO-CHINA AND LIMITED WAR

With the end of fighting in Korea in 1953 and the development of the "New Look" military policy by the new administration we reverted to the pre-Korean strategy. I do not recall this having been at any time officially acknowledged except as implied in the address of the Secretary of State to the Council on Foreign Relations in New York on January 12, 1954. In that address he said:

> So long as our basic policy concepts were unclear, our military leaders could not be selective in building our military power. If an enemy could pick his time and place and method of warfare—and if our policy was to remain the traditional one of meeting aggression by direct and local opposition—then we needed to be ready to fight in the Arctic and in the Tropics; in Asia, the Near East, and in Europe; by sea, by land, and by air; with old weapons and with new weapons. . . .
>
> But before military planning could be changed, the President and his advisers, as represented by the National Security Council, had to take some basic policy decisions. This has been done. The basic decision was to depend primarily upon a great capacity to retaliate, instantly, by means and at places of our choosing. Now the Department of Defense and the Joint Chiefs of Staff can shape our military establishment to fit what is our policy, instead of having to try to be ready to meet the enemy's many choices.

That it was more than mere implication soon became clear as the strength of the Army was drastically reduced. I was the Assistant to the Chief of Staff for Plans and Operations and later Deputy Chief of Staff of Plans during the cutback. If the initiative had been ours, and not that of the Communists, and if there had been no more "Koreas," all would have been well. Unfortunately, the initiative was not ours and the military planners were soon in difficulty again. As one of them I often thought of the lines from Stephen Vincent Benét's *John Brown's Body*. They were uttered by a disconsolate and angry Confederate as he described the frustrations of fighting the Yankees:

> (He) could whip five yanks with a palm leaf hat,
> Only the yanks won't fight like that.[16]

And so it went with us. We were a powerful nation but the Communists would not co-operate and lead to our strength.

Take Dien Bien Phu for example. To the French it seemed to offer the best tactical solution to the problem of protecting the Hanoi Delta, while at the same time providing a degree of protection to Laos. It was well organized for all-around defense. But it was static; so the tactical initiative was surrendered to the attacking Communists. At first the French did not appear to be too worried about its survival since they had almost unlimited power with which to support it. But when the battle was joined, as is always the case, it was man against man and all of the modern technology in the world could not tell friend from foe nor apply power with adequate discrimination.

There was much soul-searching and speculation among the Pentagon planners. It was important that the Army not be used, for this would be exactly contrary to national military policy. The Army itself had no illusions about the possibilities of an immaculate war, one disassociated from any other war. As soon as hostilities would start, thus tying down U.S. manpower in Indo-China, the Communists would start things up in Korea. So to the Army, if it went into Indo-China the nation would have to be prepared for a fair-sized war. This meant calling up quite a few National Guard divisions, recalling Reserves, starting pro-

---

[16] Published by Rinehart & Company, Inc. Copyright 1927, 1928 by Stephen Vincent Benét. Copyright renewed 1955, 1956 by Rosemary Carr Benét.

duction of ammunition, tanks, etc. Otherwise it would have been inviting disaster. On the other hand, why not use carrier-based aviation support? The French said that they had all of the tactical air support that they could use. Why not use SAC and nuclear support in a tactical role? We couldn't tell friend from foe and nuclear weapons would have destroyed everyone, French and Communists alike. It was a dilemma, but not uncharacteristic of every military situation with which the Communists were to confront us in the decade. It was finally decided that if anything was to be done the Army and the Marine Corps would have to do it, with the full support of the other services. General Ridgway directed a team of officers to go to Indo-China to look into the situation. Concurrently, planning went ahead in the Army staff. A proposal was finally presented to the Department of Defense. It was a statement of cost of the operation, including the steps that would have to be taken at once if the decision were made to go in. I understand that the situation was laid before the President; in any event, the decision was made not to go in.

Thus once again, the West had to accept something less than victory in a limited war with the Communists, in this case defeat. The same arguments were heard that echoed through the halls of the Pentagon during Korea. It would be the wrong war, at the wrong place, at the wrong time. It was exasperating. Wouldn't the Communists ever provide us with the right kind of a war? And we didn't want to start a war that would spread into the vastness of southern China, or Thailand, Burma or Malay. And so it went. Actually, Korea and Indo-China had one fundamental characteristic in common, one challenge that we must learn how to meet if we expect to survive. They were limited wars, in a limited area, so located as to make it difficult for either side to support profusely. There was no problem about the war spreading, unless we had to make it spread because of our inability to do anything else. We should have had the tactical means to strike and win, swiftly and severely. And, if in the past ten years we had spent even a small part of what we have spent in readying our forces for a one-strategy general war, in developing and procuring the means of dealing with limited war, we could have settled Korea and Dien Bien Phu quickly in our favor. Tactical nuclear missiles, sky cavalry, and increased assault airlift can contribute decisively to that kind of an operation. And as long as we neglect such developments we will be incapable of dealing with limited wars and we will continue to be nibbled to death.

Limited war is a more highly specialized form of combat than global nuclear war, and we had better realize it and do something about it. It makes little sense to assume that since one has the power to wage general war successfully, by using a little bit of that capability you have, *ipso facto,* a little war. A thermonuclear-equipped B-52 can contribute little more to the solution of a limited local war than a 155-mm. gun can contribute to the apprehension of a traffic violator.

To some, limited war differs from general war in that general war lasts longer. This is not true. Limited war is not a matter of time. It is limited in the objectives sought, the means employed and, usually, the area in which it is fought. Limited war may go on for many years, as Mao demonstrated in China. Furthermore, there may be several limited wars all going on at the same time. In fact, this is the most probable nature of future war: a slow, almost imperceptible transition of a bad economic and political situation into internal disorder. Arms will be provided by the Communists to the side they choose, and sometimes which side they choose is not very important. They will throw out the original leaders and substitute their own, including their own revolution of the "proletariat" at a time of their choosing. Thereafter, sufficient force will be used, until combating it no longer seems worth the effort to the West, or until the West is decisively defeated. To the Communists it is best to have several such conflagrations going at the same time, thus keeping the West preoccupied with its obligations under its collective security arrangements, and creating divisive forces in the United Nations, NATO, etc. These are the tactics of limited wars and they are carried

128

out in three dimensions. The fourth dimension, strategy, is skill-fully carried on at the same time. It is the propaganda war, for the ultimate objective of the Communists is the minds of men. Psychological pressures are built up demanding peace. Peace petitions such as the Stockholm petition are circulated. At the same time additional areas are softened up for penetration and occupation.

To cope with a Communist program of this nature requires good, imaginative, strategic planning, and highly specialized tactical forces. And they must be technically superior to any-thing that they encounter, decisively superior. Of the several functional areas in which a margin of tactical advantage may be found, mobility usually offers the greatest promise. However, intelligence, communications, and missile fire power all require special consideration. All of these subjects, in their relationship to limited war, have been slighted at best, and grossly neglected at worst, in our defense planning in the past ten years. Hence the dilemma—how to keep from losing limited wars without preparing to win them. It simply cannot be done.

H. PROJECT VISTA—"BRING THE BATTLE BACK TO THE BATTLEFIELD"

One of the early disappointments of the Korean War was the failure of our fighter bombers to provide more effective tactical air support. They had done superbly against the highly mecha-nized forces of the Axis powers in Europe and they were expected to do even better against the primitive Asiatic armies. The con-trary was the case; even horse cavalry divisions were able to move the length of North Korea and participate in the battles. At the direction of the Director of WSEG, I accompanied a small group of scientists to Korea in the fall of 1950 to look into the tactical air support situation. It was hoped that the scientists could come up with some new ideas, drawing on their unexcelled knowledge of scientific technology. Dr. Charles Lauritsen, Sr., Dr. William Shockley and Dr. Edward Bowles were the three scientists in the group. They were particularly gifted to con-

129

sider the problems at hand. Dr. Lauritsen, among other accomplishments, was a distinguished nuclear physicist. Dr. Shockley was developing the transistor for which he later received the Nobel Prize, and Dr. Bowles had been a scientific adviser to Secretary Stimson in World War II.

We arrived in Japan in early September of 1950 and after the necessary briefings in Tokyo, Drs. Lauritsen and Bowles and I joined the 7th Fleet for participation in the Inchon landings. Dr. Shockley remained in Tageu, where he developed an airborne loudspeaker for use in psychological warfare. The 7th Fleet group landed at Inchon by helicopter on D-plus-1 and thereafter accompanied the 1st Marine Division for a week. They joined the leading battalions and devoted almost their entire attention to the problems of tactical air support. The 1st Marine Division had an abundance of this support and knew how to use it. But after the initial landing opposition was rather light and we did not get to observe very many examples of its use. Following the first week at Inchon, we flew to Tokyo and then to the perimeter headquarters of the 8th Army at Tageu. The divisions in the perimeter had launched their big counteroffensive, and we spent a couple of days with the 25th, 24th and 1st Cavalry and the 1st ROK divisions in turn.

Dr. Lauritsen was particularly impressed with the task with which the ground divisions were confronted. I recall late one evening taking him to visit a forward battalion commander of the 24th Division. There was some Communist artillery fire, so we left our jeep about a mile behind the front and went forward on foot. As we did so, occasional rounds of artillery fire fell in the rice paddies off to the right. I was a bit uneasy, because the Germans had often registered their fire to the flank of a road on which you were moving, and then suddenly shifted bringing an entire crescendo down upon you. The Communist fire was obviously not so well handled and continued in random fashion in the empty paddies. We arrived at the battalion commander's location just at dusk. He was behind a slight rise of ground. By crawling forward and peering over the top, we could see a high wooded ridge about a half-mile ahead. The battalion commander had just come back from his rifle companies and he was confronted with a typical infantry battalion commander's problem. He was obviously very tired, bewhiskered and red-eyed, and he had to make a decision whether to hold his present position until morning and then jump off under daylight conditions, and in doing so risk Communist counterattack during the night, or to attempt to seize the higher ground to his front before dark. If he were to attack, darkness would probably overtake him before he reached his objective and there was a possibility of his battalion's being badly disorganized during the night, always a very dangerous situation. But the infantry lives with danger, and this was not untypical. As he gave a few minutes' thought to the problem, a soldier tried to give him something to eat from a mess kit, staff officers were answering his questions, and he obviously had much on his worried and tired mind. We asked about air support and he said he had none nor had he had any for days. His communications didn't work, and when they did and he got tac air support, it was almost impossible for the pilot to distinguish friend from foe in the rough wooded territory in which they were fighting. Obviously he needed more fire power—probably missiles, and preferably nuclear—immediately responsible to him and under his own control. Dr. Lauritsen was impressed by the situation, particularly since he knew that science and technology could offer real assistance if called upon.

We worked our way back to the division command post and then went on to other divisions on successive days, returning finally to Tokyo and to the United States about six weeks later. The group discussed their experiences for many hours in the ensuing weeks and from it we reached the conclusion that a special study group of top scientists and military men should be organized to look into the problem of tactical air support for our ground forces. Dr. Lauritsen and I had particularly in mind nuclear rocket support, although these could not be considered in isolation nor as a panacea. Tactical air support included logistical support as well as fire power support, and this involved the movement of troops as well as supplies. And when one considered troop movements, the character of equipment and weapons had to be studied also. From these discussions was born Project Vista.

Korea, initially, had a powerful impact on our military thinking. The early disillusionment of the military planners was soon followed by a rationalization of our failures. The political-military pot seethed over the right or wrong of allowing the North Koreans the sanctuary of the Yalu. But to our scientists there was a growing conviction that something had to be done to improve our capability to conduct land warfare. For the problem of Korea was not whether or not to attack China, or Russia, but what to do about the war in Korea. Of equally great concern was what to do if a similar combat pattern developed in other areas. And the feeling was beginning to grow that the more dangerous problem ahead of us was not general nuclear war, but limited war, either nuclear or nonnuclear. Europe, also, was on people's minds and for the first time we began to feel that unless something were done we might well lose Europe. Militant Communism was on the march and Korea was neither an accident nor an isolated phenomenon. From these considerations emerged a proposal that a group of outstanding scientists form a study group to look into what could be done to assist all of the services in dealing with the deficiencies made apparent by our fighting in Korea.

Project Vista was established at the California Institute of Technology in early 1951 under the joint auspices of the Army, Navy and Air Force. Its purpose was to conduct a broad study of ground and air tactical warfare with particular attention to the defense of Western Europe in the immediate future. Dr. Lee A. Dubridge was chairman of the group and he was assisted by an impressive array of scientists. Among them were Drs. William A. Fowler, Robert T. Bacher, C. C. Furnas, Charles C. Lauritsen, Clark B. Millikan, J. Robert Oppenheimer and H. P. Robertson, and many others, each distinguished in a particular field of science.

The project was well worth while and soundly conceived. We had to improve our capability to deal effectively with limited wars. By drawing upon our nation's great scientific and industrial resources we surely could do better than we had done in Korea. That there would be more Koreas there was little doubt, and probably sooner than we expected. The scientists were enthusiastic and most helpful. The services entered into the project wholeheartedly and, in prospect, it appeared that much would be accomplished. Unfortunately, the early enthusiasm of the Air Force began to wane when it was realized that increasing emphasis on tactical air support and tactical airlift would conflict with Air Force views on strategic air power. At the same time, the Air Force began to suspect the views of Dr. Oppenheimer. Earlier he had opposed the development of the thermonuclear bomb and now he was recommending a diversion of our nuclear resources to the tactical battle. There had also been talk among the scientists about air defense. This too ran contrary to the basic theory of the strategic-air-power enthusiasts; that an all-out air offensive was the only sound tactic and any diversion to defense was a waste. Dr. Oppenheimer's work with Vista came under closer scrutiny.

As the summer of 1951 wore on, the Air Force became conscious of a change in the atmosphere. The explanation was soon forthcoming: the Vista Group was conferring with Dr. Oppenheimer.

In November, 1951, at a Vista conference at Caltech, Dr. Dubridge presented a preliminary draft of its proposed report, including a chapter that Oppenheimer had written. It produced an explosion in the Air Force. Oppenheimer had transformed Vista into an exercise for rewriting U. S. strategy—an exercise introduced by a veiled suggestion the Air Force doctrine was based upon the slaughter of civilians. . . . Oppenheimer proposed that a substantial part of the atomic stockpile should be diverted from SAC to the direct support of the ground battle. . . . The objective, as stated in Vista, was "bringing the battle back to the battle field."

In December of 1951, Oppenheimer, Dubridge, and Lauritsen went to Paris and talked to Eisenhower. Norstad entered an uncompromising dissent to the Vista report.[17]

About a year or so later I mentioned the Vista report to General Norstad and he used strong language in his denunciation of it. Ironically, seven years later as SACEUR he was striving to achieve many of the goals sought in the report.

Unfortunately, Dr. Oppenheimer was in trouble, and his participation in Vista added to the aura of suspicion with which the Big Bomber advocates were now surrounding him. As *The Reporter* expressed it in an editorial some years later, in 1957:

His [Oppenheimer's] urging that ways be found to bring war back to the battlefield was considered preposterous if not treasonable. . . . They [the scientists] must protect the strongest offensive military interest in the country. There was something quite sinister in a scientist who concerned himself with defense as Oppenheimer did.[18]

The Vista recommendations had sought to improve the capabilities of each of the services. The Army was urged to adopt a lightweight tank killer, the Ontos. It has since been developed by the Marine Corps. Vista recommended an across-the-board improvement in communications, the development of tactical nuclear missiles to replace the 280 mm., and an extensive improvement in intelligence-handling systems. It finally recommended the establishment of a Combat Developments Center to test new tactical concepts with troops. This has been established.

For the Navy, among other things, it urged a step-up in our antisubmarine defenses and the development of across-the-beach cargo and personnel-handling facilities.

The Air Force recommendations were almost entirely related to improving its capability to wage tactical, nuclear or nonnuclear war. Among other things it recommended procuring 400 C-124 and 850 C-123 Troop Carrier aircraft by 1954, tactical nuclear

[17] "The Hidden Struggle for the H-Bomb," *Fortune*, May, 1953, p. 109.
[18] *The Reporter*, December 26, 1957.

weapons for use in air defense, and a significant improvement in fighter bombers, interceptors and support aircraft.

The Vista report was submitted to the Secretaries of the several services in February of 1952. It has never been officially approved.

I. DUTY WITH THE NORTH ATLANTIC TREATY ORGANIZATION

I was ordered to duty with the North Atlantic Treaty Organization in June of 1951. My first call was upon the Supreme Allied Commander, General Eisenhower, whom I had known quite well during World War II. Since I had recently attended the tactical nuclear weapons tests in the Pacific test area, we discussed at considerable length use of nuclear weapons and the contribution that they could make to NATO. He seemed very interested although, understandably, he was out of touch with some of the technical aspects of the problem. I urged that he obtain a scientist for his staff, to assist as an adviser on nuclear as well as scientific matters in general. We discussed the characteristics of the tactical weapons that would soon become available, particularly the 280 mm., and the advantages that would accrue in the use of fissionable material when we were able to replace the artillery weapons with missiles or small air-dropped weapons. There was no question in my mind at the time about the essentiality of tactical nuclear weapons to NATO's future. The problem, and it was an urgent one, was to develop the tactics and organizational structure that would enable the NATO forces to fight successfully in tactical nuclear warfare.

From Paris I then went to Naples, Italy, for duty with Admiral Carney's Southern European command. The Admiral was one of the finest men to work for that I had the privilege of associating with in Europe and the tactical problems of the area were challenging, to say the least. I had numerous opportunities to visit our faraway fronts in Turkey, Greece and northern Italy. The northern Italy area particularly adapted itself to the tactical employment of nuclear weapons since the mountains channelized an attacker. The greatest danger was in a large-scale vertical envelopment. This, however, could be dealt with by a defense in depth, specifically by organizing the Apennines as well as the Alps. Admiral Carney had recommended, on a number of occasions, the static use of nuclear weapons in the Alpine passes and they obviously had great merit. The Greek and Turkish areas, with the exception of the area immediately north of the Dardanelles, which is rolling open country, likewise offered excellent opportunities for the use of tactical nuclear weapons in defense. The Dardanelles defense required mobile armored forces in considerable numbers, matched with nuclear weapons, in order to handle the type of attack that might be expected through that area. It was evident, in the summer of 1952, that nuclear weapons would play a decisive role in the defense of the Southern European area.

In December of 1952, I received orders to take command of the United States VII Corps, then occupying all of southern Germany from the Alps north to an east-and-west line just above Nuremberg. It contained the cities of Nuremberg, Stuttgart, Munich and Heilbron. The most prominent terrain features were the open rolling farmlands of the east backed by the Swabian Alps in the west. The Danube bisected the area, running generally west to east and the Rhine River ran north and south directly across the rear of the area. The corps had been on occupation duty since the widespread tension following the opening of the Korean War. It consisted of two mechanized cavalry regiments deployed on the border, two infantry divisions behind them, and numerous supporting artillery, engineer, signal and transportation units. It offered me the opportunity that I had been seeking to develop tactical nuclear concepts for our infantry organizations. I started to work on the project at once.

The Staff developed a plan for the defense of the area along World War II lines. This was done as a map exercise, initially, and we then conducted an actual count of the troops and their supplies dispersed throughout the area in terms of quantity per five-kilometer square. A five-kilometer square was selected because it was one that would contain a circle 2½ kilometers in radius, which was the median lethal distance of a fifty-kiloton weapon.[19] When the raw data were assembled and compiled, a plot was made, showing by color gradient the density of our forces in defense. It was evident, at once, in relating this density to nuclear weapons that the Soviets could use in attack, that it would fragment badly and lead to quick defeat in tactical nuclear combat. We then turned to the problem of rearranging our deployments so as to offer the best prospect of defense against nuclear weapons, consistent with the accomplishment of our mission. Using the existing forces, we soon learned that the World War II type organizations, no matter how packaged, would not adapt themselves to nuclear tactics. The one exception was our armored divisions. Our rearranging involved a complete re-examination of the terrain and its defense characteristics, the availability of airstrips and suitable air-landing areas, and the location of extensive underground shelters, of which there are quite a few in southern Germany. At the conclusion of our studies, forces were again deployed and their density analyzed. We learned that it was entirely practicable to provide optimum defense with a quick tactical responsiveness to an attack in a two-sided nuclear war provided certain steps in reorganization were accomplished.

First, the leading elements to contact any aggressor, the "cavalry" elements, had to have a mobility differential over an aggressor. This suggested that a new type "cavalry" arm had to be developed based upon VTOL aircraft. The only ones available in the corps at the time were helicopters. Next, the area held by the infantry had to extend from a depth of about five to ten miles, which characterized World War II deployments, to about one hundred to one hundred fifty miles, with reserves further back. This suggested at once the need for the replacement of

[19] The median lethal distance is the distance from ground zero to the point at which one is as likely as not to become a fatality from a nuclear detonation. Considering the protective measures that can be taken by trained troops 2½ kilometers is a conservative figure.

conventional artillery with missiles, if our fire power was to have adequate range, and this was one of the conclusions on which all participants agreed. We would need missile ranges adequate to provide continuous fire of tremendous depth, that could reach anything in the opposing Soviet Army. We knew of nothing of this character in development at the time, but the need was quite evident. A missile many hundreds of miles in range, with an accurate nuclear warhead, and one that was mobile and immediately responsive to the decisions of the ground commander, was critically required.

Communication ranges had doubled and trebled and therefore it appeared necessary to move the communications equipment down about one echelon of command. That is, communications equipment employed by divisions in World War II would now be needed by a regiment, regimental communications by a battalion, etc. In addition, alternate command posts, always kept suitably separated, were required. This was necessary since the magnitude of effectiveness of nuclear weapons was such that a complete command post could be destroyed with one round, much the same as a capital ship could be sunk in naval warfare, and thus an alternate command center had to be available. To support such a concept logistically would require a significant expansion and development of the air logistics organization. The area of defense of the corps, which in World War II extended over hundreds of square miles, now was to be extended over thousands of square miles. If the wounded were to be evacuated promptly, ammunition flown up, and gas, oil and food provided in adequate quantities, then air mobility was the key to the solution of the logistics problem. However, the air mobility had to be in terms of the type of aircraft that could land in cultivated areas, in bad weather and darkness, and that under no circumstances would require sophisticated facilities and concrete airstrips.

When all of the foregoing was accomplished, it was evident that the infantry division itself had to be completely redesigned. Instead of deploying in a linear defense, backed by a monolithic communications and supply system, it now had to become amorphous. It had to repackage into small, widely dispersed battle groups, each one being capable of sustained combat on its own, but not one ever offering a tactical nuclear target to the Soviets. Finally, and this was most important, if the foregoing were valid in defense, then the organization to be combat-worthy had to adapt itself to immediate offensive employment. This aspect of the problem was considered also, and the final type of division selected, we were convinced, was capable of either defensive or offensive nuclear warfare. One over-all conclusion stood out clearly, although for several years it was the basis of considerable argument: more rather than less manpower would be required to fight a nuclear war successfully.

When the map studies were completed, two-sided war games were undertaken to put the concepts to the test of human decision under realistic conditions. Exercises known as "Battle Mace" and "Beartrap" followed. They were to prove invaluable, not only in testing the concepts themselves, but in instructing our tactical commanders in the type of combat we anticipated if nuclear weapons were employed. As soon as the war games were completed, extensive field exercises were planned to put the concepts to the test of realism on the ground. Already, however, commanders had begun to try out their new ideas in smaller units within the corps.

In January of 1954, I received orders assigning me to the Department of the Army, Assistant Chief of Staff for Plans and Operations, G-3. I looked forward eagerly to the opportunity that it offered, for the Army was on the threshold of a revolution in tactics, weapons and organization. If the Free World was to survive, the time was past due to put our minds to these problems.

Looking back, I realized that duty with NATO had been most rewarding. I had made many new friends in Europe and I had had an opportunity to make a direct contribution to the defense of that area so vital to the West. Unfortunately, for the few things accomplished to ready NATO for a war of tomorrow, dozens remained unaccomplished. The North Atlantic Treaty Organization needs our technical advice and material assistance to a greater degree than we have been willing to give.

The creation of the North Atlantic Treaty Organization is one of the truly great achievements of our time. It makes clear for all time that we, as a nation, have put behind us our aversion to "foreign entanglements." Now that we had reached maturity, we were willing to accept the responsibility of leadership in the world community of nations. That the first line of defense was in Europe we accepted, and we definitely committed ourselves to participation in that defense. NATO brings together, freely and impelled by the highest motives, the great nations with whom we have had cultural and economic ties since the founding of the Republic. The history of Europe contains instances of past efforts to organize the continent as one political and military entity, through the use of force and persuasion. Never before have the European nations, of their own free will, gone so far in achieving a collective organization. Now, through an awareness of the common goal, and a conviction that the needs of humanity can best be served by this instrument, NATO has been created. Finally, Western Europe contains huge resources of skilled manpower and industry, resources that undoubtedly would be decisive in tipping the scales in any contest between the United States and the USSR. NATO is by far the largest, as well as the most important, coalition that we have entered; it is "the acid test" of our system of alliances.

Many Americans see in NATO physical benefits to the United States. The shield of the Republic is advanced toward that of the USSR; the first blows of combat will, to a degree, be absorbed by NATO as they were by Europe in World Wars I and II. This is partially true, but far more important than this is the security that comes to each member from the spiritual bonds that unite free nations in the common defense. No longer can any nation survive in isolation, not with rapacious and greedy neighbors such as the

Communists have proven to be. The only security is collective security.

Collective defense is as essential to the United States as to Europe. The idea of Fortress America is as idiotically out of date today as that of Fortress Britain was twenty years ago. It is vital to the United States that she should continually foster and build up her system of alliances and maintain the balance of power in the World, as Britain did for centuries in Europe.[20]

One would assume that an alliance so conceived and so dedicated would move forward, with a minimum of internal friction, to high levels of achievement. Such, unfortunately, has not been the case. Neither dedication nor hard work on the part of its planners have brought NATO to the goals so eagerly sought. "None of the force levels of NATO which have been announced periodically with such fanfare has ever been achieved. Almost a decade after its creation, NATO is still without a force sufficient to prevent its members from being overrun by the Soviet army."[21]

I have worked closely with NATO and within NATO, almost since its inception. I have no reservations whatsoever about the soundness of the concept and the compelling need for it to be successful. And NATO can be successful, and can achieve its lofty goals and serve Western man as no other political and military creation in Western history. But this will take realism, sacrifice and courage. Mere agreements on paper and periodic high-level meetings with much attendant publicity will not give NATO an added bit of strength.

NATO strength must come, first of all, from confidence. This is absolutely fundamental. It must have confidence in the goals it seeks and it must have confidence in the technical adequacy of the means available to achieve those goals.

Confidence within NATO will best be served when we are realistic with each other. The NATO nations collectively comprise the most highly educated, sophisticated and industrialized

[20] *The Great Deterrent*, Sir John Slessor.
[21] *Nuclear Weapons and Foreign Policy*, Henry A. Kissinger.

area in the world. Its political and military leaders are outstanding. I have known many of the senior military leaders for some years, and I have discussed NATO military problems with them on many occasions. As a group of professionals, they are unmatched anywhere in the world today. I have no concern whatsoever for their performance in peace or war, nuclear or nonnuclear. However, above all, they are realistic. For their peoples have fought to defend their homeland against aggression since the beginning of recorded time. More than any nations in the world, they recognize the importance of collective security. To achieve such security in a collective manner—and this includes the participation of the United States in every sense of the word—they will reach compromises between what they know must be done and what they consider the other NATO nations are willing to do. Polite murmurs of agreement will go round the council tables and periodic communiqués will go out over the press wires, from time to time assuring an uneasy world of the potential strength of NATO and the soundness of its military planning. Privately, however, most of the senior military people are worried, for they know, as we know, that the Soviet nuclear colossus once in motion will be difficult to stop, and that if the most modern weapons are not in the hands of the NATO nations, they will be overrun in a nuclear catastrophe without precedence in human history. As the NATO military forces fall back or disintegrate, the next tactical decision confronting NATO's military leaders will be how to liberate the overrun territory. One gunpowder liberation in a generation is enough. Few of them will admit welcoming a nuclear liberation. And yet, this is what is implied in a military policy that would rely upon a "trip wire" strategy and nuclear retaliation by forces not even under the control of NATO.

NATO members must have confidence in each other and this implies mutual trust and a free exchange of information. A free exchange of technical military information provides the basis of understanding the latest trends in military technology. And in the dynamic technological age in which we live, this is of the utmost importance. A technological lag of even a few years could spell military disaster.

The members of NATO must have confidence in the military policies that serve it. This, of course, is related to NATO's awareness of the manner in which technology can serve it. Our military policies, therefore, must be those that would serve NATO and its members and not destroy them. Finally, not a small part of NATO's confidence must stem from a conviction of the thriving and promising nature of the cause they serve, and the righteousness of that cause. The member nations of NATO must have an ideal to which they may aspire that is more than the mere maintenance of the status quo. NATO must be a proponent of something, something worthy of the aspirations of the free people of all of Europe, and of the world for that matter. And it should provide a cause to which they can feel, at least in their hearts, they can rally. It therefore needs a doctrine and a military program to serve that doctrine. It needs it collectively exactly as each nation needs it separately. NATO's problem is our problem as Americans.

The free exchange of information within NATO has been one of our most difficult problems. The NATO nations have been considerate and understanding, knowing that the laws passed by the properly elected legislative bodies of the member countries sometimes preclude the free exchange of information. In some cases, an exchange may be permitted with one or two nations, but not with all. This is more damaging, in many respects, than no exchange at all since it tends to create cliques of nations within NATO itself and nothing short of Soviet penetration could be more harmful. Yet we have such a situation today. Aside from the intangible but insidious harm caused by holding back information, real physical harm is done.

We are in a technological revolution of the most profound nature. Nuclear weapons are one sign of that revolution. Nuclear weapons are here to stay and the basic problem is to learn to live with them. Nuclear weapons can now be made so small in size and light in weight as to be man-handleable and shoulder-fired. They can be employed in infantry combat, in the smallest of units. Fissionable material is becoming available in such abundance that the economics of the situation alone will soon compel its use as replacement for the tons of high explosives and steel shells used in the gunpowder era. That this information is not exclusively ours was made abundantly clear in the parade of November 7, 1957, in Moscow celebrating the fortieth anniversary of the Red Revolution. There the Soviets chose to display a family of highly mobile nuclear missiles. It is important to realize that these were the ones we were allowed to see, and even so, they included short-range infantry-support nuclear missiles on amphibious track-laying vehicles, missiles with a combat mobility unsurpassed in any Western army today. Their display included both liquid- and solid-propellant missiles, and both surface-to-surface and surface-to-air missiles. It is of the utmost importance to NATO, therefore, that nuclear information be provided to all of its members. Out of ignorance, too many still think of nuclear fire power as their ancestors of five hundred years ago thought of gunpowder: "O! curs'd device! base implement of death! Fram'd in the black Tartarean realms beneath! By Beelzebub's malicious art design'd to ruin all the race of human kind."[22] The problem in NATO is not how to avoid use of nuclear weapons, for that is a decision the Soviets will make, but how to live with them when they are used. How to make nuclear weapons the servant of NATO and how to avoid making NATO the slave of nuclear weapons—that is the problem.

Nuclear weapons are essential to an adequate defense of Western Europe. Take, for example, air defense. Time and space are such in Europe today that only missiles can provide an adequate air defense. The British White Paper of 1957 recognized this. The most exposed nation is Western Germany. It can only be defended against Soviet air and missile attack by having nuclear surface-to-air missiles. There are technological reasons for

[22] Ariosto (1474-1533).

this. The reaction time is such that manned aircraft can no longer respond quickly enough to meet an enemy threat. Neither men nor airplanes are adequate to deal with attacking missiles and rockets. Finally, the objective of a modern air defense must be to destroy the payload of the incoming missile or bomb-carrying plane. Technologically, this is possible using a nuclear missile in defense. Obviously, therefore, if Western Germany is to be defended and not abandoned immediately, she must have nuclear surface-to-air missiles. It is idle chatter and simply a waste of time to talk otherwise.

In defending against Soviet land forces matched with nuclear missiles, the NATO nations must themselves be equipped with a family of surface-to-surface nuclear missiles. For missiles are modern artillery and tactical nuclear warheads are modern conventional fire power. It would be as wrong to ask the NATO nations to defend against Soviet nuclear aggression with gunpowder weapons as it would have been to equip our own forces with bows and arrows to deal with the blitzkrieg.

All nuclear missiles should be highly mobile. The Germans learned this lesson in World War II, when their concrete bases were completely destroyed, while their mobile missile units were not harmed until overrun by our ground forces. Because of the fact that our Air Force has had primary responsibility for the deployment of our Intermediate Range Ballistic Missiles overseas, it has thought of their employment in terms of air bases and aircraft employment. I was responsible for developing the tactical characteristics of the Army's Intermediate Range Ballistic Missile, the Jupiter. It was designed to be as mobile as any piece of equipment in the present-day field army. It was designed for movement on highways to launching areas through all kinds of weather. Neither rain nor snow nor fog nor extremes of temperature can impair its launching. Furthermore, its over-all configuration is such that it can be stored in highway and rail tunnels. Mobility is so fundamental to success in combat that it is inconceivable that anyone would consider Maginot-Line-like bases as militarily sound, for they are certain to attract retaliatory missile fires that will put them out of action quickly. And they are tactically as inflexible as a one-weapons-system strategy, and as sterile of tactical potential. Unfortunately, too, their proposed employment has raised the issues of bases, and their attendant cost and risk to the civilian population. And well the issue might be raised, for firing bases as such are entirely unnecessary. If NATO must engage in prolonged base negotiations every time the need arises to move a missile, it will bring military disaster upon itself very quickly. The present IRBMs, both the Jupiter and Thor, are the largest of their size and the most difficult to move, for an attainable range of fifteen hundred miles, that we will see. With each passing month of development, their characteristics will improve and ultimately they will probably approach half their present size, or less, and with new propellants will be at least twice as mobile. At the same time, they will be capable of reaching any vital military target offered by the USSR.

Any discussion of the use of nuclear weapons in the NATO area raises the question of tactics. Due to the range and destructiveness of missiles today, the world has shrunk, in a tactical sense, to a small tactical theater. Most of the NATO region is in the forward area of the front lines. Many parts of it, the United Kingdom, for example, are too shallow in land depth to offer reasonable dispersion possibilities for missile employment, except for self-defense. To suggest placing huge retaliatory missiles in some parts of NATO, England for example, would be like suggesting that an infantry battalion commander have 155 howitzers so far forward as to be amid the foxholes of the infantry. I have known infantry commanders who asked that big guns be dug in far forward, not wanting to trade their men and land for time and wanting enough fire power to enable them to deal with anything that might come down upon them at once. In such situations, the higher tactical commander, in view of his over-all tactical plan, must have the courage to make the decision not so to expose his more valuable and more vulnerable long-range weapons. Instead of placing them in the front lines, where they will be quickly destroyed, he uses them from areas where terrain protection can be provided and from areas where they can be deployed in such great depth as not to be destroyed or overrun when the first blow falls.

Seemingly, one of the most difficult things for people to understand today is the fact that survival may well depend upon our defensive capability, more than upon our retaliatory, that is, our offensive capability. The eternal seesaw between offensive and defensive warfare still goes on and while the offensive may have the upper hand today, it may well be entirely overtaken by the defensive tomorrow. There was a time when the period of transition was a generation or more, but the dynamics of military technology today are such that the period may be a year or less, depending upon the possibility for technological breakthrough. It would be folly for a nation to assume that either the offensive or the defensive would remain exclusively valid indefinitely. Technologically, therefore, since we have given the initiative to the enemy, only a mixed solution, one containing our best prospects for both offensive and defensive combat, will enable us to survive. As applied to the NATO area, therefore, that portion of it lacking land depth should be provided with only the means of self-defense and not be considered as an area for retaliatory weapons. Great land areas or areas backed by great land masses should provide the operational location for retaliatory firings. Specifically, England and the lowland countries should not be expected to receive and protect IRBMs. Southern Europe and Greece and Turkey, backed by the extensive African land mass, should be considered as the area from which NATO would employ its counteroffensive missile firings. And these missiles must be part of completely mobile systems.

I have no concern for the defense of Western Europe if nuclear weapons are not used. Despite the overwhelming size and impressive state of readiness of the Soviet forces, without the use of nuclear weapons, they would have a long hard fight. Once they crossed the Rhine, their lines of communication would be so long and so precariously exposed to sabotage and destruction that their main armies would certainly be destroyed. The launching of a nonnuclear war would bring to bear not only the weight of Western Europe, but most of the satellites against the USSR. Germany almost single-handedly came close to defeating the USSR in World War II, despite being at war on another front and the tremendous amount of assistance that we gave to the Soviets. With all of Western Europe and most of the satellites arrayed against her, I do not think Soviet prospects of conquering Europe by nonatomic means are very bright, and they realize this.

The tactical nuclear war is the real danger, both because of the magnitude of the holocaust that would ensue and the rapid exploitation by highly mobile forces that could be made by the Soviets. The Soviets realize this and their tactical doctrine today contemplates being on the English Channel in forty-eight hours. In unmistakable language, they threaten the use of nuclear, biological, chemical and psychological warfare. In psychological warfare they are very good, as the evidence of recent years shows. The important thing for the USSR to accomplish today is to convince Western Europe of the absolute horror of nuclear weapons so that the NATO nations will refuse to allow them to be stored in their countries or used in combat; then if war comes it will be a nuclear-ready Red Army against a gunpowder NATO Army. We can expect a veritable drumbeat of propaganda on these points, while Soviet technology moves ahead to give them a capability of utterly devastating and overrunning Europe at a time of their choosing.

If an "agonizing reappraisal" is needed anywhere, it is needed now in NATO. At the outset, being unwilling to make the sacrifices necessary to provide the force essential to NATO defense, despite paper agreements to do so, the participating governments sought ways and means of easing the burden. There may have been valid economic reasons for this, but this does not justify the military policy that followed. By coincidence our own country was embarked on just such a program—"A bigger bang for a buck"; nuclear air-delivered weapons were to be substituted for manpower. The program had obvious appeal and "The Great Deterrent," as Sir John Slessor refers to it, became the cornerstone of our NATO planning. "Trip wire" and "plate glass" were used to describe the tactical concept. To be a sound military venture, it would have to be based upon the assumption that the offensive would indefinitely dominate warfare. Unfortunately, such has not been the case and with each passing day, we see the Soviet position improve vis-à-vis NATO. Hence the current preoccupation with disengagement and the search for a formula that would protect Europe from nuclear weapons employment. There may have been a short period a few years ago when "The Great Deterrent," as such, was valid, but even this I doubt. Certainly, now, the military leaders of NATO realize that the risks in such a program are becoming more unacceptable each month. They do not want to be faced with the prospect of a nuclear liberation and yet their own strategy and weapons are becoming rapidly obsolescent.

If NATO is to survive, and it must if our nation is to survive, then its survival must depend on a freer exchange of technical information than in the past. It must be equipped with modern nuclear weapons systems, and this includes the latest types of surface-to-air and surface-to-surface nuclear missiles. It must plan realistically, and in this day of nuclear missiles and four-dimensional warfare, it must realize that it is unsound to try to be offensively strong everywhere. In fact, the major portion of NATO should be entirely defensive in character. From such strength, which should be attainable without undue economic strain, NATO will gain the confidence it needs. It will know that the weapons systems available to it can serve it well, and that NATO itself can serve the loftiest aspirations of free men and provide a standard to which the Soviet satellites can rally, if the opportunity should arise.

J. THE NEW LOOK

In March, 1954, I reported to the Department of the Army for my new assignment. I was met at once with the "New Look," which was based upon increasing emphasis on our strategic retaliatory power at the expense of our so-called "conventional" forces. Testifying before the Senate Subcommittee for Appropriations on March 15, 1954, Secretary Wilson expressed the trend of the times when he said:

. . . the integration of new weapons systems into military planning creates new relationships between men and material which emphasize airpower and permit overall economies in the use of manpower. . . .

The fiscal year 1955 budget incorporates the new air force objectives and continues a rapid buildup of air strength, and the creation, maintenance, and full exploitation of modern airpower. . . .

As we increase the striking power of our combat forces by the application of technological advances and new weapons and by the continuing growth of airpower, the total number of military personnel can be reduced.

Shortly before, in January of 1954, our Secretary of State, speaking before the Council on Foreign Relations in New York, said:

We need allies and collective security. Our purpose is to make these relations more effective, less costly. This can be done by placing more reliance on deterrent power and less dependence on local defensive power. . . .

Local defense will always be important. But there is no local defense which alone will contain the mighty landpower of the Communist world. Local defenses must be reinforced by the further deterrent of massive retaliatory power. A potential aggressor must know that he cannot always prescribe battle conditions that suit him.

The way to deter aggression is for the free community to be willing and able to respond vigorously at places and with means of its own choosing.

At the time this statement caused a great deal of misunderstanding and it has since been modified. In 1954, however, the

New Look was something to be reckoned with. It seemed contrary to all of our experience in NATO, for tactical nuclear weapons would be required as much as and perhaps more than strategic weapons. And the tactical employment of nuclear weapons implied quite clearly an increase rather than a decrease in manpower requirements. The thesis upon which the New Look was based was entirely wrong, or at least it appeared to us to be. It placed the Army Staff at once in a very difficult position vis-à-vis the Chairman of the Joint Chiefs of Staff and the Secretary of Defense. The immediate problem—and it persists until today as one of the most troublesome problems to the professional military man—was whether or not in defending the Army budget before Congress, to agree to the basic philosophy of the New Look. This was fundamental, for to agree was to agree to many things other than mere reduction of manpower and the main reliance upon strategic nuclear power that had brought us to the brink of disaster in 1950. It meant agreeing to less emphasis upon the development of tactical nuclear weapons. It meant agreeing to close our minds once again to the challenges of tomorrow's land warfare, with the implied need for long-range missiles, improved radars and communications, VTOL and STOL air vehicles, and an increased Air Force Troop Carrier airlift. To disagree with the concept in testifying before Congress was to be insubordinate, and yet many of us were convinced that to agree would only once again advance our nation on the road to military disaster. I was personally convinced, too, that NATO would be badly served indeed by our acquiescence in such an unsound program. For with each passing day, as we got further along into the tactical nuclear missile age, local defenses would increase in importance and manpower requirements would increase accordingly. To me personally, it was a real dilemma—how to serve the national need while at the same time obeying implicitly the policies initiated by the Department of Defense. At about this time, Walter Millis wrote a column which expressed much of our concern quite well:

. . . a new policy which, in the name of regaining "the initiative," can tend only to retie our hands to the old pre-1950 limits, shackle us once more to a single, "retaliatory" strategy and invite the Soviets to hit us again, if they wish to, in ways to which this strategy demonstrably offers no useful reply. . . . The return to the retaliatory and strategic atom is not consonant with the argument that . . . "we need allies and collective security"; for probably the best way to lose allies is to make it clear that you no longer intend to provide them with the means of local defense. It is not consonant with the EDC policy and the statement that "rearmed Germans" must "serve the common cause"; for "rearmed Germans" must mean infantry (not atomic bomber crews) and if we no longer need American infantry for local defense how can we claim that we need German infantry?[23]

Unfortunately, the New Look soon found expression in NATO policy and a document known as MC-48 was published. It envisioned a war in which the first phase would be a brief massive nuclear exchange, the outcome of which would very likely determine the outcome of the war. Some of our most able soldiers subscribed to it, notably Field Marshal Montgomery, and his statements in support of it were widely used. In fact, they were reproduced by the Air Force Association and distributed to retired as well as active Air Force officers.

In the Department of the Army Staff, we were profoundly concerned with implications of the New Look, but we felt that subsequent events would soon make clear its unsoundness. Our concern was for the by-products of the New Look that would not be apparent for some time, but that would in the long run be very damaging to national security. Specifically, failure to support our surface-to-surface and surface-to-air missile programs, inadequate funds to support a satellite program, which we were proposing in 1954, inadequate funds for our research and development programs so essential to the development of land forces for the nuclear missile age, and finally a serious reduction in manpower at a time when the trend should have been exactly the opposite, all worried us. That our concerns were well founded soon became manifest.

[23] "Arms and Men," New York *Herald Tribune*, February, 1954.

The Decade of Dilemma: 1945-1955

When I joined the Army Staff in early 1954, the Army contained twenty divisions and seven basic training organizations with divisional numbers. In accordance with the philosophy of the New Look, a critical cut in this division strength was undertaken at once. First, the Army was directed to include the training organizations in its over-all division strength. The total number of divisions was then reduced to match the old number of combat-ready divisions, so that if you didn't examine the numbers closely you would be given the impression that no reduction had taken place. As the cut back continued, and some concern was expressed on the part of Congress, the Army was directed to regroup its nondivision personnel and thus account for more divisions. For example, forces at Fort Benning, Georgia, were grouped on paper with those in the Panama Canal Zone and called a division. Likewise, forces at Fort Lewis, Washington, were grouped with those in Alaska. To some segments of the press, these became known as "Wilson" divisions. Concurrently, Congress was assured, in the annual hearings, that our combat strength was not being reduced, that as our atomic stockpile increased, fewer divisions would be required, and that we were cutting the fat and non-essential service and support units. That the contrary was the case few, outside of the Department of the Army, seemed willing to admit.

More important than manpower cuts, however, was the inability to obtain adequate funds for the missile programs. In late 1954 it was decided that it was in the nation's interest that we develop, as a matter of high priority, an Intermediate Range Ballistics Missile, and that we undertake a satellite program. After considerable staff discussion, I personally recommended to General Ridgway in March of 1955 that the IRBM program be undertaken at a cost of $25 million. At the end of a week's time, I discussed it with him again, and he stated that he could not possibly obtain money on that scale from the Department of Defense, and that if the Army were to undertake the program, it would have to be out of the money then available to it. Since the

153

Army's budget was critically inadequate, the decision was made not to start an IRBM but to advance the Redstone from its proposed range of two hundred miles to five hundred miles. It was hoped that by the time a range of five hundred miles was achieved, the Department of Defense would be aware of the national need and authorize a longer range.

We were at the time in a most interesting situation in missile development. In 1951, the Army had undertaken the development of a 450-mile-range ballistics missile. Then at the direction of our missile "czar," Mr. K. T. Keller, a heavy thermonuclear warhead was programmed for the missile and its range, of necessity, was reduced to two hundred miles. This was a good change since it assured the country of an early surface-to-surface thermonuclear missile. At the time, however, there was no interest in the Army's missile program because evidently it was considered rather exotic and far in the future. Therefore, in early 1955, when the Army decided once again to develop a missile of five-hundred-mile range, there was little interest shown in it outside of the Army. In fact, there was a JCS agreement authorizing the Army to develop surface-to-surface missiles for tactical use, without range limits. It was not until all services became aware of the combat potential of missiles that the Secretary of Defense issued his now famous memorandum of December 26, 1956, restricting the Army to a range of two hundred miles. So, the lack of awareness of the importance of missiles in 1954 had two facets: money could not be obtained for them, and there were no limits on the surface-to-surface technical missiles to be developed and used by the Army. In effect, they canceled each other out, and the country's missile program and satellite program awaited a more favorable attitude in the Department of Defense. In the meantime Congress was being assured that all was well and that we were ahead of the Russians in our military, including missiles, programs.

General Matthew B. Ridgway had come to the Pentagon as one of the "good new chiefs" when all of the "bad old chiefs" left in the summer of 1953. He brought to the office of Chief of

Staff a background and breadth of experience unique to that office. I had known him to be a man of extreme courage, moral and physical, in combat, and soon I was to see his resources taxed to the utmost in his efforts to maintain a combat-ready army. Much has been written about General Ridgway and more will be written when the full record is available for public scrutiny. Suffice to say that the country owes him a debt that it will never be able to repay. Somehow, despite Secretary Wilson and the Chairman of the Joint Chiefs of Staff, he managed to hold together an army and to continue to ready that army for the nuclear-missile-space age. And that he was readying it for all three of them, despite a constantly shrinking budget, the record will now show.

Yet, from where I saw the situation as one of his senior staff officers, it was not the shrinking budget that was bothersome—for the Army traditionally suffers from fiscal malnutrition in peace. It was the deception and duplicity of those with whom he had to work in the Department of Defense.

Mr. Wilson tended to deal with his Chiefs of Staff as though they were recalcitrant union bosses. The thought struck me often that Walter Reuther, under the circumstances, would have been a more effective Chief of Staff than a professional soldier. I have known General Ridgway, after weeks of painstaking preparation, to brief Mr. Wilson on a problem with lucidity and thoroughness. At the conclusion Mr. Wilson would gaze out of the window and ask a question that had no relevance whatsoever to the subject of the briefing. Among his aides this was known as taking the briefer "on a trip around the world." It was a studied technique that he used when he had his mind already made up about what you were going to talk to him about. As I heard another Chief of Staff say, "He was the most uninformed man, and the most determined to remain so, that has ever been Secretary."

When the Army's dwindling divisional strength made it apparent that it would have difficulty meeting the nation's commit-

155

ment to NATO, Secretary Wilson said that we had no commitment to NATO. This was a thunderbolt, but by juggling words, and finally by a change in NATO's standards of readiness, he made it stick. As the situation deteriorated in the Pacific, following Dien Bien Phu and Quemoy-Matsu, we became concerned about the defense of Formosa. General Ridgway sent a general officer to Formosa to look into the situation. Upon his return he recommended that a sizable increase in the logistical and air-defense units be provided by the United States. This was particularly important in view of the proposed plan to put U.S. Air Force fighter aircraft on the island on a rotational basis. Due to the Army's reduction in strength, General Ridgway was extremely reluctant to go along with the recommendation but he finally felt that he had to. At the same time, however, the Secretary of Defense and the Chairman of the Joint Chiefs of Staff were assuring Congress, in reply to specific questions, that additional Army units would not be required and none were under consideration. The Secretary solved his dilemma by ordering the Army to send bodies without regular organizational designation. He even forbade the wearing of shoulder patches. But more troublesome than these seemingly trivial things was the constant pressure on funding. The technique was to suggest that another cut in funds, say 10 per cent across the board, was due. When the critical harm that would result from such a cut was pointed out the reply was polite.

"The Department of Defense understands how serious the situation is, we realize that you couldn't stand a further cut in either funds or personnel and still meet your obligations. But suppose you go back and think the thing over. Suppose you did have to take a cut, just suppose, how would you do it?"

A week later, or perhaps a few days, you would return with an outline of the implications of such a cut. After explaining it you would be greeted with:

"That is very good. I am glad to see you think that way. The program that you have recommended is approved."

Thus the burden of cutting is shifted to the Chief of Staff. If later there is occasion for a congressional query, and there always is, Congress is assured that the Chiefs of Staff recommended or concurred in the reduction. To inform Congress to the contrary would be insubordinate; in fact the Department of the Army has issued specific instructions covering this point. And so, on and on, in a never-ending game of labor bosses vs. business tycoons. I am happy to note that Secretary McElroy is trying hard to put an end to the system, and if he continues in his present methods he should succeed.

K. CONGRESS AND DEPARTMENT OF DEFENSE POLICIES

Now, in retrospect, it is well that we ask ourselves what was the significance of Korea and Indo-China. Were they accidents of time and circumstance? Or do they fit into a pattern of history? Korea was the first war that we failed to win; was it also the symptom of our decline? Did we reach the high noon of military achievement, and with Korea turn toward the long afternoon shadows of a deteriorating republic? The answers to these questions are not as simple as they may seem. But the questions deserve answers.

There is some evidence that we have learned from the Korean experience. In the field of fire power, for example, there has been a gradual shift from large nuclear weapons to small tactical weapons and with this shift there has been a growing acceptance of tactical nuclear war. The case for tactical nuclear weapons was well expressed by Mr. Thomas E. Murray, then a member of the United States Atomic Energy Commission, on April 12, 1956:

Wars in the future will be nuclear wars. This does not mean that they need be all-out nuclear wars. All-out nuclear war is no more acceptable than murder or suicide. It would be fatal to permit ourselves to drift into the habit of thinking about nuclear war only in all-out terms. The traditional moral effort of Western civilization to impose limitations on warfare must be continued even in the nuclear age. A limited nuclear war is a possibility that our consciences can face and accept.

In the different kinds of limited war that might confront us certain types of nuclear weapons have a genuine military usefulness. It would therefore be wrong on our part to deprive ourselves of these weapons.

However, our stockpile should include only weapons that are actually useful in war. Moreover, it should include only weapons that we can legitimately intend to use. I am altogether opposed to any school of thought that would move on toward weapons of ever-increasing magnitude, while at the same time disclaiming the intention of using them.

Commissioner Murray went on to recommend the procurement of tens of thousands of very small nuclear weapons, stating that, "A stockpile of this composition will support a theory of moderate and discriminating use of force against all aggression, including aggression that may be minor in degree." There is no doubt whatsoever of the need for small nuclear warheads in abundance. We know that at least four powers have nuclear weapons: the United States, the USSR, Great Britain and France. We can expect other powers to have them in time. The state of nuclear technology is such that the tactical characteristics of weapons can be improved with further testing. This means not only can they be made smaller in size and more efficient in yield, but that they can also be made cleaner and thus better suited to tactical use. Unfortunately nowhere near enough has been done, for again we conflict with the requirement for large-yield weapons for so called "strategic" employment.

It would be particularly unfortunate if we fell behind in the development and procurement of tactical weapons. Heretofore, the United States has relied in war upon its great industrial capacity. Industry responded quickly and shifted its skills to the making of tanks, trucks and airplane parts, diverting the raw materials intended for consumer use to military production. Nuclear weapons are another matter. Fissionable material is not being applied to consumer products and there will be a specific amount of fissionable material available at the outset of hostilities. We will be caught in a very precarious situation, for if nuclear hostilities commence, even in limited areas, and we find ourselves opposed by modernized land forces well equipped with nuclear weapons such as the type shown us on November 7 by the Soviets, we may well find ourselves in serious trouble at once. In order to meet our world-wide requirements, we may have to ration drastically our tactical nuclear ammunition and as a consequence we may suffer the loss of another war, this one a nuclear limited war. So the pattern of Korea may be extended into the nuclear era if we do not have the foresight to see the need and the courage to make the decisions to procure the necessary tactical nuclear weapons now. We should either procure and stockpile many more small weapons, or we must procure and stockpile fissionable material.

It is now clear that national policy on this subject has changed since January of 1954. Writing in *Foreign Affairs Magazine* in the issue of October, 1957, Mr. John Foster Dulles said:

However, the United States has not been content to rely upon a peace which could be preserved only by a capacity to destroy vast segments of the human race. Such a concept is acceptable only as a last alternative. In recent years there has been no other. But the resourcefulness of those who serve our nation in the field of science and engineering now shows that it is possible to alter the character of nuclear weapons. It seems now that their use need not involve vast destruction and widespread harm to humanity. Recent tests point to the possibility of possessing nuclear weapons the destructiveness and radiation effects of which can be confined substantially to predetermined targets.

In the future it may thus be feasible to place less reliance upon deterrence of vast retaliatory power. It may be possible to defend countries by nuclear weapons so mobile, or so placed, as to make military invasion with conventional forces a hazardous attempt.

Later, upon returning from a North Atlantic Council session in Paris, in an interview with the press, Mr. Dulles is reported to have said: "Tactical weapons such as atomic cannon are fast becoming conventional and presumably they would be used in war."

Unfortunately, there is a vast chasm between statements of policy and military capabilities. There is much to be done if this is to be bridged, for the acceptance of tactical nuclear weapons suggests an entirely different pattern of war. Missiles in many categories, extensive tactical land and air mobility, vastly improved intelligence-gathering systems and improved communications are all required. The programs of the Department of Defense today indicate little awareness of this need. The Army, which has had a great potential for missiles development and a great need for the associated components of its weapons systems for that kind of a war, has been limited by a steadily deteriorating budget, and this has been the technical dilemma. While policy appears to have changed, the military programs supporting that policy have not changed and the dilemma, that was a military-political one at the time of Korea, slowly has become technical—how to provide the missiles, mobility and associated equipment required for tactical nuclear warfare under the fiscal limitations and the artificial restrictions imposed by the Department of Defense.

Notable among the latter was a memorandum of November 26, 1956, which limited the range of the Army's surface-to-surface missiles to two hundred miles, the weight of its fixed-wing aircraft to five thousand pounds and the weight of its helicopters to ten thousand pounds. At the time the memorandum was issued, it was made clear to the Army that it was fortunate to get off so lightly, that serious consideration was being given to more restrictive limitations. Up to then there had been no limitations on the weight of helicopters and no limitation on the range of its tactical surface-to-surface missiles. Hence at the very time when it should have been encouraged to go ahead in these new fields, it was forbidden to do so. The effect of the memorandum was to close the vast area between the Army's light air vehicles and the large vehicles of the Air Force to further exploration and research.

This seems unbelievable. At a time when the challenge of the Soviets is greatest, we have, in effect, forbidden research and development in those areas. A recent authorization of another missile of greater potential range than two hundred miles was used to imply that the range limitation had been lifted, but it has not. In fact, many hours of discussion took place between the Assistant Secretary of Defense for Research and Engineering office and the Army's Research and Development office as the Department of Defense sought a face-saving formula, one that would give the impression of authorizing a longer-range missile without in fact lifting the restrictions of the memorandum. The formula was found and is expressed in a technical description of the missile. The November 26 memorandum restricting ranges and weights of Army equipment urgently needed for limited nuclear war remains in effect.

If the lessons of the decade since World War II mean anything, it is that this highly mobile mid-range missile with a tactical nuclear warhead should be developed as a matter of highest national priority, since it peculiarly meets the needs of limited war.

Strangely, the tendency to further restrict the Army's efforts to ready itself for limited war became more pronounced as the need became greater. In late '56 and early '57 there were a number of statements made by spokesmen for the administration indicating a growing concern for the problem of something less than general war. At a press conference in February of 1957, President Eisenhower said:

Of course, anything [a Soviet attack on the U.S.] is possible in this world in which we live . . . but I say this: the likelihood that any nation possessing these great weapons of massive destruction would use them in an attack, grows less, I think every year. I believe that as their understanding of them grows, then the less the chance that they would go on an adventure that brought these things into play, because as I see it, any such operation today is just another way of committing suicide.

Seemingly, more preoccupied with rhetoric than reason, and with publishing restrictive memoranda than with urging that more rather than less be done to solve the problems of limited war, the Department of Defense continued on its course out of harmony with the Executive.

161

So contrary to the national need has this course been that there is real need to ask ourselves whether or not we have been the victims of Soviet strategy. To the Soviets we are at war, and the conduct of war involves to an increasing degree its fourth dimension: strategy. Strategy includes technology, and thus the making of technological decisions. For example, we are constantly faced with the problem of how much of the national product to put into our military programs. The state of Soviet economy, its very low standard of living and its ability to get more out of its people for less investment in consumer goods, has enabled the Soviets to maintain a huge military establishment. And not only to maintain it, but to refurbish it from time to time. Compared to the Soviets, we seem constantly worried lest too much of our national product go into our military program. In fact, it was this very point that caused us finally to rely exclusively on a one-weapons system for some years. If our economy is as precarious as this suggests, then it would be an extremely worth-while strategy for the Soviets to cause us to invest in weapons systems that would not serve our need but would in fact, in the strategic sense, serve theirs. As an example, there are many well-informed individuals in intelligence circles who doubt that the Soviets have huge fleets of manned bomber aircraft. Instead they believe that the Soviets achieved a significant lead over us by jumping ahead to missiles quite a few years ago, while at the same time they led us to believe that the bomber threat was the most serious.

Within the pattern of strategy of the war in which the Soviet Union is now engaged with the West, we should expect them to devote a major propaganda effort to causing us to create weapons systems that will serve the Soviets rather than serve us. And I use the expression "serve the Soviets" in a strategic sense. Thus if the Soviets' strategy is sound, the tactical application of their power will meet with success because we have been misled strategically and are incapable of meeting the technical challenge. Hence, it seems reasonable to presume that as long as the Soviets have the strategic initiative, and our actions, as a consequence, are reactive, we should expect the Soviets to talk constantly about the danger of global war. We should expect them to deprecate any thought of local war, and we should expect their military and political leaders to boast of their most powerful long-range equipment. If they could cause us to invest a sizable portion of our national product at the proper time in weapons systems that in fact could not serve, while for what we consider economic reasons we neglect others, they will have achieved a major strategic victory.

As an illustration of this, we invested many billions of dollars in B-36s, which were never used, at the very time when we starved our missile programs and failed to acquire an adequate modern technology to deal with limited wars. I believe it reasonable to assume, therefore, that our actions have been, at least partially, reactive and stem from Soviet initiative. Our failure to provide adequate forces for limited war appears not to have been entirely our own doing. This, to my mind, is more serious than if it had been, for it suggests that our senior civilian and military leaders, whose decisions act so decisively on the weapons systems we bring into being, have not only used poor and tardy judgment, but have been *led* into bad judgment as well.

It would be well to say a word about the decision-making processes in our national government that ultimately find reflection in weapons systems. And it is the decision-making processes that have been in error. We have not lacked resources, either intellectual or physical. Our nation has had the spiritual strength to face up to the Soviet threat. We have had an abundance of national resources, although many of them have been wasted. It has been the decisions that have been, at times, shockingly in error, not only the decisions themselves, but their tardiness. And the principal object of any reorganization now should be to accelerate and improve the quality of the decision-making processes.

At the top of the pyramid is our National Security Council. The President, the Vice President, the Secretary of State and Secretary of Defense are its principal members. The Secretary of the Treasury and the Director of the Bureau of the Budget are considered "standing request" members and in fact take an active part in its discussions. The National Security Council brings together the leadership of the nation and from it have emanated basic policy papers of pre-eminent quality and soundness. The guidance coming to the Department of Defense from the National Security Council has usually been couched in such language as to give the Secretary of Defense all the latitude he needs to provide the country with the type of defense that it should have. Upon reaching the Department of Defense, however, we encounter a different situation.

National defense is today the biggest industry in the United States. Furthermore, it is by far the most complicated. Final test of the decisions in defense matters is made in the crucible of battle in which the stakes are our national survival. Battles today are so highly complex as to be beyond the grasp and control of all except those few skilled, highly educated and dedicated individuals who have learned how to deal with them. Far beyond the problems of World War II, they now involve many times greater fire power, manpower and mobility. Each of the services is confronted with very difficult problems that can only be solved by career officers of high intellectual attainment and dedication; I speak, of course, of those in the positions of leadership and responsibility. Each of the services has its resources scattered to the far corners of the earth. Each of the services deals with highly technical weapons systems that only our topflight scientists understand in detail, and the interplay of the services and the weapons systems poses problems beyond the management capabilities of the average individual American, no matter how skilled he is in making and selling automobiles, or oatmeal, or shoes, or airplanes. As a consequence, he will have to rely for a long period of time upon the advice of those closest to him. Commenting on this in the *Wall Street Journal* of February 19, 1958, Henry Gremmill said:

> . . . judgment boils down to this, Defense is really too serious and too complicated a business to be entrusted to amateurs, as it very largely seems to be. . . .

Be they lawyers, bankers, politicians or the biggest of businessmen, all have encountered in the Defense Department an assignment which in sheer physical dimensions is larger than anything they have ever tackled before (even General Motors' Mr. Wilson, who had bossed over a half million employees, had encountered new dimensions in the million working for the Pentagon). "I very much fear that these good gentlemen who come and take these positions—and they are dedicated men—take several months to become acclimated and educated to the problems," remarks the president of one great aircraft company.

The time-honored principle of civilian control of defense matters is sound and absolutely fundamental in our democracy. It must be preserved and the efforts of our military should serve its continuance. It worked particularly well through World War II. At that time the Secretaries of the separate services had competent military staffs to advise them. The civilian Secretaries made the decisions, defended their programs before Congress, and assumed full responsibility for the exercise of civilian control over their departments. That it was exercised effectively the record now shows. With the establishment of the Department of Defense in 1947, an additional layer of civilian management was placed above the services. Furthermore, by the law, military officers are forbidden to be staff officers in the Department of Defense. By its ruling they may be aides and assistants. They do not occupy executive or decision-making positions. In order to conduct the affairs of his office, therefore, the Secretary of Defense had to bring in increasing numbers of civilian secretaries. These have varied in competence from one who was recently reported in the press to have spent a few days a month in his office, to some of the most able men in public life. There has been much criticism of the large numbers of Assistant Secretaries and the manner in which they have retarded decision-making in the Department of Defense. Some of it, but far from all of it, is justified. However, there is one layer of civilian participation that is almost entirely overlooked and it is one of the most significant in the Department. It is the group of Civil Service career people who, year in, year out, work in the Pentagon. Within the Armed Forces themselves there are many able Civil Service people who contribute effectively. However, within the services the decisions and final recommendations are made by uniformed people to their civilian Secretaries. In the Department of Defense, lacking senior military staff officers, the Assistant Secretaries rely largely on the Civil Service employees. In the Department of Defense, there are over three hundred such individuals. They probably have more impact on decision-making in the Department of Defense than any other individual or group of individuals, military or civilian.

Here is an illustration of the decision-making problem, as the Department of Defense is now organized, and presumably will be organized after congressional action of the 85th Congress. If a service desires to develop a missile and is satisfied that it needs the missile under high priority, it includes a program for it in its annual budget. When the budget is submitted to the Department of Defense Comptroller by, let us say, the Secretary of the Army, the Comptroller may or may not ask the Assistant Secretary of Defense for Research his views. He may, however, and very likely will, refer it to one of the Civil Service employees of long standing who passes judgment on the need. This individual may visit forces in the field and laboratories to determine whether or not in his opinion the proposal has merit. More often than not, however, the final judgment hinges upon whether or not by adopting the new missile something can be dropped. The prevailing philosophy has been that the military establishment must consist of a limited number of weapons systems and if anything new is adopted, something must be dropped. The fact that the weapons systems have been expanding in quantity and

166

quality since the beginning of time, since man first used a fire-hardened spear, seems to be lost sight of. If the Army feels that the missile is very important, it can, through its Secretary, take the action directly to the Assistant Secretary of Defense for Research. After several months of discussion, and justification, the Assistant Secretary of Defense may approve the project. I have known cases where he has, and then many months elapsed before further action was forthcoming. It would then develop that within the Department of Defense the two Assistant Secretaries differed on their views of the missile's essentiality. Hence, although the Assistant Secretary of Defense for Research approved it, the Comptroller disapproved. In such a situation, the Comptroller is usually overriding, although he can manipulate funds in such a way as to allow its development without increasing the budget.

For example, the Army may be told to go ahead with a missile development, that the funding will be provided by the Department of Defense, and then find that the Department of Defense refuses to provide the funds, thus making it necessary to cut back other weapons. This happened in the case of the Jupiter. The Department of Defense may go one step farther and authorize it as an additional increment to the budget and then after the money is defended before Congress and procured, the Department of Defense can take the money away again, forcing the service to absorb the cost by cutting back on its other weapons systems. This also happened in the case of the Jupiter. In 1957, I was directed by the Secretary of the Army to defend a budget of $372 million. This included $17 million additional funding for Jupiter. While defending it, I was assured by members of Congress that I was being misled by DOD, that they had been told privately that the Department of Defense was not going to give the Army the money. Once again, before our final hearings, I verified through the Secretary of the Army the position that was to be taken. I was directed to program the research and development plans on the basis of $372 million, and to defend that budget before Congress. When the hearings were completed, I was told by the Department of Defense that the Army would be given but $355 million.

It is a practice fraught with danger, that of using career officers in uniform as tools to obtain funds for purposes other than those expressed in the budget. Returning to the proposed missile procurement: if none of the Assistant Secretaries desires to act upon it, they can recommend that it be referred to the Joint Chiefs of Staff. This has happened. Here it enters a situation where two against one is the rule. How the two line up on an issue depends on many intangibles. Individual chiefs may appeal to the Secretary of Defense, but during the administration of Secretary Wilson, this appeared to be of little or no significance. Usually, and I know of no case to the contrary, he took the advice of the Chairman of the Joint Chiefs of Staff, regardless of the views of the separate service chiefs. A proposed missile program may remain in the Joint Chiefs of Staff for many months and some have. In the case of the Army's Jupiter, with DOD approval and within the terms of a JCS agreement which authorized the Army to develop surface-to-surface missiles for tactical use without range limitation, the Army undertook the development of that missile. Later by two-to-one vote, the JCS expressed a view that the Army did not have a requirement for such a missile. Hence the decision was made by the Secretary of Defense to place the missile with another service. Since the other service was developing a missile of its own and was placed in a position of judging the merits of both, the future of Jupiter was very dim indeed. But, because the Army was convinced of the nation's need of an IRBM as well as a satellite, it sought almost desperately to keep the missile alive. Other funds were cut critically to continue to support a Jupiter-satellite program. But let us return to the basic problem. By the time a decision is finally made in the Department of Defense, many months, and in some cases years, have elapsed. All of the pleading and urging of those in uniform, who see national survival almost slipping through their fingers, can be of little avail if the Department of Defense declines to act. Its inability to act stems, in the last analysis, directly from the fact that hundreds of civilians, many of them lacking competence in their assigned field, have now transposed themselves between the senior civilian Secretaries of the services and Congress and the Executive.

The political-military dilemma in the late forties slowly evolved into a technological dilemma by the mid-fifties. The inertia in the decision-making processes doubled and trebled the time required for their making, and tragically, the two-against-one system of the Joint Chiefs of Staff caused many of them to be made wrongly. And thus we saw ourselves slowly being beaten in the technological race with the Soviets. How could we win with a decision-making establishment that could not make timely decisions? It could not be done. And most of the senior staff in the Pentagon realized this as 1957 came upon us with the Soviet IRBM, ICBM, and Sputniks I and II.

Thus in the governmental processes of our democracy, what had been a political-military dilemma soon transformed itself into a technological dilemma, and then soon became a personal one. For Congress had to be assured that the funds it was providing were wisely spent and Congress had to feel assured that it was exercising its responsibilities under the Constitution. An individual in the Pentagon who had taken the trouble to study the situation and who could foresee the serious dangers that lay ahead in the system of management then prevailing, found himself in a real dilemma, for the man in uniform serves two masters. The man in uniform swears in his oath of office to "support and defend the Constitution of the United States against all enemies, foreign and domestic." Upon being appointed to office, he receives a commission directing him to "observe and follow such orders and directions, from time to time, that he shall receive from [the Secretary of the Army] or the future President of the United States of America, or the General or other superior officer set over him."

The oath of office is a direct outgrowth of the Civil War experience and was approved by congressional action on July 11, 1868. The responsibility given to Congress dates from the drafting of the original Constitution. It appears to have been the intent of our forefathers to give responsibility to Congress for the nature and character of the Armed Forces. This includes the responsibility to look into the state of the Armed Forces, and to question its members as to adequacy of the existing establishment and requirements for the future. They have a right to expect full and forthright answers in view of the oath of office sworn by commissioned members of the military establishment. Our forefathers showed great wisdom in so charging Congress. It is close to the people, much closer than the Executive Branch, and history demonstrates the clear sensitivity of Congress to the national need in defense matters. There have been times when important issues have been resolved by dangerously close margins, notably the extension of the Selective Service Act by one vote on August 18, 1941, but all in all, Congress has good reason to be proud of its contribution to our national defense.

Until recent years, it had direct and full access to all elements of the military establishment. However, with the passage of the National Defense Act of 1947, a new department was set up that interposed itself between the separate branches of the Armed Forces and members of Congress. Interposed itself, in that, as a member of the Executive Branch of the government, it prepared the budget and directed its support by the Army, Navy and Air Force. It would be most difficult to argue that the Executive should not prepare the budget for submission to Congress. Nevertheless, when the defense requirements are considered and the budget is finally approved, the budget as finally received by a service is a directed one in every sense. Each service then tailors its requirements to fit the money to be provided. In the final analysis, the budget determines the strength and nature of the Armed Forces. And in its final determination, after money is provided by Congress through the Bureau of the Budget and the reapportionment process, even specific items of hardware and projects are approved or rejected by the fiscal offices of the Department of Defense through which they must pass.

The man in uniform soon finds himself in a position of defending the budget before Congress. Prior to such a defense, he is instructed as follows:

Budget amounts being defended in the hearings will be those in the President's budget and issued by Budget Division, Office of Comptroller of the Army, as the control figures and as set forth in the Departmental justification books. . . . It is improper except in answer to specific questions to make reference to other than control figures. For example, to volunteer such a statement as, "Our request for $———— was disapproved by (higher authority) and the amount shown in the budget is inadequate," is improper and will not be presented.

The budget as presented to the Legislative body by the President is that decided upon by the Chief Executive. We, as subordinate elements, are bound to support it before the Legislative body of the Government.

Under no circumstances should the witness voluntarily voice an opinion contrary to the Army position.[24]

Since he is required to obey such instructions, he is then, upon being queried by a member of Congress about the adequacy of the program, faced with the dilemma of telling a falsehood or being insubordinate. The degree of this difficulty reflects, to a large extent, the adequacy of the defense budget. When there is an abundance of money and most programs are well supported, there appears to be no great problem. However, when less money becomes available, as has been the situation in the Army for the past several years, then painful decisions must be made to delay or eliminate programs entirely. Sometimes it quickly becomes apparent that some of these programs are critical to our very survival. An individual who is aware of our military history and who is sensitive to our national need is soon faced with a very difficult choice. Should he, motivated by a growing concern for our national survival, tell Congress the truth and thus invite the wrath of the Executive hierarchy upon himself? Or should he be

[24] Department of the Army Memorandum to prospective witnesses before Congressional Appropriation Committees.

evasive and noncommittal and hope to get by without Congress asking the right questions?

The problem, also, goes much farther than merely defending the budget. Congress takes its responsibilities under the Constitution seriously and many members insist on questioning witnesses about our strategy and the adequacy of the weapons systems to support strategy. Thus they touch upon the very philosophy that provides a basis for our military planning. There is an additional problem that complicates the situation. Individual members of the Armed Forces may, if they desire, bring particular information into the open by providing questions to members of Congress to be asked of military witnesses. Congressmen in general look with favor on this system since it gives them a vehicle for obtaining information that they might otherwise be denied. But the system has wicked implications for the man in uniform since an unscrupulous individual can use it to embarrass a service or an individual for particular gain. It can be used as a technique to serve industrial and private interests, depending upon the type of information brought out. Each service is represented with Congress by a small group of able officers known as a Liaison and Legislative group. I have been frequently asked to plant specific questions through such a group, but I have consistently refused to do so, for great harm can be done both to our country and to individual witnesses.

In inquiring into the state of the military establishment, Congress goes beyond the budget and delves into many aspects of our defense programs. They soon learn that the views of senior officers differ on fundamental issues, not only between the services, but within the same service. Thus a lower-ranking officer will find himself supporting one Chief of Staff one year, and perhaps another Chief of Staff of a differing point of view the following year. Also to be consistent with the policies of the administration, a senior officer will find himself charged with defending the point of view expressed by Mr. Dulles on the employment of nuclear weapons in January of 1954 and changing his point of view to

172

support Mr. Dulles' changed point of view several years later. A key officer may appear before several congressional committees a year, each requiring several hearings. One soon learns that he must make a basic decision. One must either be straightforward and honest, speaking from personal conviction based upon study and understanding of the problems, or one must decide to become a military chameleon, an individual who changes his point of view according to the mood of the moment and the apparent pleasures of Congress or the prevailing civilian superior in the Department of Defense.

The airlift problem offers a good illustration. The Army was laggard in not forcibly expressing its requirements for airlift before Korea. Based upon the Korean experience, General Collins in a memorandum of March 2, 1951, expressed requirement for a tactical airlift of two and two-thirds divisions and a strategic airlift of one division. That is to say, he asked for an airlift that would enable us to lift approximately a division in tactical combat in each of the major continental areas. He also wanted to be able to fly one division from the United States to an overseas theater. In the light of World War II experience, the Korean experience, and the changing pattern of war with increased emphasis upon missiles and nuclear warheads, such an airlift was a minimum requirement. It was constantly supported before Congress by those of us questioned on the problem. However, with the appointment of General Taylor as Chief of Staff, he responded to the pressures of the DOD and the chairmen of the JCS and decided that the requirement was excessive. Of course, in Mr. Wilson's now famous memorandum of November 26, 1956, the Secretary of Defense stated flatly that the airlift was then adequate. We could not at that time lift a single division, either tactically or strategically.

As an example of the conflicts that can come from such a situation, appearing before a committee headed by Senator Symington, General Taylor said: "General Gavin, of course, informed me of the testimony he was going to give. I told him I respected his judgment and I know the committee did. I did not entirely agree with him." Later, in reply to a question by Senator Symington, "How can an Army be modern today when we have not enough airlift?" Secretary Brucker stated: "I take exception to the fact that we don't have enough airlift, if any statement of that kind has been made, because we have an airlift which is sufficient."

Another area of significant difference of views has been in the numbers of nuclear warheads that may be required under certain assumptions pertaining to combat in the mid-sixties. At the request of Secretary of the Army Stevens, I accompanied him as a witness before Senator Jackson's Subcommittee on Military Applications of the Joint Atomic Energy Committee in the spring of 1955. In reply to a question by Senator Jackson, I stated that the Army had a requirement, under certain assumptions, for a large number of tactical warheads on the order of about tens of thousands. I had gone into this problem quite thoroughly and I was convinced of the need. I am still convinced of it and in fact, suspect that this well may be the "Achilles' Heel" of our limited war-making capability unless radical steps are taken as a matter of highest national priority to improve our position in this field. We are many years late in realizing the importance of tactical nuclear warheads and in providing an adequate stockpile. It would have been to serve the country badly indeed to slight the problem in discussing it with a responsible committee of Congress merely because many of those in our national government had failed to keep themselves well enough informed on its importance. Closely related to the tactical nuclear problem is the strategic weapons problem. As has been the situation in other fields of military application, we seem to have concluded that we cannot have both a limited-war capability and a general-war capability, although this is now gradually changing.

That there was a reversal of the position of the administration as expressed in the "New Look" became clear in an article in *Foreign Affairs* by Mr. Dulles in October, 1957. (See page 159). Thus the witness before Congress, if he were to support the

Executive Branch of which he is a member, would have to switch his position if he were to remain consistent with administration policy. That this was not always easy to do I found in testifying before the Symington Committee on airlift hearings in the spring of 1956. The following exchange took place:

MR. HAMILTON (Counsel for Symington Subcommittee on the Study of Air Power): With reference to a preliminary question, and in connection with the general considerations you discussed in the paper that you read as your opening, is it the Army's view that in the event of a large war, the first phase of it would be an air power battle?

GENERAL GAVIN: I am not sure that I know what you mean by "a large war."

MR. HAMILTON: Assuming we were attacked by the Russians. The Committee has been told there is general agreement among the services that the first phase, the initial phase of the war, would be a struggle for air supremacy.

GENERAL GAVIN: You have already described the war in saying that the Russians would attack the United States.

MR. HAMILTON: Yes.

GENERAL GAVIN: I would say that the Army believes now that we are more likely to be involved in a peripheral war than we are in a general war.

MR. HAMILTON: Yes, I understand that, but I mean assuming there were a general war, would you agree with the view that has been expressed that the first phase of that war would be a struggle for air supremacy?

GENERAL GAVIN: No; I would not, personally.

MR. HAMILTON: What would be your view as to the initial stage of a war, of a general war of that kind?

GENERAL GAVIN: In giving my views I would have to express some understanding of the intent of the Russians, and I believe their intent, if it were to ultimately venture the risk of a large war in order to achieve an objective, they would start on the basis of a limited objective to put themselves in a better position, and perhaps ultimately cause enough deterioration of our position to where they could win without risking any attack upon the USSR.

SENATOR DUFF: I want to ask one question, if you please, sir. Senator Symington has referred to the number of lives that would be lost according to this article in *Fortune* Magazine. I would like to ask you, sir, if we got into nuclear war and our strategic air force made an assault in force against Russia with nuclear weapons so that those weapons were exploded in a war where the prevailing winds would carry them southeast over Russia, what would be the effect in the way of death over there under those circumstances, in your opinion?

GENERAL GAVIN: I will give you an answer to this and I will give you a specific one, sir, but I would like to respectfully suggest that the Air Force or a proper study group give you this answer.

Current planning estimates run on the order of several hundred million deaths that would be either way, depending upon which way the wind blew. If the wind blew to the southeast, they would be mostly in the USSR, although they would extend into the Japanese and perhaps down into the Philippine area. If the wind blew the other way, they would extend well back up into Western Europe. And I use the figure "several hundred million," which contrasts with the estimates that you have quoted in *Fortune* Magazine as being about several times lower. Again, though, there have been studies made on this I know and they are very interesting and worthwhile.

SENATOR SYMINGTON: Will the Senator yield?

SENATOR DUFF: Yes, sir.

SENATOR SYMINGTON: My figure was on what would happen in this country only. It did not have to do with the rest of the world. But isn't it also true, following Senator Duff's idea, that if this radioactive material stays in the atmosphere a long time, the atmosphere stays with us a long time; and it could go around the world and back? Doesn't the atmosphere revolve around the earth? I am out of my field now.

GENERAL GAVIN: Yes, sir. I should say to be sure there is no misunderstanding, I very strongly support a very strong SAC, a very strong Strategic Air Command. The Army's views as for its own requirements merely are part of the overall picture, and part of that contains SAC with very effective and impressive strength.

The foregoing fallout testimony was cleared for publication by the Department of Defense and I was shocked to read of it in the headlines of the papers in Naples, Italy, where I was on a staff visit in the summer of 1956. It had been given in a "top-secret" hearing. I had felt reluctant to answer the question on fallout, but I was aware of the very fundamental nature of the question. It touched the heart and soul of our strategic thinking and our attitude toward our Allies and what we, in the final analysis, stood for. That I had been opposed to a single-weapons-system strategy from the beginning was well known, but it was unfortunate that the question-and-answer exchange was published in the open press. It caused many questions to be asked by our Allies, as well it might have. And it placed me in a very difficult position with the Department of Defense. The Secretary of Defense, the Chairman of the Joint Chiefs of Staff, and in turn the Chief of Staff of the Army all required both written and verbal explanations. Somehow it brought into focus the basic dilemma once again, for in a closed top-secret hearing, Congress should have had made available to it such information if it is to exercise its responsibilities under our Constitution. On the other hand, the Executive Branch of the government is entitled to keep such information from Congress if it so desires. However, no instructions specifically denying such information to Congress had at any time been issued. The repercussions that followed were both troublesome and highly indicative of the deep feeling prevalent in the Pentagon. Ultimately I found myself the subject of a memorandum to the Joint Chiefs of Staff, charging me with misrepresenting facts based upon an article that had appeared in *Fortune* Magazine. My testimony was based upon one article, the memorandum on another. I finally wrote to Assistant Secretary of Defense Gordon Gray and asked that the memorandum to the Joint Chiefs of Staff be withdrawn and this was done. In addition to these major problems, there were a number of minor ones that arose in congressional hearings, the sum total of which made it clear that it would be best to ask for a reassignment.

The decade between 1945 and 1955 has, for our young nation, been an ordeal by experience. It has been part of our growing up, and the growing pains have been many. All that has happened in the recent years, since 1955, has been a summation of that period. We have been on our own, as a leader always is, since World War II. As a young leader will, we have made mistakes, but we have accomplished much. We have learned that there are no easy solutions to our problems. We have, or we should have, learned to respect our opponent as a tough, versatile competitor.

In the political world arena, our program of collective security has been somewhat more than a partial success. We have learned that more than mere paper agreements are needed. They must be supported by adequate strength, and brinkmanship without strength is a risky gamble. The Soviets have been contained in the East and in the West—in Korea and in Europe. They have turned the flank of our tactical front in the West by penetrating, for the first time in their history, the Middle East. They have shown evidences of being capable of turning our flank in the East by their penetration of Indo-China and Indonesia. Our collective security arrangements, although remaining in effect, are more seriously challenged than they have been since World War II.

Our technical programs have lagged behind those of the Soviets. They have achieved missiles of greater range and greater variety and greater payload than anything we possess. They have maintained a spectrum of military power adequate to support their policies; they can demonstrate a capability to wage general war and make evident, as well, an impressive array of mobile and tactical power for use in limited war. Admittedly, they have denied their people the abundance of consumer products so characteristic of our economy. But consumer products do not win wars, and the Soviets are at war. In the realm of strategy, their psychological warfare successes have been numerous and large segments of the uncommitted people of the Free World are proving surprisingly susceptible to the wiles of Soviet propaganda. The early Sputnik launching, the proposal to end nuclear weapons tests, their insistence upon a greater cultural exchange program, and their constant acclaim of peace have made an impressive impact on the minds of men everywhere. And while the past decade has been one of learning, the forthcoming decade will be one of decision, for the imbalance of power is gradually shifting to the Soviets. And by power I mean not only military power, but the weight of world opinion as well. I do not, for a moment, agree with Mr. Khrushchev, as he put it, that our "grandsons will be socialists." But if they are not to be, then they must know what they are for. And knowing what they are for, have the courage, vision and industry to be assertively for it.

6

Soviet Military Philosophy—
"We Will Bury You"

An understanding of Soviet military thinking is basic to an appreciation of where we, and the Western world, stand. The policies, intentions and capabilities of neither the USSR nor the West can be evaluated in a vacuum. They must be considered in relation to each other. World opinion, and especially conflicting opinions, polarize in these two great powers, the USSR and the United States. Our own attitudes, of course, are well known. They are well published and generally understood except in areas where the aggressiveness of Soviet propaganda has caused misunderstanding. Soviet policies, on the other hand, seem to many to be obscure at best and at worst utterly incomprehensible.

As Sir Winston Churchill said, "Russia is a riddle, wrapped in a mystery inside an enigma." It was a description that caught the public fancy, as was intended, and for this reason it is still remembered. But mere definition does not suffice. We need to know more of the substance of Soviet thinking, of what they are really capable and how they are most likely to apply those capabilities in carrying out policy. These things have not been easy to discern, not because of their absence, but because of the fog of confusion laid down by Communist policy. We seem at times to be in two different worlds, and even the words that we use, although they sound the same, may have exactly opposite meanings. I had the most fascinating discussions with senior Soviet officers in Berlin immediately following the war on the problems of freedom of the press, the organization of labor, and democracy in action.

When stories unfavorable to the Red Army appeared in the English-speaking press, and there were quite a few due to the brutality of the Soviet occupation, my Soviet opposite number in the Kommandatura would storm into a meeting with loud complaints. When I explained that our press was in fact a free press and thus could write the truth as they saw it, he would charge us with having done just the opposite, alleging that our press was only free to print lies, pointing out that the Soviet press was told what the truth was and only printed the truth. We then discussed what was the truth, and of course to a Communist the truth is what the party says is the truth, regardless of the personal conviction of party members. We never, apparently, reached a meeting of minds.

In organizing labor and starting our factories in operation in Berlin in the summer of '45, the Soviets attempted to bring in their own appointed "labor leaders." We told them that this was not the proper way for labor to achieve representation, pointing out that the workers, through their own elective process, should elect their representatives. The Soviets countered by saying that the workers themselves did not know who could represent them best, whereas the party did. The party knew who were the proper democratic representatives who could serve democracy best and therefore it should help the workers by giving them well-trained leaders. As for the word "democracy," it meant two entirely different things. To the Soviets, it was the opposite of Fascism, which we had just fought a war to destroy. They argued that being the opposite of Fascism, it was Communism. The fact that Communism in practice was as totalitarian in its methods as Fascism itself escaped them. And to suggest this only got blank stares in response. This was beyond their comprehension, for Communism by definition is a dictatorship of the people, of the proletariat. And so it went.

Fortunately for an understanding of Soviet military philosophy, we may turn to a student of warfare who served with both the Russian and Western European forces, and with each for many years. He was a profound student of warfare, and an able writer and his writings early caught the fancy of Lenin. In fact, Lenin wrote a book on them entitled, *Lenin's Notebook on von Clausewitz*. Lenin was a student of war. He was frequently referred to in the party as "The General."

Von Clausewitz was born of Polish parents in Germany in 1780. His father had served as a lieutenant under Frederick the Great and in 1793 at the age of thirteen von Clausewitz went to war for the first time. He fought with the Prussians against Napoleon until their defeat. He then joined the Russians and fought with them against Napoleon. He took part in the long retreat back to Moscow and in the counteroffensive that destroyed the French Imperial Army. He rejoined the Prussians for the final blow against Napoleon at Waterloo.

He left for humanity his monumental text, *On War*, which in its own way compares with Newton's writings on physics and Adam Smith's on economics. *On War* is in a sense the Rosetta Stone to Soviet military thinking. Through an understanding of it, we can translate the hieroglyphic-like intellectual process of the Soviets into the language of the West.

Von Clausewitz is perhaps best remembered for his statement, "War is a mere continuation of policy by other means." Of this Lenin has written, "The Marxists have always considered this axiom as the theoretical foundation of every war." After World War II, when the lessons of that war had begun to be understood, Stalin, in his personal correspondence, praised von Clausewitz, saying that he confirmed the Marxist thesis that there is a direct connection between war and politics and that war is, in fact, but a mere continuation of politics with more violent means. War and policy are inseparable to the Communists, this we must understand. And the nature and character of violence reflect solely the needs of policy. And finally, there is no such thing as war or peace as we in the West understand it, for the Communists are always at war in the interest of peace, as *they* understand it. One is reminded of the Orwellian "War Is Peace." Testimony given before a Congressional Committee on this subject is pertinent:

DR. SCHWARZ: You have to understand that their basic concept is that class war is a fact of being and that peace is the historical synthesis when communism defeats the remainder of the world and establishes world Communist dictatorship, which is peace. If you ask a true Communist to take a lie detector test and ask him if he wants peace, he would pass it with ease. He would look at you with a light in his eye and say he longs for peace. . . . Every act that contributes to the Communist conquest is a peaceful act. If they take a gun, they take a peaceful gun, containing a peaceful bullet, and kill you peacefully and put you in a peaceful grave. When the Chinese Communists murder millions, it is an act of peace. When the Russian tanks rolled into Budapest to butcher and destroy, it was glorious peace. Peace is wonderful and within their framework of ideology whatever helps their conquest is peaceful, good, and true.[1]

In furtherance of the above, Lenin has written, "History demands that the greatest problems of humanity be solved by struggle and by war." Thus the Soviets pursue a zigzagging course of aggression, and it is aggression, inexorable and relentless, as it penetrates every vulnerable spot in the armor of free men, political, economic and military. While on one hand Mr. Khrushchev says, "We will bury you," the Soviets piously preach peace, and every visitor and tourist to the USSR is told by the people of their hunger for peace. And in the same manner, while thousands of United Nations young men were dying in Korea at the hands of Soviet-inspired aggressors, the Stockholm Peace Petition was being circulated and Picasso's White Dove of Peace exploited.

Von Clausewitz wrote, "A conqueror is always a lover of peace; he would like to make his entry into our state unopposed." Lenin

[1] Hearings of the Committee on Un-American Activities, May 29, 1957, Dr. Frederick Schwarz testifying.

referred to this, with characteristic cynicism, as being "very witty." And Stalin, in an interview with H. G. Wells in 1934, made the remark: "Communists do not in the least idealize deeds of violence. They would be very pleased to drop violent methods if the ruling class agreed to give way to the working class." And again with characteristic abuse of words, "working class" had nothing to do with workers, it referred to the slaves of the Communist party.

Of course, only through a clever manipulation and play on the words of "war" and "peace" can the Communists march ahead to their objectives. It is for this reason that they use the words so interchangeably, for their fundamental objective has never changed. Lenin wrote, "As long as capitalism and socialism exist, we cannot live in peace: in the end, one or the other will triumph —a funeral dirge will be sung either over the Soviet Republic or over world capitalism." This was reaffirmed in almost identical language by Marshal Stalin before World War II and again after World War II. And it was what was meant by Khrushchev when he said in Prague in July of 1957, "We are convinced that our cause will be victorious," and later predicted that our own grandsons would "live under socialism in America, too." And socialism, as he used the term, means slavery under the Communist party. And judging by the current state of Soviet technology and military readiness, they have better reason to believe, than at any time in the history of the party, that their "cause will be victorious." Not since Karl Marx lived in severe poverty in Soho while he developed his theory of dialectical materialism have the Communists seen greater vistas of promise than are now unfolded before them. His theory was developed to appeal to the poor and the rich, to the greedy, the power-hungry and the ambitious. Lenin converted the theory, in practice, to a "dictatorship of the proletariat." And through the dictatorship of Lenin and his successors, and the enslavement and exploitation of millions of people, the USSR now threatens not only the economy of the West, but its very survival. In coal, steel, and a number of other essential elements of their economy their *rate* of increase of production now surpasses that of the United States. Addressing the United States Ambassador Llewellyn Thompson in Moscow on April 21, 1958, Premier Nikita Khrushchev said, "We will beat the capitalists. . . . When we win in this competition we will also re-educate you. We Bolsheviks are a ravenous people. What we achieved in the past is very little. We want more and more. Look out, Mr. Thompson, we are stepping on your tail."

Strangely, the Communist party represents only 3 per cent of the population of the Soviet Union. But it is the controlling 3 per cent. It is in absolute control of the government, the people and the armed forces. From birth until death, everyone in the Soviet Union is under the control of the dictatorship of the party. And it is a dictatorship, not of the proletariat, as Lenin liked to say, but of the transient Big Brother. At the moment, having arrived at this station with characteristic ruthlessness, he is Nikita Khrushchev.

Although Karl Marx may have dreamed of Utopian socialism when the party was first being conceived, it is one of the facts of our time that in order to achieve its goals, it has become completely totalitarian. In methodology, it has gone farther and farther to the right. All of the trappings of totalitarianism characterize the operation of the government by the party: concentration camps on a huge scale, complete control of the information media, regimentation of the thinking of the people, and the ever-present secret police. Elections are rigged so that only the party candidate may achieve office. These things are not only characteristic of life in the Soviet Union, but they are the principal export of the party. Wherever the party penetrates successfully and gains control of another nation, a dictatorship of the party is established under the guise of a "dictatorship of the proletariat."

As we would expect, the Communist party has complete control of the Soviet armed forces. One of the most comprehensive summaries of the relationship between the armed forces and the party is contained in a recent speech by the Soviet Minister of Defense, Marshal Malinovsky. It was given on the occasion of the fortieth anniversary of the Soviet Army and Navy on November 7, 1957, and is in effect a summary of their contribution to the party's military achievements. Malinovsky began with an account of the early days of the Revolution. Then citing the victories over Hitler's armies and the Japanese, he paid credit to the party for its contributions:

The Communist party, headed by its Central Committee, was the inspirer and the organizer of the victory of the Soviet Union in the Great Fatherland War. . . . The Communist party reared remarkable command and political cadres, a whole cohort of wonderful military commanders who bore on their shoulders the entire burden of directing the military operations of our troops in their battles against the experienced and treacherous enemy. They revealed unsurpassed military art and skill.

He goes on to praise the characteristics of the Army, pointing out that it had been "reared in the spirit of Soviet patriotism and and proletarian internationalism." It is well that he praised the party, for a failure to do so presages quick oblivion. Referring to his predecessor, Zhukov, he said: ". . . the party so justly condemned the mistakes and checked the harmful practices of the former Minister of Defense, Zhukov, who pursued a policy of abolishing the leadership and control of the Army and the Navy by the party, its Central Committee, and the government."

He attributed more to the party, however, than credit for past achievements. He pointed out the role that the party now plays, and it is most important that we realize the significance of this role, for in the final analysis the Soviet military establishment is an instrument of the Communist party. Its performance is not predictable in terms meaningful to Western military thinking, no more than the political performance of the Communists should appear rational to the Western politician. No matter what the Red Army or Air Force or Navy leaders say they might do in any situation, we must realize that they will do exactly as the party tells them. Otherwise, they will not be leaders for long. Referring to the current influence of the party, Malinovsky said, "The Central Committee of the party determines the line for the building up of the armed forces and sets the Army and the Navy scientifically based tasks at every stage of their development. The strengthening of the leadership of the party of the armed forces is the guarantee of the unswerving improvement of their fighting capacity."

There are numerous evidences of the death grip which the party has on Soviet military thinking and behavior. For example, it has always been the party line that the Soviets defeated Hitler and Japan single-handedly. Malinovsky, in referring to the Soviet armed forces in World War II said: "The Soviet Armed Forces played the decisive role in World War II, determining its victorious outcome. The reactionary ruling circles of the United States and Britain, striving to bleed the Soviet Union white, delayed in every possible way the opening of a second front in Europe. They opened this front only in the final stage of the war when they realized that the Soviet Army was capable of crushing Fascist Germany on its own."

I have recently had brought home to me in a personal way another facet of the same propaganda line. In 1947 I wrote a book entitled *Airborne Warfare*. It described the airborne operations in World War II beginning with Sicily and going through the war. In 1957, it was published in Russian, without my knowledge, with a lead chapter by a Russian Major General, I. K. Brushko. In it he states:

It is necessary to point that at the time of the carrying out of these large airborne operations, such as those of Normandy, Holland and the Rhineland, Hitler's army had been so weakened as a result of the crushing attacks of the Soviet Army that in reality it could not offer any serious resistance to the Anglo-American troops. In minimizing this and exaggerating the capabilities of the German troops, Gavin fails to give an objective appraisal of the events.

187

In *Airborne Warfare,* I concluded that "the knowledge of the existence of a well-trained airborne army, capable of moving anywhere on the globe on short notice, available to the international security of a body such as the United Nations, is our best guarantee of lasting peace." Referring specifically to this, General Brushko says:

This is the usual propaganda line of the partisans of the arms race who claim to be peace-loving and at the same time are preparing for a new war. As we know, after the end of World War II, the American imperialists employed airborne troops in a war of conquest in Korea, just as their Anglo-French Myrmidons, in their disgraceful and unsuccessful adventure in Egypt."

I was rather shocked when I first was given the party line on who won the war. It was in Berlin in the summer of '45. The question arose as to who was to lead the Victory Parade then being planned. To my disbelief, the Soviet member of the Kommandatura told me in so many words that they had won the war. Thinking back over the trail of white crosses extending from Africa through Sicily, Italy, Normandy, Belgium and Holland, right up to east bank of the Elbe, and of the 65,000 troops who processed through the 82nd Airborne Division in its almost three years of fighting, I could not believe my ears. I told him what I thought about it. He seemed a bit embarrassed and then rather grudgingly admitted that the British, French and the Americans all had something to do with winning the war, he supposed. But, I felt at the moment, my obvious unwillingness to say "yes" to the party line shocked him more than his statement did me. The point of view of the party was to him religion and under no circumstances to be questioned. It was but one of a number of fundamental differences that became apparent as our work in the Kommandatura went along. But it did seem, at times, that it must have been refreshing to the Soviets to hear the free discussion and exchange of ideas that took place between the three non-Soviet members.

In addition to the contributions that the party makes to the internal military structure of the Soviet Union, it also controls the international military program. The extent and nature of arms and technical advisory assistance to China, Korea, Syria and Egypt all reflect the policies and pattern of international Communism, in its march to world domination. Such military support is far greater than most people realize. In addition to supporting the satellites with an abundance of modern equipment, the Soviets have been able to export vast quantities of tanks, self-propelled guns, airplanes and even submarines. The London *Times* of August 27, 1957, reporting on but a small part of the military equipment going to Syria, lists the following equipment:

    200 T-34 tanks
    50 heavy self-propelled guns
    200 armored troop carriers
    140 large field guns
    100 smaller guns
    60 antiaircraft guns
    70 Mig fighters

The total aid up to that time was estimated to be in the vicinity of 150 million dollars. This military aid was accompanied by additional support such as airfield construction, technical assistance, etc. It is sizable military inventory for a country like Syria. Finally, more important than the overt well-published aid, are the covert shipments, such as those intercepted by the French en route to the Algerian Nationalists. Through the mechanism of the party and its extensive international network, it has been possible for the Soviets to carry on their successful program of international support, while at the same time they have convinced the recipients of the support, and many millions of the uncommitted people of the world, of their peaceful intentions. Being a function of the party, and thus highly centralized in its control and direction, it is subject to quick change in direction and quick responsiveness to the needs of governmental policy.

Obviously, there are disadvantages as well as advantages to their system. When the military doctrine of a nation ceases to be objective in its appraisal of the past, it contains the seeds of future disaster. Human nature and its tendency to deify past achievement play a large part in poor military judgment. If in addition, a military establishment must teach in all of its schools, and to all ranks, a party line on how war was fought and battles won, and who provided the leadership in what manner, then it soon loses its ability to understand what actually did happen. For years Stalin was the great generalissimo. I remember well, in Mecklenburg, standing up and drinking toasts with the Soviet officers to Franklin Delano Roosevelt and to Generalissimo Stalin in the euphoric period immediately following the war. The Soviet generals were extravagant in their high praise of Stalin. I often wondered what must have gone through their minds when Khrushchev so bitterly denounced him. Later it was Zhukov, who was first a great hero and then a bum. It is difficult to understand how a pattern of objective analysis of military affairs can be pursued by the Soviet students of military events in compatibility with the fluctuating party-line evaluation of what actually took place during the war.

At a time when we are preoccupied with the shortcomings of our own Department of Defense structure, it would be well to examine briefly the Soviet establishment. The Soviet high command is organized as an operational entity. At the head is the Minister of Defense, who is a Marshal of the Red Army. Immediately beneath him are four components: a general staff, an inspectorate, a political directorate and a directorate of the rear area. Beneath this top-management structure are the service components broken up into ground and naval forces, the air force of the Soviet Army and an anti-air defense force. In the next echelon are the operation commanders beginning with the military districts, then the anti-air defense districts, the groups of forces abroad and finally naval fleets and separate military forces not under any other command. The Minister of Defense exercises direct control over the military districts. Forces abroad, for example, are those in Poland and Hungary. The political directorate exercises control over the elaborate political system in the Soviet military establishment. The directorate of the rear area provides logistic support for all forces. In summary, it is a truly unified establishment managed from top to bottom by professionals. It has representatives of the party in all echelons and thus is both sensitive and entirely responsive to the party policies. It appears to be an efficient operational structure, and at least at the top echelon one that can make decisions and get results quickly, and furthermore take prompt corrective action if results are not forthcoming.

Despite the apparent efficiency of its organizational structure, the Soviet military establishment has had problems. The Finnish War was a disaster of the first magnitude. And it was fortunate for the Soviets that the deleterious impact of the party on the military forces was uncovered before the war with Germany, for out of the crucible of the Finnish War came many lessons and many changes, and Soviet military leadership improved steadily thereafter. Often overlooked, but of considerable significance, was the unending Russo-Japanese War in Manchuria. Particularly in 1938 and 1939 they engaged in extensive hostilities in that area. Essentially, however, they were fated to keep that war a limited military action, take limited military risks and apparently content themselves with limited objectives.

Under the impact of the initial German assault of June 22, 1941, the Soviet Army and Air Force disintegrated badly. Despite the many warnings which the Kremlin had received, the Germans achieved complete tactical surprise, as German General Halder reported:

Tactical surprise of the enemy has apparently been achieved along the entire line. All bridges across the Bug River, as on the Rhine River frontal, I see undefended . . . that the enemy was taken by surprise is evident from the fact troops were caught in the quarters, that planes on the airfields were covered up and that enemy troops faced with the unexpected development at the front, inquired at the Hqs. in the rear what they should do. A Gp. center reports wild flight on the Brest-Litovsk-Minsk road. Russian command organization in complete confusion.[2]

One defeat after another was their lot until the turning point at Moscow and Stalingrad. As an indication of the magnitude of the disaster at Kiev, which lasted for ten days beginning on August 25, 1941, the Germans captured 665,000 prisoners, 884 tanks, 3,718 field guns and 3,500 motor vehicles. By that date, the Germans had captured nearly a million and one-half Russians and over seven thousand tanks. And while the Soviet Army was being decisively defeated in battle, Soviet industries were moving to the east preparing for the long-drawn-out war that they fully expected to win. And then, in the pattern of the history of war within Russia, the severe Russian winter of 1941-42 began to be felt. German casualties began to mount and the high tide of the war had been reached. By its end, the Soviets had developed a family of armored vehicles as good as or better than anything that the Germans could produce—and the Germans had splendid combat armor. The J-3 Stalin tank and the T-34 both technically surprised the Germans. The Germans, in accordance with the intuitive strategy of Hitler, who did not want to surrender an inch of territory once captured, attempted positional warfare. The Soviets developed a form of deep fast-moving armored envelopments. They out-blitzkrieged the blitzkrieg. The Soviet forces that we met in the summer of '45 were lean, tough, well equipped and thoroughly professional, and while we may have been critical of their poor medical service or their lack of administration or their ill-kempt appearance, they had fought a first-class foe and fought very well.

Since World War II, the Soviet military establishment has shown a definite infatuation with its victories in that war. The techniques in its service schools continue today to emphasize the deep fast-moving armored penetrations, double and single envelopments, that characterized their successful offensive of 1945.

[2] *Halder Diaries,* entry of June 22, 1941.

Soviet Military Philosophy—"We Will Bury You"

In a recent critique, Marshal Zhukov criticized the Russian troop leaders for not moving more aggressively and for not showing more initiative, saying that the Russian armor could be on the English Channel in forty-eight hours in case of war. While their pattern of military thinking seems akin to that of World War II, they have completely re-equipped and have begun to show an interest in nuclear tactical warfare.

The problem of nuclear warfare appears to have been as perplexing to them as it has been to the West. For a number of years, senior Soviet officers claimed that there was no such thing as tactical nuclear weapons, claiming such a limitation in their use was not possible. The Soviet ground forces journal, *Military Herald*, in March, 1955, said:

All the discussion of the "tactical use" of nuclear weapons is necessary to the propagandists of atomic war in order by consecutive steps to lead public opinion to a recognition of inevitability of the use first of tactical atomic weapons, and then of strategic ones. It is quite clear that the first attempt to use this "tactical" weapon would lead to the mass use of atomic and hydrogen bombs.

Similar views were expressed by other Soviet spokesmen at that time. Major General Talensky, writing in 1955, in describing modern war, said:

In modern war hostilities extend over huge areas. The zone of combat operations, and, consequently, of the use of armaments, includes a frontline running for hundreds of thousands of miles and extending to a depth of at least 300 to 440 miles on both sides of the front, from the line of direct contact to the troops. The aggressive elements who are preparing atomic war do not intend to wage it in the deserts of Arabia, the pampas of Argentina, or even in our Siberian taiga. They are preparing to carry it on in Europe with its dense population, which in some areas reaches 200 and even more people per square mile. Can it be imagined that in these conditions war and atomic attacks would be limited only to the zone of operations of the troops and would not affect the civilian population?

It is interesting, in passing, to note that essentially the same points were being raised by some of our Western military people who were not technically well informed on nuclear matters. As in the case of the West, a general change in Soviet attitude slowly began to become apparent. Marshal Zhukov in 1957 said that "tactical atomic weapons, if they are not barred, will in the next few years be introduced into the organic armament of the troops in place of conventional weapons."

In the meantime, while the senior Soviet officers were slowly coming around in their thinking to the inevitability of nuclear weapons being employed tactically, the training of the Soviet Army in such matters was undertaken. In 1954 and 1955, a series of articles appeared in *The Red Star,* a Soviet service paper, describing the characteristics of nuclear explosions and the measures to be taken in self-defense. At about the same time, regular radio broadcasts were made on the same subject over the equivalent of our own Armed Forces Network. These were translated by the Rand Corporation and I found them quite interesting. They contained a great deal more technical discussion than we would consider appropriate for dissemination to all of the troops. And much of the information appeared to have come from our own published data. A series of manuals were developed describing appropriate behavior in a nuclear environment. These encompassed everything from individual behavior to the tactical handling of the field army in tactical nuclear warfare. In 1956, Marshal Zhukov informed the Twentieth Congress of the Communist Party, "In recent years considerable work on the training of troops in the art of conducting combat operations under conditions of the use of atomic weapons and other new weapons in the ground forces, aviation and the navy has been conducted." It is interesting to note that the Soviets have come to the conclusion that the key to the solution of the tactical problem in atomic warfare is mobility. "Under conditions of employment of atomic weapons, troops will in general operate dispersed in order to save men and material, collecting into a striking concentration only at the time of the attack." And finally, a spokesman for the general staff, a Lieutenant General Krasilnikov, stated that nuclear warfare "calls not for the combatants, but for the logical further increase."

While Soviet doctrinal development and training in nuclear warfare has been carried on, a research and development program to put this doctrine into action has been aggressively pursued. That it has been done with imagination and energy, and considerable investment of resources, is now quite evident. The family of tactical nuclear missiles displayed on November 7, 1957, cannot be matched anywhere in the Western world at this time. One may take a single warhead or a single missile without a launcher, or even a specific motor vehicle and claim superiority for the West. But this would be a labored effort, and as anyone who has carefully studied the Soviet programs during the past ten years must admit, their readiness to engage in tactical nuclear warfare, or in limited nonnuclear war, far exceeds that of the West at this time.

Unlike the West, which currently appears preoccupied with the problem of limited war, the Soviets seem to take all war for granted. To them war is war and it may take any form and any degree of violence, depending upon the situation. To categorize it as limited or unlimited seems not to be officially recognized, even though it is in keeping with the teachings of Communism. Actually, if one is to believe the official "party line" of the Communist party, if there were a war, it would be an all-out war in every respect. This is echoed in the public statements of the senior officials. Nikita Khrushchev, in an interview with Bob Considine, reported by INS in November of 1957, stated:

If war should break out—and it could be started only by the United States because no other nation would dare—this could lead to a great war.

Your cities and bases could be stricken from the face of the earth. This, I repeat, is not a threat. It is simply that we are obliged by circumstances to take the defensive.

And remember, your overseas bases are yours but they are surrounded by the peoples of those countries. You will see, one day they will awaken from their slumber and recognize the folly of depending on NATO and such alliances for their protection.

On another occasion, Marshal Zhukov stated that if war does come, it will involve the use of nuclear, radiological, biological and chemical weapons, as well as rockets and missiles. Another Soviet officer, a Major General Pokrovsky, stated in early 1955, "The era of local wars is over," and he said further that if Europe became an arena of war, "the war would inevitably develop into another world war."

Since the Soviets are now at war, this point of view must be evaluated within the context of war. In that context, it appears to be psychologically sound and good strategy for them to insist that any war will be an all-out war. Thus, while the strategy requires that this be the party line, they supply arms and wage war by proxy where it appears to be to their advantage to do so. Korea was an excellent example of this. I have personally seen hundreds of North Korean weapons, tanks and motor vehicles and without exception they were Soviet-manufactured equipment, much of it brand-new. In emphasizing the horrors of war, the Soviets cast themselves in the role of a gangster who intimidates and threatens the community by pointing out the frightful things that would happen if his criminal aggressions were opposed. Then when they are, the blame is shifted to the citizens of the community who are attempting to protect themselves. In simple terms, this is the current pattern of Soviet military thinking about limited wars. An examination of their military history makes quite clear that they have no hesitancy about engaging in limited war, either directly or by proxy, when it is to their advantage to do so. For years they fought in Manchuria against the Japanese. For many years they supplied arms to Mao, who fought a long-drawn-out series of battles, alternating with periods of quiet, which he has described in his book, *On Protracted War*. The Finnish War was likewise a limited one. And I suppose to the Red Army, the reconquest of Hungary in 1956 was clearly a limited war.

In summary, therefore, we should expect their writings and public statements to reflect the von Clausewitz view that in war there is no justification for the use of anything less than all-out force. They will repeatedly bring to the attention of the world their abhorrence of war, their love of peace, and the horrors that war would inflict upon humanity. In the meantime, they will continue their pattern of aggression in accordance with the teachings of Lenin. The Red Army and Navy, as instruments of the Communist party, will behave and express views fully in consonance with party leaders and, hence, with the state.

An understanding of Soviet military philosophy can be found in the writings of Lenin and von Clausewitz. This philosophy permeates all of their military planning. Their military establishment is equipped and trained with the most modern weapons systems in order that it can achieve at any time the objectives of the Communist party. In size and quality, its Army is un-excelled in the world today. Its Air Force is equipped to work with the Army and Navy in achieving party objectives. Its Navy, having early embarked upon a nuclear-missile submarine program, is readying itself for the naval wars of tomorrow. And while the physical resources of their armed forces are indisputable, their spirit and sense of dedication are likewise of high quality. There may be, and there is good reason to suspect there are, reservations in the minds of many Soviet military men about the efficacy of their system with its ever-present commissar and rigidly centralized control. Nevertheless, to the military men the achievements of the party to date justify the continuance of the system and it promises great accomplishments for them for the future. Short of a series of military defeats, in local and possibly general war, they will continue, proudly and confidently, in their march toward world conquest. Their armed forces will be equipped with an abundance of tactical and thermonuclear weapons, and soon they will have sufficient to equip their satellites and their Chinese ally with such weapons. When this time comes, the West will be confronted with an impressive array of power.

The Soviets will have, in the van, a missile and space program well ahead of anything the West is capable of for many years. Under the canopy of fear created by that impressive display of global power they will be prepared to further the aims of the teachings of Lenin by instigating and carrying out many types of local aggression. It will take different, and sometimes unrecognizable forms—support of dissident nationalists, agrarian upheavals, and exploitation of the transient economic fluctuations so characteristic of our Western economy.

The challenge is without precedent to the military planners of the United States and the West. Whether or not our resources of spirit and mind are adequate to the challenge remains to be seen. Whether or not Korea represents the beginning of the decline of the West or the dawn of an awakening awareness of a need for greater sacrifice and effort likewise remains to be seen. The challenge with which we are confronted, however, is greater by many orders of magnitude than anything in our history.

7

The Decade of Decision: 1955-1965

A. WHAT ARE WE FOR?

America is a young nation with power beyond human understanding at its fingertips. It has come to world leadership at a time when man has for the first time pried open the Pandora's box of nuclear power. Power and leadership are inseparable and as we learn to lead we must learn to use power in a manner that will serve and not destroy us. The time is short. "We do not have a century in which to learn how to be a world power; we must crowd into a decade all the experience Britain drew from a hundred years. . . ."[1] And while we learn to lead in a problem-ridden world, a world in which one nation is avowedly committed to the use of unbridled power, we must learn the meaning and proper uses of power. Our nation's responsibility is beyond anything known in the history of mankind. As Henry Kissinger has expressed it, "Our generation has succeeded in stealing the fire of the gods and it is doomed to live with the horror of its achievement." But power is a poor arbiter of differences among men and nations. Our leadership must demonstrate an awareness of this and take the firm position that power will only be used to serve humanity and to protect it from enslavement. If it is to be used in this manner, we need a doctrine upon which we may base its employment. Of all of the challenges that confront us, eco-

[1] Dr. Henry Steele Commager.

199

nomic, political, technical or even military, the most challenging of all is philosophical. Without an understanding of the goals to which we as a nation aspire, we can never create the resources that will serve those goals. This is fundamental. This must be understood by all of us before we can define the form that our leadership should take or the uses to which power may be put.

One hundred years ago, Abraham Lincoln saw the nation drifting toward the brink of a disastrous civil war. He sensed that the need for a national understanding of where the nation was going was fundamental to finding a solution to its problems. Now we are drifting again toward a crisis, and his counsel in 1858 is as applicable today as it was then: "If we can first know where we are, and whither we are tending, we can better judge what to do and how to do it." Where are we today and how did we get where we are? What is America and what does it stand for at this moment when it is at the crossroads of destiny? What are our aspirations and our goals?

Has democracy, as some would have us believe, reached its greatest hour of fulfillment? Are we so preoccupied with the enjoyment of the physical comforts it has brought us that we are now simply against anything that would challenge that enjoyment? Max Lerner in *America as a Civilization,* suggests this:

> The crucial question about America's destiny in the world frame brings us back to the tests of America's strength as a civilization. It is hard not to feel that while America is still on the rising arc of its world power it is on the descending arc of its inner social and moral vigor; that it has allowed itself to be switched off from the main path of its development into the futile dead ends of the fear of ideas and the tenacious cult of property.

This expresses very well one point of view toward our present situation. Nevertheless, while this author finds it "hard not to feel" that the conditions are as he describes them, I do not for a moment agree with the implications he suggests. The revolution of man that found expression in the new nation founded on this continent is deeper-seated and more lasting than the evidence of its physical achievements. Because it is essentially an idea, an idea that has enflamed the hearts and minds of men whenever it has touched them. It is an idea that is identified with being an American. It is what Americans have stood for since Europeans first set foot upon this continent and to understand it is to understand America itself—not only America of today but America in its beginnings.

There is no one answer to the question, "What is America?" There have been many theories as to why America is unique. Foremost among them is that it is blessed with an abundance of natural resources. But there are other nations equally as blessed. Then there is the theory that, protected by two great oceans, we have been spared the scourge of war. But we have had the bloodiest of all wars on this continent, our own Civil War. Or there is the theory that our nation from its inception had an expanding frontier and each generation had to meet the challenge of the unknown from its infancy. Consequently the nation developed men of great self-reliance, determination and courage, men who sought the challenge of the unknown for the sake of the challenge itself. They had to develop these qualities in order to survive.

I believe that America is all of these things, although it could not be any of them without men. And the men who first came to this continent were men who were willing to give up everything in the Old World and strike out on their own, accepting every risk that the future offered, in order to live as free men. They established settlements on the Eastern seaboard and created a civilization out of a wilderness and out of their hearts and minds. They soon gave expression to their loftiest aspirations:

. . . to form a more perfect union, establish justice, insure domestic tranquillity, provide for the common defense, promote the general welfare and to secure the blessings of liberty to ourselves and our posterity.

To establish and preserve a system based on the concept of the dignity of the individual.

The republic that they created expanded across the Appalachians and the Alleghenies, down the Ohio and across the Great

Plains. Few Americans have captured the moving spirit of that period of our history as well as Stephen Vincent Benét when he wrote:

> Oh, paint your wagons with "Pike's Peak or Bust!"
> Pack up the fiddle, rosin up the bow.
> Vamoose, skedaddle, mosey, hit the grit!
> (We pick our words, like nuggets, for the shine,
> And where they didn't fit, we make them fit,
> Whittling a language out of birch and pine.)
> We're off for Californiay,
> We're off down the wild O-hi-O![2]

It was more than a physical expansion, it was a spiritual growth and expansion. As our democracy grew, communities within it grew, and within them institutions of their own creation to serve them. To be American was to be a symbol of what free men were for. Optimism, buoyant energy, and drive for a new challenge all have been used by historians to describe these men. They were *for* something and while they might have had difficulty describing it, there is no doubt that they were intensely and fiercely proud of it. It was and is democracy, a dynamic living entity that lives for the morrow.

It has been written that when our frontiers reached California and the Pacific, one of a group of pioneers said, "It is too bad, we wanted to go on." They did go on, they and their sons after them. They went on, ultimately to the beaches of Okinawa and Iwo Jima and the 38th Parallel in Korea. We seemed to have difficulty in explaining what we were for at the time of Korea. Perhaps we lacked a Tom Paine, or we had just simply forgotten. Certainly those who had been touched with fire in an earlier war, World War II, knew.

The division of which I was a member in World War II arrived in the small town of Ludwigslust, Mecklenburg, just as we met the

[2] From *John Brown's Body*, published by Rinehart & Company, Inc. Copyright 1927, 1928 by Stephen Vincent Benét. Copyright renewed 1955, 1956 by Rosemary Carr Benét.

Russians early in May of 1945. The night of our arrival the Burge-
meister and his wife and daughter committed suicide. I was quite
concerned lest our soldiers had mistreated them. But the reason
for their suicide pact became known to us a day later. Several
kilometers from the town we discovered a concentration camp. It
was a desolate assemblage of primitive buildings in a forest clearing. It could be smelled long before it could be seen. I never knew
the exact number of its inmates, but we buried about a thousand
of them. It took great care to separate the living from the dead, so
alike were they. In one corner of the clearing there was what
appeared to be an old quarry or excavation. On its edge stood a
bulldozer that had been used to shove the daily pile of cadavers
into the pit. Scattered about the camp were groups of inmates
more dead than alive. The chalk-green skin stretched over their
bony frames was revolting to see, but not nearly so revolting as
the odors and sounds that came from them. It seemed incredible
that man could be so inhuman to his fellow man and to all of us
who liberated that camp it will forever remain in our memories
as a symbol of totalitarianism. If there ever had been doubt about
what we were fighting for or what America stood for, at that
moment it was removed forever from our minds. It was to rid the
earth of man's inhumanity to man, to protect and foster the way
of life of free men, and, if necessary, to fight for that way of life.
It is too bad that so many must see in order to believe.

Now, once again, we are confronted with a new form of totalitarianism. It is not enough that we merely be against it, or be
satisfied with its containment. "We live in a time of danger and a
time of great hope. Whoever offers us complacency blinds us to
one and denies us the other."[3] If the Communists are not to
"bury us," then this heritage that is ours needs new reaffirmation.
It is time that we took counsel, not from our fear of Communism,
but from our aspirations and the promise of democracy. Our country will never be truly secure until our people hold clear convic-

[3] Adlai Stevenson, Fresno, California, February, 1956.

tions on some fundamental issues, and hold them closely and fiercely. Among these convictions should be a respect for the truth; a belief in the dignity of the individual; a belief in government by law, not by men; a belief in honesty and fair play, among nations as well as individuals; and a belief in man's right to worship freely, and to climb as high as his talents will lift him and his ambitions drive him, held within the bounds of consideration for others and the knowledge that the common good must be served above all else.

It was these things that inspired our forefathers. And as our nation grew it was a belief in these ideals that sent them

> Across empurpled plain and precipice
> And whispered in the starlit tamaracks
> Where travelers told of freedom in the West
> Around the fires of hopeful bivouacs;
> The vision of a mighty purpose, pressed
> By all the peoples of the earth, to make
> The hidden truth within them manifest.[4]

The way to freedom was not easy. Nature and recurring war combined to test our physical mettle and spiritual dedication. Even the most bitter test of all, a war between brothers, was to put us to trial. And from the crucible of our experience came a stout conviction of the righteousness of our cause. It took us to the far corners of the earth, through two world wars. It took us to the 38th Parallel, to physical conflict with Russian-inspired aggression. Well over one hundred years ago a Frenchman visiting America foresaw the inevitability of that conflict. Alexis de Tocqueville was amazingly prophetic when he wrote:

The American struggles against the obstacles that nature opposes to him; the adversaries of the Russian are men. The former combats the wilderness and savage life; the latter, civilization with all its arms. The conquests of the American are therefore gained by the plowshare; those of the Russian by the sword. The Anglo-American relies upon personal interest to accomplish his ends and gives free scope to the

4 From *My Country*, Russell W. Davenport, published by Simon and Schuster, Inc.

unguided strength and common sense of the people; the Russian centers all the authority of society in a single arm. The principal instrument of the former is freedom; of the latter, servitude. Their starting-point is different and their courses are not the same; yet each of them seems marked out by the will of Heaven to sway the destinies of half the globe.[5]

And now well over one hundred years since those words were written, the people of the world look to these two great powers for leadership, the United States and the USSR. The history of our people makes abundantly clear that we possess the basis for leadership. No material wealth and none of the physical achievements of democracy can substitute for what is in men's hearts. Nor should we allow anyone to cause us to suspect for a moment that physical comforts have replaced spiritual values in our civilization, for our spiritual values are held as high as they have ever been. But they need reaffirmation. We must be aggressive advocates of what we are for. It is not enough merely to be against an ism, specifically Communism. It is a delusive belief that the world crisis that lies ahead can be resolved merely by resisting Communism. The only acceptable alternative to Communism is dynamic and articulate democracy. It is not the status quo, nor is it another form of authoritarianism.

Democracy is a living, flexible, political thing. It is sufficiently flexible to serve the needs of mankind everywhere. It is a living entity and this means it is changing as the way of life of people changes. It is neither static nor passive. And in order to continue to serve, it must be aggressive and assert itself. "The great nations in the history of the world have been the nations which proposed, the nations which asserted, the nations which conceived."[6]

We are entering a decade in which we will either make manifest the meaning of democracy or we will fall forever. We will regain our lost momentum and we will assert ourselves as proponents of freedom, or we will drift toward slavery. Sixty years ago Theodore Roosevelt said:

[5] *Democracy in America*, Alexis de Tocqueville.
[6] *The Conquest of America*, Archibald MacLeish.

If we stand idly by . . . if we shrink from the hard contests where men must win at hazard of their lives and at the risk of all they hold dear, then the bolder and stronger peoples will pass us by, and will win for themselves the domination of the world.[7]

Time is running out and we must make up our minds now to make the sacrifices necessary to create and maintain a military establishment adequate to serve the needs of democracy and of the West, and by adequate I mean adequate in over-all strength as well as in breadth of capabilities. For if democracy exists to serve the needs of people, then the weapons systems that it creates must serve it. They must be able to apply power with discrimination anywhere in the world, as the need arises, at any time. We must be able to control space, through the United Nations if possible, but if not, as an instrumentality of the West.

There will be those who will argue that since power cannot resolve differences of opinion, it should exist to deal only with general war. This is unrealistic, for when reason can no longer prevail, as anyone who has lived abroad for any length of time knows, power in being is important as a basis for stable government. Following World War II we were naïve in our belief that the people of the satellite countries could establish democratic governments under Soviet occupation. Into the vacuum that was created immediately following the end of the war, the Soviets poured the Red Army. They appointed party leaders to take over key positions in the government and saw to it that local officials were replaced only by devout Communists. At that moment democracy ceased to exist and no amount of dedication and intensity of purpose on the part of the people could prevail against the Red Army. As the Soviets were to demonstrate later in Hungary, human flesh and bone is no match for the Stalin tank. South Korea, too, is a good example of a miscalculated effort to take over a free country.

So force must be present, and in being, for two fundamental purposes. First, to make unmistakably clear that aggression will

[7] "A Challenge to Americans," *The Reader's Digest*, March, 1958.

be resisted at once, and second, to inspire confidence in the people and in the government of their free choice. Military force exists in the Free World community for the same reason that it exists in the city community. The policeman on the beat must by virtue of his reputation and appearance maintain law and order. He must have power available to him that can be applied quickly. The law-abiding citizens of the community can, by maintaining such a police force at minimum cost, go about their daily pursuits confident that the civic government of their choosing will administer their affairs well. In the world community similar power, although of a much greater degree, must be available. This must be backed by highly mobile reserves geographically placed so as to be immediately available to resist criminal aggression. And finally, such "short-range" forces—for that is what they are—must be backed by "long-range" forces, the Free World's major reserves of power. Preferably, these should operate through the United Nations. In addition, the United Nations should also operate a special space force to control space for peaceful purposes.

If adequate strength exists, then people will take counsel from their aspirations and not from their fears. Democracy will be more assertive, and it must be if it is to prevail against Communism.

This immediately raises the question, what about the satellites, specifically Hungary? I do not believe that the Free World can endure many more "Hungarys"—not and remain free. It cannot continue to stand by and watch a freedom-seeking nation be destroyed before its very eyes without doing something about it. A repetition of this will surely lead, ultimately, to the destruction of the West. What could we have done? Actually, in the predicament in which we found ourselves, we could not have done very much. But we certainly could have done more than we did. In the first place, we should be organized to anticipate the occurrence of such an uprising. With some warning, we can then prepare to do everything possible. In the case of Hungary medical assistance and food should have been flown in at once. The wounded should have been flown out. If necessary, military force should be used to protect such an operation. Next, we should have sufficient force in being to enable the West, preferably as an instrument of the United Nations, to move into such a situation. The object of such an operation would be the restoration of law and order and the supervision of the establishment of a government representative of the people's wishes—not one superimposed by Moscow with armored divisions of the Red Army. We were critically lacking the type of military force that would have been required to support action in Hungary. And before one even considers the use of force there is the question of national will or national attitude.

It is difficult to reconcile the statements made by our leading public officials with the actions taken. Unless, of course, the statements were made with the very best intention, while the neglect of our military establishment made it impossible to do anything about the situation when the events in Hungary developed as they did. Speaking to the American Legion in New York on August 25, 1952, Mr. Eisenhower said:

> We can never rest and we must so inform all the world, including the Kremlin, that until the slave nations of the world have, in the fullness of freedom, the right to choose their own path, that then and then only can we say that there is a possible way of living peacefully and permanently with Communism in the world. We must tell the Kremlin that never shall we desist in our aid to every man and woman of those shackled lands who seek refuge with us. Any man who keeps fanning among his own people the flame of freedom and who is dedicated to the liberation of his fellows . . .

This was followed by a campaign speech in Philadelphia on September 4, 1952. In developing the idea of the need for allies and our attitude toward the satellites, he said:

> The fifth step in this program is to aid by every peaceful means, but only by peaceful means, the right to live in freedom. The containing of Communism is largely physical and by itself an inadequate approach to our task. There is also need to bring hope and every peaceful aid to the world's enslaved peoples.

Several months later, as Secretary of State designate, in speaking to the General Assembly of the National Council of Churches of

Christ in Denver, Colorado, on December 11, 1952, Mr. John Foster Dulles said:

> . . . then freedom will again become the force that puts despotism to route. Then a new era of liberation will be ushered in. During the recent political campaign there was discussion about the policy of "liberation." Some were frightened by this idea, feeling it meant war. That fear illustrates the degree to which even free people have come to think in Governmental and Military terms. Our nation, from its beginning, has stood for liberation.

Finally, in the President's Inaugural Address on January 20, 1953, he expressed ten principles by which his administration would be governed. Principle No. 8 stated:

> Conceiving the defense of freedom, like freedom itself, to be one and indivisible, we hold all continents and people in equal regard and honor. We reject any insinuation that one race or another, one people or another is in any sense inferior or expendable.

Thus the record of intention seems clear. We recognized the fact that freedom was indivisible and that a barbed-wire fence or a geographic boundary could not divide people into those who were free and those who were slaves, that the world cannot continue half slave and half free. This has always been our view of freedom, and from its beginnings democracy has supported this view. In the period during World War II and immediately following that war, we referred to it as the right of self-determination. This right still exists and mere absence of power on our part should not cause us to deny it. Sufficient power should exist in being to enable us to support it. From a military point of view, we were far from being capable of supporting the Hungarians. It must have been a bitter lesson to the people of the satellites who aspired to freedom.

Let us take the measures now that will provide us with the strength in being so that there will be no more Hungarys. If people are willing to expend their lives for this concept of democracy, then we should be willing to support them, not only willing but capable. And furthermore, we should have the moral courage to face the issue for what it is, a challenge to our democratic way of life. Hungary, in a small way, was a challenge as significant and as great as any challenge to the United States from the USSR. We cannot shrink from such a challenge, or deny the challenge, if we are to survive.

Closely associated with the future of democracy is foreign economic aid. In many respects this may be more important than direct military assistance. For low standards of living, hunger and impoverishment offer the fertile fields in which the seeds of Communism flourish. We must continue to contribute technical and economic assistance to many uncommitted countries in need. Not only should our national programs be continued, but we should consider the possibility of participating jointly, through the United Nations, in programs with the Soviet Union. The success of such programs would go a long way toward the accomplishment of the goals of democracy. It may be, as Willard R. Espy has expressed it, at least a start on "A Way to Sheathe the Sword."[8]

On a basis of equality in terms of strength, we should encourage cultural exchanges. Students, artists, scientists, industrialists and agriculturalists should be encouraged to visit each other's country so that they may learn to understand and appreciate the viewpoint of each other. I have found Russians that I have met to be very friendly and desirous of peaceful relations with our people. I can see nothing but good to come from a free exchange of visits, and an exchange of ideas. Let the Soviet leadership find the basis for concern of harm that may come from such an exchange if any is to be found. Certainly we should have none. There is no reason to believe that our democracy placed side by side with Communism in practice will do anything but triumph. It will unless it is weak, reactive and apprehensive.

Obviously the creation of an adequate establishment to support such a concept will not be inexpensive. There will be those who will argue that the measures needed to provide such a military establishment, particularly its cost, will be so heavy a burden upon our economy that we would lose to the Soviets in the realm of

[8] New York *Herald Tribune*, March 1, 1958.

economics. This simply is not so, as has been demonstrated by a number of studies. The National Planning Association, for example, estimates that we could increase our national defense expenditures by one-half without endangering our economy. From the viewpoint of requirements Dr. Ellis A. Johnson of the Operations Research Office of Johns Hopkins University, who is as well informed on such matters as anyone in the United States today, estimates that we should increase our defense expenditures by a rate of fifteen billion dollars more per year for an indefinite period. Of course, mere expenditure increase is not enough. We must, in addition, improve our decision-making processes in the technological areas and reduce our lead times, thus obtaining better results per dollar invested than we are now realizing.

In the final analysis, the real challenge comes down to having the vision of democracy so clearly before us, and the courage necessary to support that vision, that we can with assurance build the size establishment needed—in effect, make a sacrifice and create the military establishment adequate to the challenges of the space age without losing sight of the fundamentals of democracy itself. It will take leadership on the part of our statesmen and some degree of sacrifice on the part of our citizens. In the long run, however, we will either make the necessary sacrifices to create the type of military establishment that can serve a positive, forward-looking concept of democracy or we will succumb to the march of Communism.

B. TACTICS IN AN EARTH WAR

The literary output of recent years dealing with policy, strategy and survival is of a high order. There has been an abundance of books on these subjects and they are, with few exceptions, of good quality. Much that has been written so far deals with strategy and policy on a global and national scale and rarely, if ever, gets down to the realities of tactics. This is understandable, since the dynamic nature of today's military technology makes it quite difficult to predict tactical trends with a high degree of accuracy. Only by being intimately associated with the military forces themselves, particularly with the research and development programs of the Armed Forces, may one venture the prediction of tactical trends. But for strategy and policy to be meaningful, we must understand the realities of the tactical battle itself. Strategy is the thought, tactics are the tools. In order to understand strategic thinking and concepts of operations, one must first understand the tools and techniques of combat in the missile-space age.

Combat tactics is the technique of employing the resources of war in battle. The actual functions performed in war are quite simple. They are the same whether it is one man engaged in mortal combat, a carrier task force, a field army or a bomber wing. Hence, the simplest weapons system of all is man himself. An effective weapons system must locate its target, transmit its behavior characteristics through a central communications system, set in motion the force available to destroy the target, follow with an evaluation of the results achieved, and prepare for the next action. In their simplest forms, these functions may be defined as a communications system, fire power and mobility. Their application in battle may become highly complex. A battle will appear entirely different to different participants. It has been said that combat to a soldier is a trade, to a commissioned officer a profession, and to a general an art. It is all of these things. Battles may extend over vast areas of the globe and involve ultramodern communications systems, hundreds of nuclear weapons, and split-second timing of decisions. Obviously the reaction time for many of the decisions are beyond man's capacity and he must entrust them to machines.

For example, in a defense against missiles, from the moment the enemy missile is launched until it strikes us we may have but few minutes, depending upon its range and time of travel, in which to react. This reaction must include an evaluation of the target, whether or not it actually is a missile or a decoy, a determination of its trajectory and thus its destination. Next, we must determine with accuracy where it will be each fraction of a second during its travel, so that we can transmit instructions to our own missile exactly where in space to intercept the incoming missile. Based upon a very rapid and accurate calculation of these factors, instructions are given to our defensive missile and it is launched. It may continue to receive information during flight thus enabling it to conform to changes in the behavior of the incoming missile. All of this must be done in minutes—in some cases in seconds—and all of it must be done through electronic systems. Some decisions only man can make, and he can only make them when he understands the technical performance of the tools that he is using. Nevertheless, as complex as tomorrow's battles may appear, on analysis, the functions performed are identical with those performed in battles since the beginning of time. It is for this reason that students of warfare will often say that while tactics may change, the basic principles of war do not. We can compare the basic functional elements of battles in the past and through a knowledge of technology of the future, we may predict future battle patterns. And when we are able to predict the future pattern that battles may take, we then may define with some accuracy the role of strategy. When we know the tools, we may develop concepts for their use.

Contrary to popular belief, battles are not always won by the stronger opponent. Some of the most decisive battles have been won by the numerically inferior force. It is for this reason that an understanding of the tactics of battle are of such great importance. Mere weight of metal, yield of explosives, or masses of men are never in themselves decisive. It is their combination into a combat-efficient weapons system, cleverly employed, that brings decisive results. One of the first great decisive battles in history was that in which Alexander the Great defeated Darius and thus established Greece in control of the known world. It was fought at Arbela in 331 B.C. Alexander's forces numbered about 47,000; those of Darius exceeded a half-million. Equally decisive was a battle fought over 2,200 years later. The United States fought a naval engagement with Japan, the outcome of which was to determine the mastery of the Pacific Ocean and thus the ultimate destiny of both nations. It was the Battle of Midway.

It was one of those rare battles in which a numerically inferior fleet suddenly snatched victory from a superior force, and thereby changed the course of war. The destruction of two-thirds of Japan's fleet carriers knocked the bottom out of her grand tactical scheme to hold the Pacific by means of "hedgehogs" and mobile forces, and it threw her on the passive defensive. For the remainder of the war it secured the central Pacific for the United States. . . . it struck a mortal blow at Japanese prestige.[9]

History provides us an interesting study of the growth of the battle area. The size of the battle area is a function of the radius of effectiveness of the weapons involved, the mobility of the force engaged, and the ability of the commanders concerned to control those forces. A good analogy is that of the sword and the shield. The sword is designed to penetrate to the vitals of an opponent. To defeat the sword, it was necessary to develop a shield. As the sword became increasingly effective, so did the shield. And as men organized in groups to fire team-launched weapons, they organized in groups to provide more depth to their defense. As man went through transition from hand weapons to gunpowder to nuclear weapons, the depth of the shield, thus the depth of the battle area, had to increase in relationship to the danger of the threat. And as the depth of the battle area increased, man sought to exploit new forms of mobility to make the sword more effective. As man went from foot mobility to animal mobility, to land vehicle and then air mobility, the area covered by a battle increased at an exponential rate. The Battle of Arbela did not cover much more than a dozen square miles. The Battle of Midway extended over an area of several million square miles. The Battle of Zama (202 B.C.), in which the Roman Scipio decisively defeated the Carthaginian Hannibal and thus gave mastery of the Mediterranean to the Romans, extended over but a few square

---

[9] *A Military History of the Western World*, J. F. C. Fuller.

miles. It was one of the decisive battles of history and it led to Roman rule of the known world. The Battle of Normandy, the decisive battle for a lodgment on the Continent of Europe, fought thousands of years later, extended over 100,000 square miles.

This vast increase in the size of the battle area had a regenerative effect: commanders insisted upon more effective means and weapons systems to cope with the expanding battle area, and as they became available, they in turn caused the battle area to increase further. An understanding of the impact that these weapons systems have had upon the battle area will give us some clue to the battle area of the future. Take for example, the range at which fire power is delivered. Man's first weapon was a fire-hardened, hand-carried spear. This he soon learned to throw effectively. In time he learned to add to its range by using the tensile strength of animal fibers, and while individuals retained their hand weapons, they grouped together to use team weapons. The ballista[10] was among the first and this has grown through a family of artillery weapons to today's ballistic missile. In the recent period of its growth, man used an air vehicle to deliver a bomb, then the air vehicle as a platform from which to launch a missile, and ultimately, with surface-to-surface ballistic missiles, will rely upon the air vehicle solely for logistical support. Considering the range at which a powerful blow could be struck against an opponent, one may express the relationship between the nineteenth and twentieth centuries as a proportion:

$$\frac{\text{Range, 19th Century Weapons}}{\text{Range, World War II Weapons}} = \frac{5 \text{ miles}}{500 \text{ miles}}$$

[10] The following description of the ballista is given in *A Dictionary of Classical Antiquities* by Dr. Oskar Seyffert, first published in 1891:
"*Ballista.* See Artillery.
Artillery. The machines used for sending large missiles to a great distance were supposed to have been invented in the East, and appear in Greece since 400 B.C. . . . Ballistae . . . shot stones, beams, or balls up to 162 lbs. weight, at an angle of 50°. The average range of the ballistae was from about 293 yards to about 503 yards." Energy for tossing the missile was acquired through "twisting strong elastic cords, the sinews of animals, or the long hair of animals or of women."

This assumes nineteenth-century weapons to have begun in the Napoleonic period and concluded with our own Civil War. Thus, for comparative purposes, the weapons began with the smooth-bore gunpowder weapons and ended with the rifled barrel, repeating-action weapons. One may take exception, on the basis of specific weapons, but for the purposes of comparison, the figures are valid. In the nineteenth century the average ranges that a tactical commander had to consider were of about three to five miles. In those battles, he could with his own eyes see the entire battlefield and thus he could make decisions based upon personal observation. In World War II, the ranges of weapons extended to hundreds of miles because of the availability of the air vehicle. This in turn made it possible for a tactical commander to employ his forces decisively against an opponent over an area of thousands of square miles.

While the ranges of weapons increased, their associated mobility also increased. From the foot soldier and horse cavalryman of the nineteenth century, we went to the bombardier, the paratrooper, the tanker and the amphibious Marine of the twentieth century. Thus the relationship of the average mobility may be expressed as follows:

$$\frac{\text{Mobility, 19th Century}}{\text{Mobility, World War II}} = \frac{6 \text{ mph}}{300 \text{ mph}}$$

Tactical commanders seek to gain a quick decision. At the same time, they take all possible steps to deny the enemy the opportunity of quick decision. In defense this takes the form of a maximum dispersion of all resources consistent with good control and high degree of responsiveness. In attack this takes the form of increased mobility and depth of penetration consistent with good control and a capacity to survive countermeasures taken by the defender. Thus, again, the tactical theater continues to grow. Now with the greater ranges and unprecedented fire power of nuclear weapons and the hypermobility of missiles and supersonic air vehicles, the area of the tactical battle has

216

increased beyond anything even dreamed of in the past. Let us examine the same functional factors and in doing so relate those to a war in the early sixties, to include 1965.

It will be the first truly Earth War. The bomber of World War III will be the ICBM. The fighter bomber will be the IRBM and long-range artillery. Artillery will, in its larger weapons, exceed one thousand miles. It will also include a family of highly mobile, quickly responsive, shorter-range missiles, missiles ranging from several hundred miles to several thousand yards. Communications will change radically. No longer will we be able to depend upon manned aircraft for deep battle reconnaissance. Instead, drones of exceptionally high speeds and of minimum speed will be used for target acquisition. They will be made of plastics, fiberglass and similar nonradar reflecting materials, insofar as possible. They will cover the speed spectrum from several times the speed of sound to zero—that is, to hovering drones that can remain over target areas for prolonged periods of time. In addition to drones, such as those operating within the atmosphere, drones will operate in space as part of the ICBM systems. The first military application of satellites will undoubtedly be as reconnaissance vehicles for the ICBM system. Not only will the satellite provide accurate, timely information for an offensive ICBM strike, but it will also provide early warning in defense. A family of reconnaissance satellites will enable a nation to keep extensive areas of the earth under almost constant surveillance. When fully developed, with associated ground data-handling equipment, they should be able to transmit at once evidence of enemy missile launchings. Thus they will become part of a nation's early warning system. They should also be able to transmit photos of enemy launching preparations as well as to perform poststrike reconnaissance of specific areas.

General war in the ICBM age will, therefore, be a war involving the entire earth as a tactical theater. Up to the present, wars have attained the scale of being intercontinental in character. But the ranges of reconnaissance vehicles and of weapons, and

217

man's ability to use them anywhere on the earth, bring us for the first time to the threshold of an Earth War. In such a war comparative ranges and mobility in general terms would be as follows:

$$\frac{\text{Ranges, World War II}}{\text{Ranges, Earth War}} = \frac{500 \text{ miles}}{5{,}000 \text{ miles}}$$

Mobility is somewhat more difficult to estimate. If we assume that man and all of his resources for war would move by air in decisive tactical engagements, then mobility may be expressed as follows:

$$\frac{\text{Mobility, World War II}}{\text{Mobility, Earth War}} = \frac{300 \text{ miles}}{600 \text{ miles}}$$

The mobility of man's resources in war is indicated in terms of high-speed air transport. In expressing mobility in this manner, we assume that missiles, by themselves, will not be decisive within the time frame under consideration—by 1965. To be decisive, missiles should be combined with exploitation forces. These latter should be entirely air-transported, and this includes all of the missiles accompanying them. A revolutionary change in tactical mobility is in prospect. The Army's exploitation forces should be built around new forms of air vehicles now being called "sky cavalry." They must be matched with highly mobile nuclear missiles and they should be able to operate over many thousands of square miles and be capable of gaining tactical decisions in a few hours.

It should be apparent from the foregoing that the world has shrunk to the area of a tactical theater. The world that was beyond man's comprehension in the time of Alexander the Great, that was considered the theater of grand strategy in World War II, will have shrunk to a tactical theater by 1965. Men will be able to launch weapons from any point within the United States and to strike any point within the USSR and vice versa. Shorter-range weapons can be employed tactically from close proximity to an opponent, for example from five to fifteen hundred miles. Thus, the employment of power in combat on this earth undergoes its final transition from strategic power to tactical power and thus strategy enters a new dimension, the last frontier: space and the mind of man.

An interesting example of a quick shift from a strategic to a tactical role took place in our own Civil War. On March 9, 1862, reports reached President Lincoln of the existence of an ironclad in Hampton Roads. It was the Confederate *Merrimac*. Upon appearing, it sank two Union vessels and drove a third aground. As the Secretary of War considered the situation with the President, he foretold the destruction of Boston and New York and suggested that the *Merrimac* would come up the Potomac, shell the capital and disperse Congress. The Confederates had in their hands an innovation so unique that it could not be opposed. Its employment in a strategic role was considered by both sides at once. Fortunately for the Union, a Swedish inventor had been experimenting with a cheese box on a raft, the *Monitor*, and with much skepticism it was sent forth to challenge the *Merrimac*. In the engagement that followed, the *Merrimac* was forced to retire to Norfolk. Thus what appeared for a short span of time to be a new strategic naval weapon turned out to be after all but another tactical weapon.

Our own Strategic Air Command has undergone a similar transition. When in the mid-forties we alone possessed nuclear weapons, and SAC to make possible their air delivery, we thought of them in terms of strategic employment. In the pattern of Hiroshima and Nagasaki, and in the philosophy of Douhet, they were to strike terror into the heart of an enemy by razing his cities and industries. Hence we planned in terms of urban bombing and the destruction of his industry and war-making capacity. Even after we knew of the existence of the Soviet long-range bombing force, we continued, for some years, to adhere to our original concept of SAC as a strategic striking force. Only recently have we come to the full realization that its first aim, if it is to contribute in the most decisive manner possible to the outcome of a general war, must be to destroy the Soviet long-range bomber command. And the reverse is true: the first target of the Soviet bomber command must be the Strategic Air Command. Thus in effect, both forces become long-range tactical air commands. Now that the Soviets have an inventory of ICBMs, these will constitute their long-range striking force, the long-range artillery in the Earth War of tomorrow. In passing, it is of interest to note that in the exchange that took place in late April of 1958 between the two governments on the subject of H-bomber flights over the Arctic, Mr. Gromyko had this to say: "If an American bomber armed with nuclear weapons violated the Soviet frontier, the necessity would arise to send rockets to repel the imminent menace." And he added, "and rockets cannot be turned back."[11] The significance of this comment, that rockets would be used in retaliation, should not escape us.

As the area of tactical combat has expanded, it has encompassed all four media: land, sea, air and space. Weapons used in an Earth War will certainly cross the media associated with the three services, the Army, Navy and Air Force. Thus their identification as such is of diminishing importance. Far more important are the weapons and tactics that men employ to win an Earth War regardless of the media of their origin. And overshadowing all three is the problem of space. This is not to say that man's natural habitat, the land, is not still of overriding importance to him, for it is. But to exist on land as a free man and to establish a government of free men and their institutions, he must control the media that surround him, the sea, the air and space. Since he has largely within his grasp the means of control of the sea and the air, and since space is virtually unexplored, it becomes of great significance to man's future.

Space is the theater of strategy of tomorrow—space and the human mind. Obviously a discussion of the strategy of space war is somewhat premature until we have a better understanding

[11] The Washington *Post*, April 30, 1958.

of the tools. I will discuss space strategy later, but here I would like to consider the basic tools of space war. First, considering the satellite in general terms, it will provide us with a vast amount of basic information most of which will have, sooner or later, a significant impact on military space combat. The obvious problems of the environmental influence of space upon man's behavior must be solved. Already much information on heat insulation and absorption, and tolerable temperature control within a satellite has been learned from Explorer I. The Soviets have learned much about blood pressure, heartbeat, body temperatures and the general physical reactions of an animal in space flight. The effect of cosmic rays, of prolonged periods of weightlessness and the over-all psychological problem of human existence in an entirely new medium all need further study. The answers to these problems will be of direct application to space combat.

Of immediate concern to us are the special uses of satellites today. The first and obvious use of the satellite is as a reconnaissance vehicle. As pointed out earlier, no ICBM weapons system is complete without a reconnaissance element. Although few people realize it, there is no way today to give information to a missile in the United States that will cause it to arrive with accuracy at a specific geographic point in the Soviet Union. This is because the exact relation of specific points in the Soviet Union to the United States is not known except in the case of the few observatories that were in existence prior to the Red Revolution. Obviously, if we are going to great expense to build sophisticated guidance systems in ICBMs we must be able to give equally sophisticated information to the missile at takeoff. And good accuracy is important since without it we would waste a very expensive weapon. It must be able to destroy its target even though the target may move from time to time. This requires knowing with a high degree of accuracy where the target is. Existing cartographic data is simply not that accurate, in fact for some areas of the USSR it is virtually nonexistent. Even close to home, in the West Indies, for example, we found major errors in the assumed location of some of the islands when we first surveyed the Cape Canaveral missile range. One of the first uses of a satellite, therefore, will be to conduct a survey of the major land masses of the earth, refining the data received and transmitted back to the earth as the satellite improves in performance. I am personally convinced that the targets that will be of the greatest importance to the West, and that will be worth the investment of a very expensive ICBM, will be the targets that threaten our own existence most. These are the Soviet long-range missiles. And these, either in whole or in part, are now mobile, and they will be entirely mobile as propellants and techniques for launching increase in efficiency. Thus, to employ profitably an ICBM will require accurate and timely intelligence and this can only be secured through the use of a reconnaissance satellite. As the reconnaissance airplane had to serve the bomber, a reconnaissance missile will have to serve the ICBM. They are complementary and essential ingredients of a complete system. And finally, the most efficient type of reconnaissance missile at this time appears to be one that accurately orbits a useful satellite.

The first requirement of a reconnaissance satellite is to accomplish a rough survey of the earth's surface. Thus we will determine with accuracy the over-all shape of the earth. Next an accurate determination of the relative location of major land masses must be made. Finally, in the very near future it will be possible to place a satellite in orbit that will be able to conduct detailed photography. Its accuracy should be such that it will be possible to distinguish separate aircraft on an airfield. Satellite photography will require the development of ground handling and processing equipment and this may be far more difficult and expensive than the launching of the satellite itself. With a satellite circling the earth roughly every hour and a half, thousands upon thousands of photographs, many of them of little value because of cloud cover, will have to be processed. Automatic systems for accepting or rejecting any portion of the photographs will have to be developed so they can be handled quickly.

In addition to reconnaissance satellites orbiting at a speed that will bring them over the United States with some frequency, there will be a need for satellites that remain stationary relative to a given point on the earth. Although it may take considerable development effort, it will be possible to place in orbit a satellite moving at the same speed as the earth's rate of rotation. It will no doubt have to possess a small propulsion capability of its own so that once in orbit it can, in response to signals from the earth, adjust its position in space. Such a satellite should maintain its orbital station for an indefinite period of time. It will be so far from the earth's surface, however, that it appears unlikely at this time that it could be useful for reconnaissance purposes. A family of such satellites properly placed could provide a network of radio and TV stations for world-wide program relays.

The military and commercial uses of a satellite for communications purposes are most attractive. At the present time, the frequency spectrum of our terrestrial radio communication networks are very crowded. Communications facilities, such as cable systems, are very costly to maintain. It appears to be economically worth-while to undertake the development of a communications satellite. Overflying major communications centers, let us say Paris and Washington, on an accurate time schedule, it could pick up and store an enormous volume of communications. These would be automatically played back over the receiving station, again let us say Washington. A similar communications service could be provided anywhere on the earth. Our industrialists now believe that this would be an economically profitable way to communicate in the future. From a military point of view it has tremendous potential.

Currently there is much speculation about the possible uses of a satellite as a weapons carrier. Obviously the mere release of a warhead will accomplish nothing since it will cruise along in orbit with the platform. However, by giving but a little propulsion to the warhead, it could be directed back into the earth's atmosphere. At this point the problem of re-entry would become as severe as that of an ICBM warhead. The solutions applied to the ICBM warhead problem will apply to the orbital re-entry body. Since we intend to place a man into space and bring him back to earth under tolerable and accurately controlled conditions, these problems must all be solved. When they are solved there appears to be no reason why a warhead could not be placed on the earth with the accuracy with which we intend to return man.

Next, one can foresee the day when a manned orbital vehicle will be able to transmit guidance signals to a returning object so as to guide it with some precision into a selected target area. Thus, although it is far from feasible now, we cannot afford to overlook the possibility of an orbital vehicle launching an attacking warhead. It will be argued, with ample substance, that the earth is a far better launching platform. It is, and it will no doubt remain so for some time. However, when we reduce the antimissile-missile problem to manageable proportions, the ability to launch objects from a satellite may well play a part in the effectiveness of our over-all system. In summary, therefore, we cannot afford to dismiss the possibility of an object's being launched from a space vehicle as being of no significance.

This brings us to the next aspect of space combat—whether or not we should develop a satellite to intercept a satellite. It raises some delicate legal problems that deserve much more study than they have been given so far. The subject is treated comprehensively and well in *Spacepower*.[12] It is inconceivable to me that we would indefinitely tolerate Soviet reconnaissance of the United States without protest, for clearly such reconnaissance has an association with an ICBM program. It is necessary, therefore, and I believe urgently necessary, that we acquire at least a capability of denying Soviet overflight—that we develop a satellite interceptor. On the basis of studies that have been conducted so far, this appears possible, although it will be quite a difficult problem

[12] *Spacepower* by Donald Cox and Michael Stoiko, John C. Winston Company, 1958.

until man himself operates on a platform in space.

Military operations on the earth—not only tactical operations but strategic planning—are very much affected by weather. Excess rainfall and prolonged droughts have a definite effect upon a nation's economy and thus affect its war-making capacity. It appears at this time that much could be learned about the weather patterns on the earth through the use of weather satellites. It has been suggested that man may be able to control the weather at some time in the future. In the meantime we should undertake a study of global weather patterns through the use of satellite vehicles.

Finally, if we are to control space, we must undertake the exploration of the moon and the planetary system as a matter of highest national priority. A preliminary step in such an undertaking is the establishment of a manned space station. There have been numerous proposals about how to do this. Most agree that the basic problem is to develop a main thrust unit of large enough size that big payloads of lightweight construction material can be placed with accuracy in orbit. Man can then build his station and when it is complete and inhabitable, use it as a platform for further space exploration. The military significance of being able to establish and maintain an inhabited space station is obvious. The tactics of space warfare must begin, therefore, as usual with survival. We must acquire sufficient knowledge and equipment to protect ourselves, specifically a capability to intercept a satellite. We must develop the equipment and train the men to operate the equipment in space regardless of any obstacle, man-made or otherwise.

I am of the personal conviction that the space age offers for the first time a real prospect of lasting peace, for despite all that has been written so far about the tactics of space combat, if this planet is to remain inhabitable by man, a space program must be developed under the United Nations. We should establish, as a matter of high priority, a United States space command directly under the Department of Defense. Its full utilization should be made available to the United Nations. We should ask that our Allies and the Soviets also contribute to such a UN program to the extent of their ability. If the exploration and control of space can be carried out under the auspices of the United Nations, we will not have to concern ourselves with space war; instead, the exploration of space can be conducted for the peaceful purposes of mankind.

In the handling of earth forces, the problems that confront the military tactician are tremendous. Mobility will change radically. Missiles offer us a new order of mobility, particularly for high-priority cargo. For quite a few years, the need for missiles for purposes other than transportation will be so great that the transportation field will probably not receive the attention it deserves. It does seem clear, however, that initially a combination of chemical and missile propulsion systems should enable man to move high-priority cargo, say from Washington to London, in about thirty minutes. Between now and 1965, however, the form of mobility of most significance to us will be air mobility. We have hardly begun to exploit the combat potential of the airplane. Tactical decisions will be won or lost depending upon how well we learn to understand the uses of the air vehicle in the immediate future. It is essentially a vehicle of transportation and every missile and every gram of fissionable material must be flown. "Fire brigades," of course, must be flown, for in dealing with limited wars the amount of force required is a function of reaction time. The quicker one responds, the less the force required. Long delay presages a long and costly war. The air vehicle should be used tactically to provide the means for dispersion and quick reaction.

The Army has a peculiar requirement for the air vehicle that is just beginning to be understood. It is sky cavalry. Since the beginning of recorded history, man has sought to gain a mobility advantage over his opponent in land combat. The Greeks demonstrated this in their basic tactical organizations, as did the Romans after them. Perhaps the greatest demonstration of the

226

potential in war of a mobility innovation matched with ruthless aggression was that of Genghis Khan. In our time, a new form of land mobility has been developed, the gasoline engine. Among the few who foresaw its potential were members of the German Army in the 1930's. Hence the blitzkrieg that destroyed Poland in a few days, despite the predictions of the experts, overran most of Europe and came to the brink of defeating the West.

Now we are in the air age and as the potential of the air vehicle becomes understood, we can foresee its marriage with tactical nuclear fire power giving us an innovation without precedent in military history. We can foresee it, but doing something about it is another matter. Tragically, in the years between World War II and Korea, we neglected it. If we had had the vision to see, and the courage to venture in our research and development programs, we could have had a tactical mobility in Korea that would have enabled us literally to run circles around our opponents. As General Walker's armies moved north towards the Yalu, blindly going from road bend to road bend and hill to hill, they were ambushed by an army that depended largely upon foot and horse mobility. Technically, this situation was inexcusable. Tactically, with the equipment at hand, it was unavoidable. Even at the time of the Inchon landing, when MacArthur established a lodgment near the vitals of the North Korean forces, it took a week for them to link up by tank and foot with the remainder of the 8th Army going north from Tageu.

One of the most striking aspects of man's military past is his persistent search for the technical means to get an edge on his opponent in mobility. When he was successful, and especially when he could organize elements of varying mobility into a cohesive combat team, he was successful in combat. When he failed to solve the technical problem created by his needs, he failed in combat. Mobility offers greater promise of innovation than any of the other functional areas of tactics. I know of no area in our military programs that deserves more attention at this time. Hypermobile forces matched with tactical nuclear weapons, from the shoulder-fired infantryman's weapon to medium-range missiles, supported by long-range missiles, will be the key to the control of the land masses on this earth. Sky cavalry teamed with drone surveillance forces offers our military establishment the greatest innovation in tactical combat since the beginning of history.

Nuclear fire power will, to an increasing extent, complement mobility. As our research continues in making "cleaner" weapons the military usefulness of nuclear weapons will increase. Likewise, as their size diminishes they will be more combat-worthy. We can see quite clearly now that the time is not far distant when tactical nuclear weapons will be in every echelon of the military establishment. Then the West will need ten times the ten-thousand figure of tactical weapons that has been frequently quoted. It will, if it is to control its own destiny in the space age.

So far, this discussion of tactics as a function of earth power has dealt mainly with land warfare. Obviously with by far the largest part of the planet consisting of sea, sea power is of at least as great or possibly greater significance. Rapidly increasing in importance is our submarine program. While a member of the Weapons Systems Evaluation Group some years ago, I became very impressed with both the importance of submarines and with Russian progress in submarine development. With the valor of ignorance, as a soldier, I suggested then that all combat vessels should be submersible. I still believe that they should be and that our Naval Research Program should concentrate on the submarine-missile problem. It is not going to be as easy as much of the current press output would lead one to believe. For a submarine is quite vulnerable. Present detection systems can locate and track submarines at very great distances. They must move to live and while moving, they are detectable. Furthermore, the effects of nuclear weapons under water are, in some respects, greater than on land. The Soviet submarine threat and our own awareness of current technology suggest that we should concentrate a great deal of our naval research effort in this field. The control of the seas is essential to our collective security policy and thus to our survival.

Admitting the importance of mobility and fire power, and of man's ability to control both of these on the earth and in space, we still must recognize that the most important factor of all is man himself. Our weapons systems will never be a bit better than the men who design them, make them, and man them. And more men rather than fewer will be required in the missile-space age than in the past. Writing on this problem in the *Army-Navy-Air Force Register* of May 9, 1957, William H. Stoneman said:

It is possible that more troops would be needed to supply and operate a larger number of individual units than were needed to run an army on the old divisional system.

The firm stand taken by General Lauris Norstad, supreme commander of Allied forces in Europe, against further cuts in NATO ground forces on the continent indicates that he and his advisers think the answer to the big question may be "more troops."

Several months later in an article in the *United States Air Force Times* entitled, "Missiles to Need as Many Men as Bomber Units, Planners Say," the author concluded:

The whole success of the mission and the possible outcome of the "pushbutton war" hinge on the ability of thousands of technicians to do their individual jobs right before the count down. Ironically, planners say, the most mechanized war the world has ever known promises to be the most demanding too on human capabilities.

Unpalatable to many as the conclusion may be, clearly we will need more men, and better scientifically trained men, in the future than in the past.

In conclusion, in the missile-space age the earth will become a tactical theater, and combat in space will have begun. Missiles will be the dominant form of fire power and air mobility will provide the key to tactical success in land warfare. Through air mobility we must discover the innovations that will give us the margin of advantage we need to win in land combat. Control of the seas, so essential to our collective security program, must be achieved through an effective submarine-antisubmarine program. Space will be of overriding importance and we must exploit the military potential of a comprehensive satellite program as a matter of highest national priority. Finally, more men and better scientifically trained men will be needed than in the past. And our achievements in the field of applied tactics will be no better than the men who create our weapons systems and the men who man them.

C. STRATEGY AND SPACE

"All warfare is based on deception."
—SUN TZU

"Mystify, mislead, and surprise."
—"STONEWALL" JACKSON

The first object of strategy is to make tactical battles unnecessary. The measure of success of strategy therefore is the degree to which battle becomes unnecessary. The second object is to have one's resources so disposed as to win if battle does occur. Since most writing on strategy has been done by soldiers, there has been a tendency toward preoccupation with battle itself. To many military writers, strategy is considered hardly more than the interrelationship of battles. In its simplest form, a defensive battle may be fought in one area while an offensive strike is made in another. A generally accepted definition of strategy that reflects this point of view is: "As a rule, strategy concerns itself with those larger-scale measures which serve to bring the forces into play at the decisive point under the most favorable conditions possible, while tactics relates to what is done in the engagement itself. Strategy might be called the science of generalship, while tactics is that of handling troops."

The idea that a successful strategy is one that makes physical battle unnecessary is not new. J. F. C. Fuller, in describing the durability of the Eastern Roman Empire that lasted for a thousand years, attributed it to its military organization, pointing out that the emperors, "in their manuals, the Strategicon and Tactica, gave the armies of the Empire a stability utterly unknown in the West. War was looked upon from a practical and not an heroic point of view. Battles were avoided rather than sought, and to sacrifice lives in attempting to achieve by valor what could be gained by cunning was considered the worst of bad generalship." Even this form of strategy, however, can be overemphasized and with the end of the Eastern Roman Empire, war gradually devolved into an exercise in geometric patterns. The object was to maneuver one's forces so as to make it demonstrably not worth while for an opponent to fight, and while the aim was laudable, continued idolatry of it caused the military forces to deteriorate to the state where they no longer had the capability of fighting effectively. In the seventeenth and eighteenth centuries, generalship improved in quality and Napoleon demonstrated that personal leadership and valor could be as important in battle as all of the preliminary maneuvering of generalship. Von Clausewitz, who recognized the elements of war besides physical force, wrote: "The object of a combat is not always the destruction of the enemy's forces. . . . Its objective can be obtained as well without combat taking place at all." For many centuries strategy consisted of what we would consider today hardly more than a higher form of tactics. Gradually, as war became more technical, and thus more elaborate, preparations for its conduct had to be made and strategy encompassed many other things. In Napoleon's time, the problems of sustenance for men and animals, money, the attitude of other states toward the war and particularly the movement of forces, all had to be carefully considered before tactical battle was sought. And as war became more complex, the realm encompassed by strategy became greater.

Now in the mid-twentieth century, we have come to the state in the evolution of warfare where the world is hardly more than one large tactical theater. As the realm of tactics has expanded, so has the realm of strategy, and many more factors must now enter into strategic planning and strategic warfare. National attitudes, national resources, technology and lead times in creating new weapons systems all have a decisive bearing on national strategy. The economic, psychological and technical factors all weigh more heavily on the outcome of a combat between nations than applied physical force itself. And now that we have entered outer space, a nation's plan for the strategic exploration of space and the knowledge gained in such exploration, may have a more decisive bearing on the outcome of a contest between nations than any tactical engagement on the earth.

If we are to believe the statements made by the Soviet leaders, from Lenin to Khrushchev, then we are at war now. If this is the case, and I believe that it is, the Soviets are far beyond the planning stage in their strategy. They are in the field of application. Of course, planning goes on concurrently in anticipation of forthcoming events. But the Soviets have a strategy plan in execution today, the object of which is to so weaken the West psychologically, economically and politically that battle will be unnecessary. Thus a Communist can avowedly insist that his sole aim is peace and believe it himself, since it accurately reflects the Soviet strategic concept. Nothing would please the Communists more than lasting peace and this is the object of their strategy—lasting peace on their terms.

The evidence is now abundantly clear that the psychological element of the Soviet strategy is, at the moment, a decided success. We have had numerous examples brought to our attention, the most recent being the Soviet exploitation of the Sputniks' success at the expense of the West. Even the frequencies selected for transmitting a signal to the earth by Sputnik I were not those agreed upon for the International Geophysical Year, but were those that could be received by home radios in most of the countries of the world. The direction of launching was such as to place the satellite in orbit over a major portion of the Eurasian-American land mass. Their propaganda was organized to exploit their launching the moment the satellite was in orbit. By contrast, even after Explorer I was in orbit, our own USIA lacked information on its characteristics and in fact was unaware of the time of its launching until it was in orbit. I say this not in criticism of the USIA or the DOD but to point out the shortcomings in our system of co-ordination to achieve maximum psychological impact. Following Sputnik I, we widely publicized our intended Vanguard launching in December when most technically well-informed people knew that the probability of a successful launching was slight, if not nonexistent. Its failure was a grievous blow to our prestige. Likewise, the Soviet offer to ban nuclear weapons after they had completed a series of tests was a psychological victory for the Communists. From the viewpoint of the United States we are absolutely right. Tests must be continued, and it is in the interest of humanity that they be continued. For we must learn to direct fission to useful ends and not allow it to destroy us. Despite this, and our forewarning of several weeks that the Soviets would propose a ban of tests, we took no measures in our own behalf and once again we were victims of Soviet psychological warfare. Senator Hubert H. Humphrey used sharp but not overdrawn language in describing the situation: "This morning our nation has been delivered a terrible propaganda blow." And Senator Theodore F. Green is reported in the *New York Times* of April 1 as saying: "The fact still remains that we are once again thrown on the defensive. The fact still remains that our own policy has permitted the initiative for peace once again to pass to the Soviet Union."

Our record of setbacks in psychological warfare is dreary and repetitious. A recent survey of public opinion in the uncommitted areas makes overwhelmingly clear the Soviet successes, and merely decrying the Soviet acts as "gimmicks" and "propaganda stunts" not only does not help our position, but in many cases harms it. As reported in the *New York Times* of March 6, 1958:

A recent poll in New Delhi turned up the following percentages on its question, "Which is doing more to help peace in the world, Russia or the West?" Russia, 54 per cent; West, 18 per cent; don't know, 28 per cent. Note the ratio: three-to-one for Russia.

The same poll asked citizens of twelve world capitals, "Who is ahead in the cold war, Russia or the West?" Russia was rated ahead in ten capitals—in some cases by four- or five-to-one among those who gave definite answers—and the West in only two.

The dilemma confronting our government is a real one. Secretary Dulles described it well at a news conference on April 1, 1958:

Now we operate, I think, under some disadvantages from a propaganda standpoint. We operate under conditions that are totally different from those which surround the Soviet Union.

We operate, as is visible right here, in terms of a free and independent and highly intelligent press. If I came before you with something that was a phony you would recognize it in a minute and tear it apart publicly.

We operate in terms of an opposition political party, which is alert and prepared to expose, here at home and for reporting abroad, anything which does not seem to be thoroughly sound.

We operate in terms of an American public opinion which is highly intelligent and properly critical of its Government—when I say 'critical,' I don't mean necessarily antagonistic, but which holds government up to high standards.

And we operate with allies who have to be consulted—they are not just dummies that we can lay down the law to, like the Soviet satellites are.

Now all of those conditions make it very difficult for us to carry on a type of propaganda such as the Soviets carry on.

Obviously we do not want to embark upon an effort to control our free press, but without doing so, we can do more than has been done. From the viewpoint of one who has seen and been part of the interworkings of our government in Washington, there is clear and compelling evidence of lack of co-ordination on the psychological aspects of important national projects. Notable among the most recent, as I have already pointed out, were the failure to appreciate the psychological importance of an early satellite launching, the failure to appreciate the damage that would result from a highly publicized failure on our part when this could have been avoided, and the failure to make the most of our own early launching. And these failures are as serious as failures in tactical battle since they represent to the Soviets victories in strategic warfare which if repeated often enough will lead to strategic victory and thus the tactical battle may be avoided, or if unavoidable, certainly won.

The object of war in the abstract, of strategy, is the disarming of the enemy. The best illustration of this strategy in practice today is the insistence that our NATO allies, specifically Western Germany, not be given nuclear weapons. Now nuclear weapons are as much a part of today's arsenal as gunpowder was yesterday. In fact, no modern air defense is possible without the use of nuclear weapons. Furthermore, the realization of the importance of nuclear weapons to a modern military establishment, on the part of the Soviets, is quite apparent in the weapons that they now display and in the statements of their military and political leaders. They insist, however, upon the denial of nuclear weapons to Western Europe, and also at times on a ban on missiles. In a trade visit to Bonn in the spring of 1958, Anastas I. Mikoyan, the Kremlin's No. 2 man, said: "If the Bonn Federal Republic is free of atomic weapons and missiles . . . the Soviet Union, even in the event of the outbreak of a war in which the Bonn Republic is a participant, will refrain from employing nuclear weapons and missiles against . . . the Bonn Republic." And while the Soviet propaganda line has hammered home the horrors of a nuclear holocaust in Western Europe, they have preached abroad the likelihood of a nuclear war being inadvertently triggered by placing weapons in the hands of the West Germans. At the same time, their own military establishment continues to receive nuclear weapons in abundance and in many categories. The impact of their propaganda line has not been without results and as responsible a paper as the London *Economist* on April 12, 1958, in a reference to NATO strategic planners wrote: "In the particular case of Germany, the military advantage of having the new weapons in German hands looks minor, while the political arguments against it appear decisive." In the light of history, if the Soviets succeed in denying nuclear weapons to the strongest ground force in Europe, the German forces, they will have achieved one of the most remarkable strategic victories in military history. It is rare indeed that a strategy has been so successful as to disarm an opponent. Yet, in this case, it could happen and if the German forces are denied nuclear weapons, Marshal Zhukov's boast will certainly come true: the Soviet forces will be on the English Channel in forty-eight hours, well equipped with an abundance of tactical nuclear weapons.

Americans are innately confident that they can win any psychological battle with the Soviets. Sooner or later, most of us are convinced, the truth will come out, and adherence to the truth and avoidance of gross lies, even for momentary propaganda advantage, is the best policy. After all, Hitler and Goebbels were masters of the big-lie technique and we brought them to their end. This may be true, but our success or failure in this realm of strategy will not be known until either system triumphs. We must do more now.

There is another element of strategy, however, that is finite and measurable now. It is technology. As war becomes increasingly complex, technology becomes more and more important. In fact, if the strategy of the Soviets or of the West were to be decisively successful without tactical battle, it would be in the field of technology, for technology contains all of the elements short of war itself. Economics, natural resources, decision-making and lead time, and superior weapons systems themselves are all part of technology. Each, if not properly understood and carefully planned, could directly contribute to strategic defeat.

Let us first consider economics. It has been said that we are pricing ourselves out of survival, just as we are pricing ourselves out of the world's markets. Our high standard of living, with accompanying high wages, is fine at home, but places us in a bad position in competitive world markets. In comparison, with their low standard of living, the Soviets have been able not only to produce thousands upon thousands of tanks, armored personnel cars and other conventional weapons, but they have been able to beat us in the jet-airplane development race and in the missile-satellite race. In the meantime, our own weapons systems have become so costly that in order to support but a few, we have had to deny ourselves many. Speaking to a group of businessmen in Washington on March 4, 1958, Assistant Secretary of Defense W. J. McNeill said:

These new weapons and equipment, the products of scientific and technological progress, are much more powerful and have much greater combat capability than the items they are replacing but they also cost a great deal more.

The average cost per aircraft . . . has tripled over the last six or seven years. During World War II, for example, the cost of aircraft averaged about $10 a pound. For the very high performance aircraft to be delivered two or three years from now, the cost per pound will probably run from $70 to $80. The complexity of high performance combat aircraft may be measured by their cost per pound compared with the cost of silver which is less than $15 per pound.

The heavy bomber at the end of World War II was the B-29 which cost about $600,000 each . . . the all jet B-52 intercontinental bomber costs about $8 million each.

He went on to say that the most advanced type of aircraft now under experimentation, the X-15, would probably cost in excess of *$100 million per plane.* Comparable cost increases prevail in the missile field. For example, an Atlas deployed will cost about $17.5 million, including a proportionate share of the fixed launching base cost. A short-range mobile missile, the Pershing, of about five hundred miles range will cost one-half million dollars. Since it is generally agreed that we cannot exceed investing a certain amount of our gross national product in national defense without doing harm to the national economy, it becomes of overriding importance that we make our technical decisions well and that we make them quickly. Failure to do so could well do critical harm to our economy and failure to do so in time will give us weapons systems that are obsolete, and thus we may lose without a shot being fired.

There is considerable evidence to support the belief that we could increase our present rate of defense spending without hurting our national economy. The National Planning Association in a press release of December 29, 1957, stated that "defense spending, if necessary, can be increased to approximately $54 billion[13] by 1960 without the need for increased taxation to balance the government's budget." The National Planning Association report found "that even if national security spending increased from $42 billion in 1957 to $54 million in 1960, there would remain in the economy sufficient normal production capacity to enable business to increase its capital formation in response to the greater capital requirements of enlarged defense programs, consumers to increase their consumption at a rate slightly higher than that of the past decade, and governments—federal, state, and local—to make some expansion in their services." By increasing the tax rate, the defense expenditures could be raised to $64 billion and provide a program that would "expand the stepped-up program of air-power and guided missiles and would permit a significant increase in strength for all the other national defense forces and possibly a comprehensive civil defense program, including industrial relocation." Actually, some of our most important missile programs have been slipping steadily because of the diminishing value of the dollar and the increased cost of labor and scientific help. It appears, therefore, that an increased investment of our gross national product into our defense establishment is both necessary and possible without disrupting the economy of the country. However, this is but a small part of the problem. Far more important than dollars invested are the decisions made, and the timeliness of these decisions, and decision-making

[13] Statement made by the President at a press conference on September 3, 1957: "I have come to believe that a very fine and adequate defense for the United States can at present prices be sustained—with an expenditure program, if it can be planned in advance, at about $38,000,000,000."

in military technology is a very complex business. For, again, technology is part of strategic warfare and the decisions are just as complex, and the results that depend upon them just as critical as any battle decisions ever made.

In making a decision to create a new weapons system, we must consider many things. Foremost among them must be national military policy, enemy weapons systems, our resources, our economy and the state of technology. All of these are variables that occur in many combinations in the decision-making process.

Let us consider the first: national military policy. It reflects national political policy and if our political policy is positive and affirmative in its view, then this factor is not too difficult to weigh. On the other hand, if national policy is passive and committed exclusively to containment, it is by its very nature reactive. The initiative is with the enemy and we tend to respond to his programs. This is very dangerous in the strategy of technology. For technological initiative in the hands of an enemy enables him to deceive, mislead and ultimately surprise us. Mere deception itself can be tolerated if the other factors are preponderantly in our favor. That is, if we have an abundance of natural resources compared to an enemy, and if our economy is in a much better state, we can afford the loss of the initiative without too great a concern.

Our natural resources situation is far from favorable. From a "have" nation, we are rapidly becoming a "have-not" nation. We have less than 7 per cent of the world's population occupying 8 per cent of the world's land area, yet we consume almost half of the Free World's natural resources. And this rate is rising. Prefacing an excellent analysis of our situation in the *New York Times* in December of 1957, Mr. Richard Rutter wrote:

America is living dangerously. Every time a car is driven, a coal fire is made, a meal is cooked with natural gas, a tin can is thrown away, something is gone forever. That something is a bit of a natural resource.

Day by day, year by year, the bits add up to an enormous drain on supplies of vital raw materials.

The survival of the nation is involved. An assured supply of iron ore, petroleum, natural gas, metals, coal and a host of other materials is essential to the strength of the American economy. Without these, the great industrial machine would come to a halt. It would be impossible to match or excel the Soviet Union's dramatic technological advances. The national security would vanish overnight, the standard of living would collapse and the United States as we know it would be no more.

So great is our dependence upon foreign supply that there are but two metals that we have in sufficiency, magnesium and molybdenum. Iron, tin, tungsten and petroleum are among the critical items for which we must depend upon foreign supply to meet our needs. Eighty-five to 90 per cent of the world's reserves of tungsten is under the control of Communist China. Seventy per cent of the known petroleum reserves is in the highly sensitive and vulnerable Middle East. And finally, this situation, rather than improving, will get worse with time. Thus, an awareness of it imposes serious limitations upon our decisions.

Our high standard of living, with an accompanying high cost of production, makes abundantly clear that our decisions must be made with considerable care since we cannot afford many of the things that we would like to have. Thus, operating within a fixed budget, we are particularly sensitive to deception since the harm that we could suffer would be much greater than that which we could inflict upon the USSR.

Finally, the lead time in the technological race has been increasing and this is alarming. Dr. Ellis A. Johnson, Director of the Operations Research Office of Johns Hopkins University, has written: "During World War II our lead times were about 2½ years. Now the Russian lead time is five years. Our lead time is ten years."[14] In a paper published by the Stanford Research Institute, *The Lead Time Race*, the statement is made: "The central problem in the survival of the United States today is the lead time race with the Soviet Union for weapons superiority." Thus it would appear quite clear that in the technological decision-

[14] *U.S. News and World Report,* January 31, 1958.

making processes of strategy, we are at a great disadvantage. The Soviet lead time is decidedly shorter, and their controlled economy gives them greater freedom in allocation of resources in support of decisions. And finally, having the initiative they can, in "Stonewall" Jackson's words, "mystify, mislead, and surprise."

For example, there is a considerable quantity of intelligence to support the view, a view held by a number of people in the intelligence business, that in the competition to develop Long-Range Striking Forces, the Soviets have led us to believe that they were building a sizable long-range bomber force, whereas, in fact, they were investing most of their national product for their long-range forces in long-range ballistic missiles. The Soviets merely built and displayed before Western observers sufficient long-range manned bombers to cause apprehension, and consequent reaction on our part. We in turn embarked upon a very expensive long-range manned bomber program. If this actually has been the Soviet strategy, then billions of dollars have been invested in aircraft that will never be used in combat. If we had spent those billions on missiles and satellites, we would be well in the forefront of the missile-space race today. The canceled Navaho program, amounting to 700 million dollars, and the discarded B-36s suggest that there may be some validity to the theory. Of course, we could not afford to ignore the bomber threat entirely and this is not to say that we should not have built bombers, for it is likely that the Soviets would have moved with much greater freedom if they believed that we lacked a capacity to retaliate by bombers. But there is a considerable amount of evidence to support the view that Soviet displays and Soviet statements have been cleverly made with a view to cause us to continue to invest in a weapons system that they themselves know to be obsolescent. In this connection, Mr. Khrushchev, after announcing in 1957 that the manned bomber belonged in a museum, reversed himself and a report to the *New York Times* from Moscow on March 21, reports: "Nikita S. Khrushchev has substantially amended his stated position on the relative roles of manned aircraft and missiles in modern arsenals." The question remains unanswered, whether or not he was still engaging in technological strategy. The odds are that he was.

Technological strategy offers us one of the most interesting challenges that we have ever known. This is a technological age and the mastery of technology will determine our fate in the future. It is absolutely fundamental that we understand technology, and the war of technology, and plan carefully for participation in this kind of war if we are to survive.

World War II brought to our attention a number of examples of the role that technology can play. We came close to defeat in antisubmarine warfare but our scientists and our Navy won that technical battle for us. In the field of mine laying alone, the competition was very close and as we went from magnetic to acoustic to influence mines, the scientists on both sides sought to mislead and outmaneuver each other. In an AP report from London on January 24, 1958, an account is given of British success in deceiving the Nazis. Although it is applied technology rather than strategy, it gives a brief account of some of the work done by Professor Reginald Jones, Chief of the Scientific Intelligence Section of the Royal Air Force:

In this job, he ingeniously bent a German radio beam guiding bombers to London so they flew out over the Irish Sea.

He hoaxed the Germans into believing the British anti-submarine radar detector worked by infrared rays. So successful was this hoax that U-boats later were found painted with an anti-infrared paint.

Perhaps his most important feat was the J-beam hoax.

A radar navigation device the RAF was working on, called the C-beam, fell into German hands when the bomber trying it out was shot down. Jones set out to convince the Germans they had something else.

He conjured something called J-beam, which supposedly worked on a radio beam principle. He planted stories about it which were picked up by Nazi agents, built several phoney J-beam stations, and convinced the Germans that they had really captured a J-beam device.

"When our bombers started using the C-beam, the Germans were caught completely by surprise, and it took them five months to work out a way to jam it," Jones says proudly.

"And then—when they had decided that the whole J-beam business was a complete hoax, we actually started to use the J-beam. What started as a hoax ended up a serious reality. The Germans didn't know what was going on."

It would appear to be entirely possible for a nation to develop and carry out a well-conceived strategic plan in technology that could cause an opponent to waste vast amounts of critical resources.

War has become much more complex since World War II and it has reached the stage where technology is a special field of applied strategy. It deserves special treatment at our highest scientific and military institutions. For example, we should bring together a group of our topflight scientists, industrialists and military people for the purpose of conducting two-sided technological war games. This could be done at our National War College, let us say, during the summer when a regular class is not present. The group should be organized into three subgroups: a composite science-industry-military team representing Nation "A," a similar team representing Nation "B," and an umpire or control group. The control group should be picked with care and they should do considerable preparatory work before the meeting. The team representing Nation "A" should be organized with a team leader and it should be physically separated from Nation "B" during the conduct of the war game. This is an important point, for many of our present so-called "war games" on scientific matters are conducted on blackboards with all participants present and indulging in a free exchange of ideas. The element of competition and human judgment in decision-making is badly slighted.

Once the teams are properly placed, they should be given situations out of our past history with which to deal, for example, antisubmarine warfare. The control group should provide the teams representing Nations "A" and "B" with actual historical data, following the exact situations that developed during the war. When both sides understand the problem, variables can be introduced, requiring different solutions. The next phase would be the presentation of current problems in technology. When the teams are working well, either nation may then provide the other, through the control group, with false information to cause the other to make bad strategic decisions. The team representing each nation should be required to make decisions in the light of information given it by the control group. Computers would be used for much of the calculations, but the elements of competition and human decision should be ever-present. Such training should be projected as far into the space age as it is possible to go, for sooner or later it is in the realm of space that the great battles of technology will be won or lost.

From such a technological war game, much can be derived. Among other things, it offers us a prospect of recovering the technological initiative and this we must do. We will never survive if we continue to be exclusively preoccupied with the technological initiative of the Soviets. We must think for ourselves and this is a practice that we can only acquire through training, and if we are to develop a sound strategy of technology, our considerations must transcend the problems of any service, or of science, or of industry. It must bring them all together.

A technological war game such as this can be conducted under the auspices of the Weapons Systems Evaluation Group. There may be those who would say that this is being done now in the Weapons Systems Evalution Group. This is not quite so. Numerous symposiums, conferences and summer study groups are held, but none of them has the element of competition between select teams representing science, industry and the military. Far too many of them merely consist of round-table discussions, forums and just plain talk sessions.

The following are examples of the type of problems that lend themselves to study. Let us begin with the problem closest to us —self-defense, defense of the United States against missile attack, launched from either land or sea. An analysis of a Soviet missile program should give us our first clue to the type of target with which we must deal. We must make an analysis based upon available intelligence and then make our own estimate of what Soviet technology might be able to accomplish. Based upon this we can then determine the technical programs needed to provide an adequate defense. We must then place ourselves in the position of the Soviets and in the light of the defense measures that we are planning, introduce variants in the Soviet system to mislead and defeat our defensive measures. In the case of a defense against Soviet long-range missiles, these are many and highly complex. They can include for example decoys, spoofing,[15] countermeasures and finally counter-countermeasures. If all possible measures were taken to defeat an ICBM attack without a thorough evaluation of the over-all defense problem, we could expend a major portion of our defense budget on this problem alone and still fail to provide an adequate defense. The DEW line is an example of a defense that was established, but which because of the time lost in decision-making, and because of the lead time, proved to be too late for the purpose intended. Designed to provide defense against manned bombers at specific altitudes, it has become operational at a time when our greatest threat will be Intercontinental Ballistic Missiles. This is not to say that the investment was a total loss, for it was not. Much that was learned can be applied to our antimissile-missile defense and many of the facilities can contribute directly to that defense. However, with the advantage of hindsight, we see now that we should have thought of defense and foreseen the need for a DEW line many years earlier, or given more attention to the problems of defense against the missile and less to the manned bomber.

The problem of defending against submarine-launched missiles

[15] Spoofing consists of making attacks against a defense system to cause it to react, thus disclosing its characteristics and enabling an enemy to take appropriate countermeasures to defeat it.

is equally as challenging as that of land-based missiles. At the present we appear to be relying upon our own submarines to detect Soviet missile-carrying submarines thus hoping to defeat them at sea. Our own nuclear-propelled missile-carrying submarines will be very expensive, and all things considered, they will be as vulnerable at sea as the Soviet submarines themselves. It would appear obvious that it would be to our advantage to examine the feasibility of using surface-to-surface missiles associated in a weapons system with land-based sonar detection systems to defeat Soviet missile-bearing submarines. Since our IRBMs and mid-range missiles will be in storage, it would be of little additional cost to have a number of them so placed that they could be used against hostile, threatening submarines. Thus from not too many locations—on the capes and on the islands in the oceans bordering the North American land area—we could provide surface-to-surface missiles coverage of most of the Atlantic and a large portion of the Pacific. Under such protection, our own submarines could have considerable freedom of action. The economic, technical and military soundness of this proposal deserves the most thorough technological evaluation. Science, industry and our military should all be brought together to war-game technological challenges such as this. Again, it would be possible to invest mistakenly a sizable portion of our national product in a defense against such missiles with little actual return.

So far, this discussion of technological strategy has concerned itself with measures to be taken in our own defense. A nation's technological strategy, however, must go beyond this if it is to win. We must develop a strategic plan of our own. We must project our thinking into the future so far that we can foresee technological patterns that we must follow if we are to survive. At the same time, we must develop plans that will cause a would-be aggressor to be misled and make bad technological judgments. Hence, if our plan is successful, we can survive without physical battle. This is the real challenge and yet one entirely in keeping with the forward-looking concept of democracy itself.

It is particularly applicable to space, for in space we bring together all the problems of psychology, economics and applied military power.

An interesting illustration of a Soviet technological decision exists in Sputnik III. Prior to the launching of Sputnik III, there was a great deal of speculation among our scientists and military people about what the Soviets would do next. Based upon the size of Sputnik II, it was evident that the Soviets had a missile engine with a thrust much greater than anything that we had in operational use. Under the assumption that Sputnik III would be an improvement over Sputnik II in size and performance, it was thought most probable that the Soviets would go to the moon. Many believed that they would either circumnavigate the moon or impact upon it. Since they presumably had the capability of doing so, but instead launched a much larger satellite with a predictably short life, this had considerable significance. It would appear that their decision was to develop a reconnaissance satellite for military purposes, for psychological as well as tactical reconnaissance, rather than expend their resources on a moon probe at that time. We will be faced with similar decisions.

But if we are strong enough and wise enough to avoid World War III, we shall continue to engage the Soviets in an ideological race in which the stakes are the minds of men of the uncommitted nations. In that ideological race, outer space may well be the proving ground on which the uncommitted people of the world will judge whether the democratic free enterprise system or the communist system is superior.[16]

In order to win, the strategic initiative must be ours. We appear to be losing it, but we can regain it by proper study and the selection and training of imaginative and farsighted scientists and officers. We can develop a strategy of technology that will regain the technological initiative for the West. With an all-out effort,

[16] Testimony of Dr. J. Sterling Livingstone, Senate Preparedness Investigating Subcommittee, December 16, 1957.

it could be done, possibily in five and certainly in ten years. But it will take an all-out effort. Of one thing we may be sure, the nation that first achieves the control of outer space will control the destiny of the human race.

Military and Political Thinking in the United States

To be complete any discussion of strategy should consider service attitudes. Judging by the questions they ask, and much that they read in the newspapers, many people seem to believe that service attitudes contribute more to the molding of national strategy than any other single thing.

The problem of service attitudes and differences of opinion on the fundamentals of military policy must be perplexing to the average American. "Overwhelmed with conflicting facts, figures, theories, predictions, and arguments from generals, admirals, congressmen, the State Department, and the Alsops, the intelligent layman tends to view defense policy as a confused and impenetrable chaos in which the real alternatives of policy are known only to the initiated few."[17] To add to the confusion in the minds of the public, generals and admirals differ among themselves. Each draws upon his own experience and quotes his own statistics to prove the correctness of his point of view. Finally, within the services themselves, senior officers frequently disagree. The Tactical Air Command people often are at loggerheads with the Strategic Air Command, and those who would concentrate the Navy's effort on an underwater Navy conflict directly with those who desire a carrier Navy. The Army has its partisans also and there are those who would emphasize air mobility at the expense of everything else, while others would put our emphasis on sustained combat and heavy armored equipment. Overshadowing the interests of all the services are the problems of missiles and space. There is little wonder then that the average citizen has

[17] Samuel P. Huntington, "Radicalism and Conservatism in National Defense Policy," *Journal of International Affairs*, Columbia University, Vol. III, No. 2, 1954.

difficulty understanding the fundamentals of our national defense policy, the differences of opinion that exist and the real reasons therefor.

National defense policy presents to the intelligent layman a challenge significantly different from that of domestic policy. Give the informed citizen the names of Robert Taft, Leverett Saltonstall, Harry Truman, Hubert Humphrey, and Norman Thomas, and he will have no trouble in arranging them in a politically rational progression in terms of their respective viewpoints on domestic policy. Not only that, but the informed citizen will also have no difficulty in locating his own position in this progression. We have all grown accustomed to thinking of domestic policy in terms of a right-left, conservative-liberal continuum.[18]

Military policy covers as broad a spectrum and encompasses comparable divergencies of view as our political policy. This should not be surprising, since after all, military policy merely reflects political policy and, in application, is a continuation of politics. Therefore, with an understanding of our military policy, one should be able to place the names of Radford, LeMay, Twining, Burke, Taylor and Bradley in a rational progression in terms of their respective viewpoints on military policy. And having done so, one should be able to locate his own position within this progression with a reasonable exactness.

Many people believe that each service develops and follows a party line, and requires its members to adhere to that party line. As a friend of mine said not long ago, "Scratch a member of the Air Force and out comes an airman, they are all of the same point of view and say the same things." This is not so. Within each service there are strong differences of opinion on many of the fundamental issues. I have had long service in the Department of Defense and in joint commands where I have had occasion to discuss exhaustively many of our fundamental military problems. With few exceptions, men in uniform think for themselves and in the higher staffs they give you their best objective judgments. If I were to generalize on this problem at all, I would say the more intelligent the individual, the more objective he is. Further,

[18] *Ibid.*

if I were to place our military spokesmen in categories, I would group them as liberals and conservatives, for it is quite evident that the differences of opinion tend to polarize into such schools of thought. If, for example, one were to question an individual of any service on one or two of the following points, one could without difficulty place him in his proper place in the progression of views on military policy. Generally speaking, the two categories, and their points of view, are as follows:

LIBERAL	CONSERVATIVE
War, if it does occur, will begin first by economic and political penetration. This will be accomplished by appropriate diplomatic maneuvers to place us in a position from which it would be difficult to respond with force. Thereafter, force would be used by the Soviets to the degree necessary to achieve their objectives, and these will normally be limited. The ultimate objective of the Soviets, and ever-present in their thinking, planning and actions: world domination.	War, if it does come, will be an all-out and devastating air strike at the source of strength of the Western world—the United States. Since we concede the initiative to the Soviets, it is most logical to assume that they will take advantage of it. With the advantage that surprise affords a ruthless aggressor, the war could be won by the Soviets in minutes if we are not prepared for it, or if we did not launch an anticipatory attack of our own.
Our nuclear resources being fabricated into weapons should be made in such size as to be useful against military tactical targets in precise application. All services have a need for nuclear weapons and we need tens of thousands of them.	Our nuclear resources should be fabricated into weapons of the largest yield possible. Thus in one blow we can maximize the damage inflicted on any potential aggressor, or aggressors. Nuclear resources should not be wasted on weapons that may not be used and that are less efficient than the biggest weapons.
Our national military policy should reflect our national diplomatic policy. NATO, SEATO, the Baghdad Pact and the many other	Maximum investment should be made in our atomic retaliatory forces. We cannot afford to squander our limited resources in pack-

The Decade of Decision: 1955-1965

LIBERAL	CONSERVATIVE
commitments should be supported fully with forces in being, as far as our budget will allow.	ets all over the world. We should provide the atomic retaliatory forces and let our Allies provide "conventional" forces, or whatever they can provide.
Planning in our military programs should reflect our continued close association with our overseas Allies and even when ICBMs and IRBMs are in our inventory we should maintain a frontier of freedom, physically supported in part by our own forces, contiguous to the boundaries of the USSR and its satellites.	We should continue to develop weapons of increasing range and refueler jet tankers to the end that ultimately there will be little need for overseas bases and facilities. They are too costly and too vulnerable to continue to maintain in this missile age. We should be prepared to withdraw them as soon as possible.
A sizable Troop Carrier lift should be maintained in being and should be flown regularly. This is necessary if we are to support our foreign policy and military programs in support of those policies.	A minimum investment should be made in Troop Carrier lift and Troop Carrier resources should be considered, in first priority, as logistical backup for the atomic retaliatory force.
The control of the seas must be maintained and our Navy must be fully supported in this effort. If this means bigger and more aircraft carriers, then it is for the Navy to judge and if it believes it needs these, they should be provided.	Aircraft carriers, particularly of the super type, are a waste of our national resources. They duplicate the land-based atomic retaliatory forces. The only real need for naval forces are submarines to deal with the Soviet submarine menace that may threaten our commercial shipping, and threaten the U.S. with missiles.
The nation must have an adequate reserve force and National Guard and an effective Industrial Mobilization Plan. War, if it comes, may extend over a long period of time and it would be	Only the forces in being will be effective. War will be over too quickly for the participation of large reserve forces. There is little value, therefore, in maintaining such an establishment and in

LIBERAL	CONSERVATIVE
prudent to be prepared in every respect for war of long duration.	funding an industrial mobilization program.
Civil Defense is the responsibility of civilians. The military should assist to get it started but the Reserves and National Guard and the Regular Army establishment must be free for immediate overseas commitments in support of military plans.	Civil Defense is the responsibility of the Army, including its Reserve and National Guard. Since the war will be over quickly there is no place for the Army to go and it can best be used in Civil Defense.
The budget should be big enough to provide the forces necessary to meet requirements. These requirements include a spectrum of capabilities that makes possible a flexible strategy to support a flexible, responsive foreign policy. War may take any form the Soviets choose, from very limited use of power to an all-out war. We should be prepared for anything they launch. In the meantime, our actions and plans must inspire our Allies and maintain their confidence, for the very thought of a preventive war is immoral and abhorrent.	The budget must be limited carefully or we will lose the war economically. Pick the best weapons system and put your money on it. Reduce all others to a minimum. There is only one kind of a war, a general war, and we had better be prepared to win it. We should not shrink from the advantages of attacking first; an anticipatory-retaliatory war.

The foregoing represents two very definite schools of thought that now exist within the military establishment. Officers of all services are scattered throughout both. However, in general the Army and Navy associate with the liberal school and the Air Force with the conservative school. There are, of course, many combinations of the above but the majority of officers are intellectually committed to either of the two schools. Finally, there are extremists who depart from either. On the liberal side there are some who would have a much greater commitment to our

252

Allies of all types of weapons and resources than we can possibly afford, and among the conservatives there are those who would favor a preventive war right now, a "destroy them in their nests" anticipatory-retaliatory war. It is interesting to note that there is, in general terms, a political party affiliation with these military groups. Generally, the liberals and the Democrats side with the liberal military group and, again generally, those far to the right politically and the Republicans tend to side with the conservative military group.

Closely akin to any concept of what a military establishment in this country should be are the doctrinal attitudes of the services themselves. Much has been written about service attitudes, interests and interservice rivalry. And a great deal has been said and written about the over-all management of the nation's defense establishment. They deserve a word.

Interservice Rivalry

Interservice rivalry, long a subject of discussion and speculation, has come in for much more attention since the Sputniks. Some columnists have attributed our failure to beat the Soviets into space to interservice rivalry, a view in which they frequently get support from people in the Department of Defense.

In the first place, this is a competitive system—the American way of doing things. From the cradle we are taught to be competitive, as were our forefathers. Competition is the essence of our democratic system which stems from a way of life that encourages the individual to develop himself as fully as his God-given talents will allow, consistent with due respect for the rights and feelings of others. When he becomes a member of a group, be it social, athletic or business, he becomes a loyal team player. As a member of the team, he accepts and supports enthusiastically the competitive role of the team.

Few establishments in this world, perhaps none, are as intensely competitive as American industry. For this reason it has always seemed strange to me to find experienced businesmen, new to the Department of Defense, horrified by evidence of rivalry between the services. It would be a very poor Army, Navy, Marine Corps or Air Force that was not fiercely proud of its own service, and at the same time just as proud of its ability to serve as a team player with its sister services. And this they do well and have done extremely well, as our record in war has shown. Most interservice rivalry that I have become aware of has been productive of good results in the nation's interest. I have discussed this frequently with members of the Armed Forces and have read the congressional testimony of uniformed members of the Armed Forces on this subject and they generally support this point of view.

On the other hand, one is given the impression in Washington, particularly by statements made by civilians in the Department of Defense, that interservice rivalry is out of control and extremely harmful. A corollary to this is that more would be accomplished if it were not for interservice rivalry and that only through the intercession of the higher-echelon civilians in the Department of Defense can progress be made. If this were true, then our military joint commands overseas would be ridden with interservice bickering since they lack the calming control of any civilian superiors. The contrary is the case. Whether the overseas command is headed by an admiral or a general makes no difference. They are efficient working teams and if there is any interservice feeling, it expends itself in athletic competitions and cocktail chatter, and much of the interservice competition is friendly and helpful to our nation's interest.

The question remains unanswered, Why all the talk of interservice rivalry in Washington? On analysis it seems to be a handy thing to have about on which to blame failure for proper decisions in defense matters. About a month after the turbulence and criticism following in the wake of Sputnik I, I discussed congressional attitude with a member of the Army's Legislative and Liaison group. He informed me that Congress was being told by

254

members of the Department of Defense that our failure to launch a satellite first was due to interservice rivalry. This was shocking because it was entirely untrue. Subsequent discussion on The Hill, including references to harmful interservice rivalry in the President's "chins-up" talks, tended to support this. It was for this reason that I decided, in my appearances before Congress, that I would make as clear as circumstances would allow the facts on our satellite-missile failures.

There is one aspect of interservice competition that is unquestionably harmful, and it is an aspect that frequently comes to public attention, and yet there is little that the services can do about it. Essentially, it is industrial competition. Industry, through extravagant advertising claims and lobbying pressures on Congress and civilian members of the Department of Defense, can place uniformed members of the Armed Forces in a difficult position. Industry can make extravagant claims for their products and convince Congress of the accuracy of these claims, even though they are not valid. If a service will go along with industry it means an increased budget and money to spend, sometimes on things not directly associated with the industry-supported product. It is difficult for a service to resist such pressures since by going along they can rationalize their position in terms of the over-all good that can be accomplished with more money. The amount of money that is spent on nation-wide advertising, by industry, for hardware that is obsolete is sizable, and the pressure that industry can place through lobbies in terms of employment, payrolls and effect upon constituents is impressive to Congress. Finally, when such forces come into play in the committee system that presently characterizes the decision-making processes of the Department of Defense, they can become very harmful. It is at this stage that they assume the appearance of interservice differences although fundamentally the problem is an industrial and not a service one. This gets to the heart and soul of a type of competition that leads to results that are, at times, alarming.

If we believe as we profess to believe in the superiority of our competitive system, and thus believe that American industry reflects this competition at its best, then our military services should be intimately associated with American industry. Thus, in theory, as industry through its unique competitive and free enterprise system, quantitatively and qualitatively surpassed the state-controlled industries of a totalitarian nation, a military service would benefit and should expect to be equipped with the latest and best weapons systems. In fact, on even brief analysis, it would appear that such a marriage between the Armed Forces and industry would appear to be not only advisable, but absolutely essential. Experience, however, points out real pitfalls, for industry competing for dollars will insist that its products be used long after they become obsolete. Lobbies and pressure groups will use every means conceivable to cause the Department of Defense to invest in their obsolete weapons systems, and they will insist on a continued investment in those systems, even though the best interest of the country and the service concerned is not being served. They rationalize their point of view in terms of possible unemployment that may be caused by cancellation of orders. They point out the disastrous effect that unemployment might have on the economy of the country, finally arguing that though prepared militarily, we might well lose the decision to the Soviets in the arena of economy.

It takes the judgment of Solomon and no little political fortitude to make decisions on problems such as these. Unfortunately, they are not always made in time and hundreds of millions of dollars have been and are being spent on obsolete weapons systems. At the same time, the Armed Forces are placed in a very difficult position when they realize they are being denied weapons systems, not because of a limited budget, but because industrial pressure is causing decisions to be made in favor of systems that are already obsolete. And ever-present, through all of the maze of committee meetings, industrial discussions and congressional hearings, is what appears to be intense interservice rivalry whereas in most cases it is fundamentally industrial rivalry.

Pertinent to this discussion, in the unclassified and published record of the hearings before the congressional committee looking into the satellite and missile programs, there is a section entitled: "Inter-service Rivalries."[19] It consists of an exchange between a Senator and a witness and the witness's reply to a question is devoted entirely to the problems of industry and their willingness to exchange information with each other.

The rivalry among the services that I have seen has not been harmful; on the contrary, from the nation's point of view it has been helpful. The uniformed members of the Armed Services in Washington work well together and they keep the nation's interest foremost. There is far more interservice co-operation than there is competition.

D. ORGANIZATION FOR DEFENSE

"A major purpose of military organization is to achieve real unity in the defense establishment in all the principal features of military activity. Of all these one of the most important to our nation's security is strategic planning and direction. . . ."

—PRESIDENT EISENHOWER'S STATE OF THE UNION MESSAGE,
January 9, 1958

Unity of purpose is fundamental to survival. However, purpose is one thing and accomplishment is another—and the gap between may be wide indeed. The divisive forces that bear upon decision-making in the Department of Defense are many, industrial interests, political pressures, professional competence or lack of it in committees, personal prejudices, and service interests. All work against unity of purpose. And all are, and will remain for the indefinite future, part of our planning processes. The object of a national defense organization therefore should be twofold: to restrain these divisive forces so that they do a minimum of harm to our defense readiness, and to provide the means

[19] "Inquiry into the Satellite and Missile Programs." U.S. Senate Hearings, Part I, p. 36.

whereby the best scientific, industrial and military judgment can be brought to bear in decision-making.

No organizational arrangement, no matter how skillfully conceived, can by itself solve our defense problems. It takes people and resources to solve them. But the best of people, regardless of the resources made available to them, can be thwarted and frustrated, and finally made ineffective, by a poor organization. The evidence of the first ten years of the operation of the office of the Department of Defense abundantly supports this. Some of the most able and most intelligent Americans in public life have sought to bring order out of the decision-making maze of the Department of Defense, only to fail. It has been the organization that has defeated them. Interminable delays, caused by committees pyramiding upon committees and unfortunately very often containing individuals not well qualified to deal with the problems under consideration, have characterized the organization of the past decade. Further, despite the desire for "clear and unchallenged civilian responsibility"[20] uniformed members of the Armed Forces have successfully sponsored the development and procurement of weapons systems of which their civilian superiors, had they been given all of the facts, undoubtedly would have disapproved.

The Joint Chiefs of Staff

Civilian control means civilian decision-making. It does not mean decisions that are made by the Chairman of the Joint Chiefs of Staff, then confirmed by the Secretary of Defense. If the Secretary of Defense is going to make the decisions, he needs the best possible professional military advice upon which to base them. As Walter Lippmann has expressed it,

> But then we arrive at the real question. How are these great decisions to be made? It is all very well to say that they should be made by the Secretary of Defense. But Secretaries come and go. They are chosen

[20] President's Reorganization Plan, submitted to Congress on April 30, 1953.

from lists of politically available men. They come from banking, from law, from professional politics, from the automobile business and the soap business. How does a man who has spent the first fifty years of his life far away from strategic problems go into the Pentagon, hang up his hat, sit down at the Secretary's desk, and make the decisions which he is supposed to make?[21]

The answer is given by William R. Kintner in *Forging a New Sword*. "At the present time the Secretary of Defense obtains his advice from an array of civilian assistant secretaries and the Chairman of the Joint Chiefs of Staff. In our conflict with the Soviet Union, Soviet professionals are stacked up against United States amateurs at the decision-making level."[22] The answer might appear to be that the Secretary can obtain professional military advice from the Joint Chiefs of Staff. But the Joint Chiefs of Staff do not work like that. As long as a Chief of Staff is responsible for the leadership and morale of a service, he cannot be expected to be party to decisions in the Department of Defense that deleteriously affect his own service. In the final analysis, the Joint Chiefs of Staff corporate attitude and expressions of opinion reflect the two-against-one situation that prevails. The record of the last ten years makes this abundantly clear. During that time we have had some outstanding Chairmen, notably General Omar Bradley and General Nathan Twining. All of their wisdom, fairness and exceptional professional competence could not prevail against an organizational structure that has established us in second place in the technological race with the Soviets.

Recently I heard a distinguished member of the United States Senate describe in a few words the evils of the *modus operandi* of the Joint Chiefs of Staff. He was speaking to a senior general:

"The trouble with the Joint Chiefs of Staff, General, is it just simply doesn't work. If Congress sends you five billion dollars, you decide to buy five more supercarriers and five more B-52 wings."

[21] New York *Herald Tribune*, May 8, 1958.
[22] *Forging a New Sword*, William R. Kintner.

I intervened and said, "Nothing for the Army?"

And the Senator replied, "Yes, that is right. Nothing for the Army." Which tells the story tersely and well. Of course it could possibly be the Army and Navy against the Air Force or the Air Force and Army against the Navy. However, the Chairman, in the event of a sharp difference of opinion, may act as a spokesman for the Joint Chiefs of Staff in presenting the problem to the Secretary of Defense. Regardless of the law, or of the intent of Congress, the Chairman of the Joint Chiefs of Staff under its present organization has tremendous influence on the development of our future weapons systems. He can wield far more power than any chief of a general staff could possibly have. As an illustration, the former Chairman of the Joint Chiefs of Staff, Admiral Radford, was a proponent of supercarriers. The position that he took in the B-36 hearings in which he bitterly opposed the growth of SAC at the expense of the supercarrier program is well known. During his tenure of office as Chairman of the Joint Chiefs of Staff, the supercarrier program received unprecedented support. And, as Representative Cannon observed in February of 1958, "We are ahead of the Russians in supercarriers, tomahawks and scalping knives. No one questions our pre-eminence in any of these three categories."[23]

The workings of the Joint Chiefs of Staff must be positively bewildering to a military student. For example, in the fall of 1954, the Joint Chiefs of Staff published a document in which it was unanimously agreed that, among other things, there would be no range limitation placed upon the surface-to-surface missiles employed by the Army in a tactical role. This paper had been under discussion for over a year, it was well thought out and all services agreed to its publication. This was sound and exactly the type of guidance the Army needed, for the Soviets were then intensifying their missile development program. As our Armies overseas experimented with tactical nuclear warfare formations, they began to realize that they would need missiles of great range. At the

[23] Congressional Record—House, Vol. 104.

same time, all intelligence indications pointed to the Soviet Army developing long-range missiles also. As a matter of urgency, therefore, the Army cut back its other research and development programs in order to support an intensified surface-to-surface missile program. It had had approval for a missile of approximately five-hundred-miles range since 1951. It seemed clearly in the nation's interest that it accelerate its missile programs and it was obviously a tactical necessity for the Army to have missiles of many hundreds of miles range as quickly as it could develop them. In 1956, the Chairman opposed the Army's development of the missiles it so badly needed. Despite the pleas of the Chief of Staff of the Army, the other chiefs and the Chairman decided that the Army didn't need a missile of greater range than two hundred miles. At the time, and it was the time of Suez, the Soviet Army had operational missiles of 750-mile range.

Thus the Joint Chiefs of Staff reversed its position on such a fundamental problem and this in the face of demonstrable need. The economic factors alone are compelling. The estimated cost of an operational ICBM is about $17.5 million, an IRBM $6.4 million, and a mid-range missile of the type under consideration, one-half million dollars. A mid-range missile is invaluable in limited-war-type operation because of its high mobility and quick responsiveness to tactical requirements. Finally, at the time the decision was made to deny its development, no other service expressed an interest in filling this vacuum into which the Soviets were moving very rapidly.

The problem illustrates one of the fundamental shortcomings of the Joint Chiefs of Staff system. The Chiefs must wear two hats, one as a member of the J.C.S. and another as a member of their own service. In a larger sense, they should keep the national interest paramount. But one cannot disassociate the two. And, in fact, the record will show that interest in the particular service usually prevails, although entirely in a patriotic sense, since their background, loyalties and responsibilities all suggest that in this manner the national interest is best served. It is obvious, therefore, that the responsibilities must be separated. One solution that should work quite well would be to appoint the Chiefs of Staff to a Senior Military Advisory Group upon the termination of their tour of duty with the service. In the latter group they would act as an advisory group to the Secretary of Defense and fill a role comparable to the Joint Chiefs of Staff. Thus their military background and valuable counsel could be brought to bear on our national defense problems without their having to serve an obligation of leadership to their own particular branches of service. With the separation of the "Joint Chiefs" from the joint staff that had been created to serve them, the joint staff, numbering over two hundred officers of all services, could be made available to serve the Secretary of Defense. It would then, in effect, become the military staff of the Department of Defense, serving subordinate to the Secretary and Assistant Secretaries of Defense.

A Military Staff

Considerable opposition to a military staff for the Secretary of Defense exists today. There is frequent reference to the horrors of a "Prussian General Staff." I am not sure that many people who use that expression know what they mean by it, but they use it so frequently that it has come to assume some meaning. For example, in a talk at the National Press Club on April 10, 1958, in discussing the proposed Department of Defense reorganization, Secretary of Defense McElroy took care to point out that, "It does not set up a Prussian-German type general staff." That assurance contains all of the bad words: "Prussian," "German," and "general staff." Members of Congress seem to share the Secretary's abhorrence for them.

Appearing before Mr. Vinson's committee in the spring of 1958, I was asked a question by a member of the committee that contained the implication that we surely did not want the kind of staff that Germany had when she lost the war. I pointed out that Hitler did not have a general staff. This seemed to fluster him for a moment; however, he quickly recovered. His attitude is shared by many. Nevertheless, the fact is that in the last two world wars Germany did not have a German general staff. In World War I, the German Army and Navy were completely independent and no staff existed to co-ordinate their efforts. In World War II, the failure of Germany to achieve a quick victory has been attributed to its failure to co-ordinate its Army and Navy efforts.[24] At the beginning of World War II, Hitler exercised control over three entirely independent and un-co-ordinated military services—Army (Reichswehr), Navy (Reichsmarine) and Air Force (Luftwaffe) —through a small personal staff. This staff, entitled the Armed Forces Supreme Command (Oberkommando Der Wehrmacht), was generally known as OKW. The OKW never actually in any way operated as a unified general staff for the co-ordination of the three services. Although composed of Army, Navy and Air Force officers, the individuals on this small personal staff of the German dictator were picked not for their military knowledge, but because of their loyalty to Hitler and to the Nazi party.

The historical evidence is clear that there was in Germany no pretense toward unified staff control of the three armed services during either World War I or World War II. Whatever co-ordination of effort was accomplished among the services was due to the initiative of individual German officers. One of the most telling indictments of this lack of co-ordination through some kind of unified central control has been made by General Bobo Zimmermann of the German Army:

It is a matter of irony that Eisenhower, the servant of the great democracies, was given full powers of command over an armed force consisting of all three services. With us, living under a dictatorship where unity of command might have been taken for granted, each of the services fought its own battle. Neither Rundstedt nor Rommel, try though they might, succeeded in changing this state of affairs in creating a unified command. The result was that the German Army fought singlehanded against all the armed forces of the Allies.[25]

[24] *Der Seekrieg: The German Navy's Story, 1939-1945*, Friedrich Ruge. U.S. Naval Institute, 1957, pp. 22-24.
[25] *The Fatal Decisions*, Seymour Freidin and William Richardson, eds. Sloane, 1956, p. 238.

Memoirs of German military leaders of World War II are replete with complaints of lack of co-ordination of military efforts. The fact that there was inadequate understanding of sea power evidenced in top-level German military decisions can in no way be used as an indictment of centralized military control. Quite the contrary, such evidence of lack of proper evaluation of all military considerations is clear proof that this, like other failures in military co-ordination, was due to the lack of a single German staff where all aspects of all military problems could have been considered in a logical, thorough manner.

The German Army, of course, had a staff that could be compared with the U.S. Army staff. As in the case of the United States, however, this staff was an Army staff only and in neither World War I nor World War II did it have any responsibility for over-all interservice co-ordination. There is no basis in history, nor in logic, for an assumption that a military staff composed of American citizens wearing the uniforms of the different services, would have more sinister objectives, or be less responsive to civilian control, than has been the Army's General Staff for more than fifty years.

In summary, Germany did not lose both wars because of a well-organized efficient staff system, for that is what a general staff is and that is what we had. She lost it, among other reasons, because she lacked this very thing. On the other hand, the staff system developed in the United States is far more efficient than anything created by any nation, to my knowledge, in military history. It has managed military affairs and brought victory to our arms in the far corners of the earth. Sir Winston Churchill, in referring to the American staff system in World War II, has said:

To create large armies is one thing; to lead them and to handle them is another. It remains a mystery as yet unexplainable how the very small staffs which the United States kept during the years of peace were able not only to build up the Army and Air Force units, but also to find the leaders and vast staffs capable of handling enormous masses and of moving them faster and further than masses have ever been moved in war before.[26]

[26] *The Hinge of Fate,* Sir Winston Churchill, p. 387.

Good staff organization exists now under Admiral Stump in the Pacific and General Norstad in Europe. A good staff can bring competent professional advice to a commander and serve him and the nation's interest well. There is no comparable staff in the Department of Defense today.

Technical Trends and Changes in the Services

Before considering an over-all organizational concept to meet our future military needs it would be well to examine the tools that will become available to us. Let us make an estimate of the form that our separate services may take by 1965. Certainly change, perhaps drastic change, is inevitable, if the present technical trends continue.

Nuclear weapons will become conventional fire power. This will be true in the armed forces of NATO, including the United States, and of the USSR and the satellites. They are conventional now, of course, in forces such as SAC and the Soviet Long Range Bomber Forces. To say that they will become conventional means that they will be in the hands of all military organizations including, for example, the smallest infantry units.

The United States and the USSR will have in their stockpiles an abundance of large-yield thermonuclear weapons. More significant than these, however, will be the stockpiles of small, precise-yield weapons suitable for tactical employment. Their number, size and performance will be critical to the outcome of any future limited wars.

Nuclear weapons will become conventional for several reasons, among them cost, effectiveness against enemy weapons, and ease of handling. By 1965 the cost of nuclear weapons will be far less than present high-explosive weapons of equivalent yield and effectiveness. Many millions of dollars spent in the manufacture, shipping, storage and handling of high-explosive projectiles and bombs will be saved through the use of nuclear weapons moved by air to combat areas. This is not to say that all high-explosive ammunition will be replaced by nuclear ammunition—far from it. Many of the smaller tactical targets will require high-explosive ammunition, but the large artillery concentrations, for example, will be replaced by atomic weapons.

An immediate consequence of the employment of nuclear weapons will be widely dispersed targets on both sides in any tactical engagement. Hence, weapons of far greater range of effectiveness will be required to gain tactical success. Nuclear weapons will meet this need.

From a technical point of view, only a nuclear weapon will provide defense against an incoming nuclear warhead, whether from a manned aircraft, missile or satellite. The object in such a defense must be to completely destroy the incoming weapon and carrier. This a nuclear weapon can do. And finally, while the problem is rather complex in a technical sense, the handling of nuclear weapons is far simpler than the handling of the many million rounds of high-explosive ammunition required in past wars. Tactical nuclear weapons will be used by individuals in defense against, for example, tank concentrations. In this they may be shoulder-fired. They will be fired from track-laying vehicles and from aerial jeeps of the type used in sky-cavalry organizations. In air combat they will be used in air-to-surface missiles and in air-to-air missiles. By 1965 it will be possible to place nuclear weapons aboard satellites for either offensive or defensive use. Finally, nuclear weapons will be used in submarine warfare. In the latter role, they will be used in air-launched missiles against enemy submarines as well as in submarine-launched missiles, and in land-to-sea antisubmarine missiles.

Complementing this evolution in fire power will be an evolution in mobility. By 1965 the use of missiles and huge jet transports should have a decisive bearing upon all tactical operations. By that time, jet transports should be operational in large numbers on a global scale and missile mobility for high-priority cargo should be in development. Global air movements for highly specialized military forces will be normal. All missiles and fissionable material used in overseas areas will be flown. The air transportation of missile and fissionable material is not only tactically desirable but administratively essential. This is because missiles, even as late as 1965, will be highly sensitive to obsolescence. It will not be practicable to supply missiles as we have manned aircraft and trucks in the past, as items that could be placed in long lines of supply. Technology will be so dynamic that constant changes and modifications will have to be made, and missiles may not spend several months in a long supply line. Furthermore, there will no doubt be an insufficiency of some types of missiles for the indefinite future. This is also true of their nuclear warheads. Hence we should no longer think in terms of huge stockpiles of nuclear ammunition scattered throughout the world much as we thought of piles of cannon balls in the Civil War and acres of 105-mm. ammunition and bombs in World War II. There will not be sufficient nuclear ammunition or missiles to allow such waste in storage. Both the nuclear warhead and missile will be too sensitive to deterioration to allow prolonged storage. To meet the Western world's requirements in the missile-nuclear age, therefore, it is absolutely essential that both of these be moved by air at all times. This suggests the need for a number of special types of aircraft suited to this particular purpose.

Far less exotic than jet transports, but perhaps more important to winning tactical battles will be the small air vehicles of the land forces, both Army and Marine Corps. Tilt wings, tilt engines, ducted fans, deflected jets, and a number of other developments now make it quite clear that air mobility will give select portions of our land forces a tremendous advantage over an opponent, provided this is understood and properly exploited.

Comparable changes will take place in sea mobility. An outstanding American authority on submarines, Vice-Admiral C. B. Monsen, in a recent issue of *Look*, wrote:

The day is not far off when submarines will be almost completely silent, and will travel at speeds of 60 knots or better and at great depths unheard-of a decade ago. How long before that is a reality? Certainly no longer—less, I believe—than the period it took us to move from 450-mile-an-hour Mustang fighters in World War II to ballistic missiles roaring 5,000 miles through space in 30 minutes.[27]

[27] *Look*, May 13, 1958.

Naval combat vessels, and all the combat elements accompanying them—supplies, cargo, missiles and fighting units of the Marine Corps—will have far greater mobility than they have had in the past.

Improvements in fire power and mobility would be of little combat value if we were not able to make comparable improvements in our means for controlling them. Earlier warning times, more accurate target data at far greater distances, and a minimum of reaction time must be realized. These appear to be attainable. Through drones, eyes can be provided for our combat missile units. The most interesting reconnaissance vehicle, and perhaps the most promising, is the satellite. Combat formations of all services will be equipped with combat surveillance units containing a variety of useful drones that will be absolutely essential to missile-space age combat. Such drones should be adapted to submarine warfare as well as land warfare. Thus, they could conduct a reconnaissance of possible missile sites and other types of tactical targets for missile-launching submarines. But mere observation by drones will be far from sufficient to our combat needs. A highly responsive system of handling the data they obtain is required. Reaction times will be so short that computers will be needed to determine target locations and time of firing, and to transmit launching and firing signals to weapons. This will be particularly necessary in defense against missiles in which the problems of analysis, evaluation and determination of when to fire are far beyond man's ability to solve in the few minutes or seconds available to him. All the communication devices touched upon so far in their simplest forms will tell us where a target will be, where our own weapon is, and in some cases provide a solution to the equation—that is, tell the weapon when to fire.

Nuclear warfare will introduce an additional problem. If surface-burst weapons are used, serious fallout may occur. Practically all tactical weapons now under consideration are intended for air bursts, both for reasons of increased effectiveness and self-defense from fallout. However, some surface bursts will take place either through accident or intent. Thus in a tactical nuclear battle it will be necessary for a tactical commander to have available accurate and timely information, in readily understandable form, of fallout patterns. By 1965 accurate fallout data, properly presented, should be available to tactical commanders as well as to those responsible for home defense. Closely related to fallout prediction is weather data. By 1965 the control of weather, even to a limited degree, may have a significant bearing upon combat operations. Hence, accurate weather data must be available to those responsible for combat decisions, since it may become a tactical weapon.

Military establishments have never overanticipated technical trends and the impact of these trends upon future military organizations. Quite the contrary; the normal pattern has been to underestimate changes that may take place. There are a number of reasons for this. By their very nature, military organizations must be conservative. They must prepare to win a war today with the resources at hand. Even when given more resources than may be required to win in battle, they are inclined, as insurance against defeat, to overinvest in contemporary weapons. Wars are usually infrequent and the thinking of the younger generation of officers is critically contaminated by the veterans of past wars. Thus they frequently find themselves preparing feverishly to fight the last war better.

These conditions could be tolerated in the past since the time between the opening of hostilities and the final decision was sufficient to enable a nation to revamp its military establishment and its thinking to produce new weapons to match new concepts. Technology, too, was slow to change. The undulating pattern from offense to defense that has characterized warfare through all history shows a span of several hundred years between peaks of offensive power, until this century. Now these peaks are but a few years apart. Hundreds of years elapsed between the time gunpowder was first used in Europe until its use in machine weapons in the battles of attrition in World War I. But a fraction of that time elapsed between the discovery and development of the gasoline-petroleum engine and the fast-moving blitzkrieg that brought the Free World to the brink of defeat in 1940. Now, the time of change is but a fraction of that fraction. Nevertheless, it is the time, brief as it may be, in which an understanding of missiles and their associated nuclear fire-power mobility may bring defeat or survival to a free people. The changes that must take place in our military organizations to adapt to this violent evolution are many. And they must be made. However, we must not allow ourselves to become so mesmerized by the wonders of tomorrow's technology that we spend most of our time, effort and resources endeavoring to adapt our military establishment to it. Instead we must have the imagination and vision to foresee the military requirements essential to our self-defense in the future and then make demands upon technology to meet them. I think that it is important that we understand this precedence.

Let us now examine some of the significant changes in the services themselves. These are the tools with which the tactical battles of tomorrow will be won.

The basic combat tool of the Army is the fighting division. It is the smallest unit that combines administration with all of the fighting elements and thus it can, in theory, fight an independent action. As conceived, it contains all of the supply services necessary for the support of its fighting elements for at least several days. In its original form, its structure was based upon horse mobility. In the memory of many still in the Army, wagons carried rations, ammunition and baggage for an infantry regiment and these were backed by the long wagon trains of the infantry division. Generally, the automotive engine changed the internal structure from a quadrilateral to triangular division but did not change the fact that it was a self-contained administrative unit. As a consequence during World War II and Korea the division was burdened with truck trains and vast tonnages of supplies. Until the advent of tactical nuclear weapons, this could be tolerated. In the nuclear age the division cannot continue in its present form as an administrative unit. Supplies will have to be moved far to the rear, out of division responsibility. The combat units within the division must be reorganized to enable the division to survive under the impact of nuclear weapons and react to win in tactical nuclear combat. A trend to accomplish this has been apparent for some years and it has manifested itself in the creation of battle groups and combat commands in place of, generally speaking, reinforced battalions and reinforced regiments. This trend will continue. The "division" designation, should be retained. The next higher organization, however, should combine administration with fighting units. It should be designated as a Battle Command. This would eliminate the old corps. The next higher command above the Battle Command would be the Field Army.

The Army has recently adopted the pentomic division, which reduced the strength of the division from roughly seventeen thousand to thirteen thousand men. However, the pentomic division is seriously lacking in missile fire power and adequate reconnaissance, both sky cavalry and drones. These should be added to it and more of its administrative personnel moved far to the rear. All divisions in the Army except those for highly specialized tasks, such as mountain and jungle warfare, and the sky-cavalry division for reconnaissance, screening and exploitation, should be armored divisions. Armor protection should be provided for all fighting personnel engaged in sustained combat. They will then be able to operate in a nuclear environment with much greater effectiveness than in the present type divisions.

The airborne division is an outgrowth of the combat need for a hypermobile force in World War II, and the available commercial air transport to provide that mobility. Although its fighting effectiveness has been of a high order, on analysis, its functional performance has left much to be desired. Now, with surface-to-air missiles available in abundance in the hands of an enemy, the airborne division can no longer carry out the type of airborne operations of World War II and Korea. As rapidly as the Army can do so, it must convert the airborne divisions into sky-cavalry divisions. The parachute capability should be retained. It will allow for combat and administrative flexibility. With this capability airborne divisions may be delivered in the combat zone without the need for landing on long airstrips.

The Army has recently created missile support commands. This trend should be continued and by 1965 missile divisions should be in being. A missile division would contain its own target surveillance drones, armored or sky cavalry for ground protection, surface-to-air missiles for air defense, as well as its own surface-to-surface missiles. This concept would envision a grouping for tactical purposes of highly mobile long-range missiles fired from hundreds of miles behind our own forces. They should be readily capable of intercontinental air movement in a reinforcing role. They should be used in defense of land areas against submarine-missile attack in close co-operation with our own naval forces.

Surface-to-air nuclear weapons should be available in sufficient quantity to provide the degree of independence of operations on land that our Army and Marine units require. This is now possible against an enemy equipped with manned aircraft. It will be far more difficult against an enemy equipped with surface-to-surface missiles. Antimissile-missile systems will be required to deal with the long-range ICBM, particularly within the United States, as well as missiles to deal with shorter-range missiles to be used against our forces deployed in vital overseas areas. By 1965, both types of missiles should be in being, although they will still be in need of considerable improvement. The threat to land operations from space will be quite serious by 1965. Up to that time passive measures probably will be adequate. By then, however, as man's capability to fight in space improves, the problem of defense against attacks and reconnaissance from space will become impressive and challenging. A satellite to intercept a satellite should be available.

272

The present trend in the Navy of shifting from surface vessels to submarines will be continued. By 1965, we should have a growing submarine-missile capability. The carrier and surface vessels that we have should be completely equipped with missiles, drones and assault landing air vehicles. Their value, however, will decrease rapidly with the increase in the numbers of Soviet missile-carrying submarines. One of the most interesting organizational problems is that of the United States Marine Corps. At present it appears to be showing schizophrenic tendencies, not knowing whether to become an all-out sky-cavalry type of organization or whether to retain heavy sustained combat equipment. I believe that by 1965 the sky-cavalry trend will have given the Marine Corps a very effective capability to extend naval operations on land in keeping with their role and their best fighting traditions. By 1965, major fighting units of the Marine Corps should be movable by submersible vessels. In proximity to their objective areas, they will have the capability of surfacing and launching an attack by air. A sizable portion of the Marine Corps will continue to operate out of surface craft in their traditional amphibious role, especially in limited types of actions. By 1965, however, the trend toward submersible craft will become dominant.

The Air Force faces some challenging and fascinating problems in this decade. Its long-range striking force will be equipped with an ICBM fired from fixed installations. By 1965, however, it will be apparent that adequate ranges can be obtained from missiles of much smaller size. By that date they will be converting to mobile ICBMs, or planning such conversions. For example, with the extensive railroad network that we have in the Rocky Mountain areas and the labyrinth of tunnels and deep canyons through that area, we should be able to develop a highly effective, comparatively invulnerable ICBM system for firing off railroad cars. Moving from concealed tunnels to firing sites, they should be able to fire with a minimum likelihood of detection. Warheads and fuel can be prestockpiled in the most likely firing areas and the system can be fully mobile. The shorter-range missiles, the IRBM, should be entirely mobile to be combat-worthy.

All missiles deployed overseas should be supported by an air supply system exactly as in past wars we have supported our combat forces by an adequate naval supply system. This implies need for several highly specialized types of aircraft—for example, aircraft capable of servicing missiles and nuclear warheads en route to operational areas; aircraft of such size, configuration and floor strength as to enable us to move "fire brigades" rapidly to any point overseas; aircraft especially equipped for medical evacuation and to some extent surgical care en route; and aircraft adapted to the many combat needs that will still remain, such as air-to-surface missile launchers as well as early-warning aircraft. It would appear that many of the functions suggested by the types of air vehicles should be grouped into operational type units. This tendency exists today and by 1965 we should have missile support wings, combat support wings as part of our long-range and short-range striking forces, and medical evacuation wings.

By 1965, the Air Force will have placed men in orbit and it will be acquiring a capability of conducting combat operations in space. A manned space station should be in orbit and plans should be under way for interplanetary exploration.

It should be quite evident from the foregoing that while each of the services continues to specialize in the type of combat that can be won in its own medium, the capabilities of all services will overlap. Their organization within a theater of operations, therefore, should be completely integrated. Let us look briefly at several of the possible theaters of operations.

In describing the military characteristics of the major geographic areas of the earth as they would appear during combat in the mid-sixties, I intend merely to suggest concepts. No plans exist to organize areas in the manner suggested nor does the intent, to my knowledge, exist today. I realize that a malicious person could see in these ideas a basis for charges of aggressive intent, but I can assure him that this is not the case. Actually, if the Free World is to survive, it must anticipate the events of tomorrow and give some thought to what might happen if it must fight for its survival. It must consider the earth as a tactical whole and its segments as theaters of operations. And having done so, it must at least give thought to what measures must be taken in the interest of self-preservation. If doing this makes one vulnerable to the charge of aggressive intent, then this is a risk that elementary self-interest demands that we take.

Europe—Africa

Europe and Africa are part of one tactical theater. Africa, in fact, is the key to the defense of Europe.

Referring to map 1, we can see that the European-African area divides itself into two parts: Western Europe consisting of a little over one million square miles of densely populated land, and Africa consisting of eleven and one half million square miles containing in its entirety less population than the European peninsula. Two major waterways cross the area: in the north the English Channel, no longer a barrier to military aggression, and farther south the Mediterranean Sea, a formidable obstacle to land movement, but readily crossed by missiles and aircraft. To the east is the land bridge connecting Europe, Asia and Africa. This fact alone, that it is a land bridge, highlights the importance of this area. The Northern European area consists of rolling flat country containing an extensive network of east-west roads and railroads. Numerous major waterways flow south to north, all of them easily crossed by modern amphibious equipment. To the south, the mountain masses of the Vosges, the Alps and the Pyrenees dominate the area. Farther south, in Africa, the Atlas Mountains dominate the western and north African area. Then come the vast stretches of desert, and below them the tropical rain forest and savannas of Mid-Africa.

The measures taken to defend the European-African area in the 1965 period will be determined by available resources and the geographic nature of the area itself. Obviously the shallow depth of the northern area suggests that only weapons that will insure its defense should be placed there. Retaliatory weapons would be in danger of immediate destruction and should be placed farther south where there is adequate concealment and land depth.

The basic requirements for the defense of Western Europe are, in order of priority: first, the best surface-to-air missile defense obtainable; next, the best surface-to-surface missile defense matched with highly mobile, nuclear equipped land forces. Because of its vulnerability, none of the area of Northern Europe should be considered suitable for a base for counteroffensive operations. The effectiveness of surface-to-air and surface-to-surface nuclear weapons in the 1965 period, however, should be so great that a defense of this area would be entirely feasible. If the forces in the NATO area are sufficient in strength and properly equipped with nuclear missiles in all the necessary categories, the Soviets would pay a very high price, and even then fail, if they sought direct aggression into the NATO area. Italy, Spain and the islands in the Mediterranean and the African land mass offer the best location for retaliatory missile forces. These missiles should be highly mobile, both in the air and on land. Missile units should be deployed in considerable depth and moved forward by air under cover of darkness to provide the close supporting missile fires that will be needed in the event of aggression. There is no military need for long-range missiles being placed in UK. Missiles from Kenya, the Middle East and Southern Europe can accomplish as much in defense as missiles fired from UK. At the same time, they will be far less vulnerable to being destroyed by Soviet missile counterfirings.

Present Army and Air Force units are inadequate for NATO's defense. General Norstad has recently asked for an increase to thirty Army divisions. This would be a minimum and would be adequate only if surface-to-air and long-range surface-to-surface missiles are also provided. In addition, there should be, by 1965, submarine-launched missile support. This is particularly important

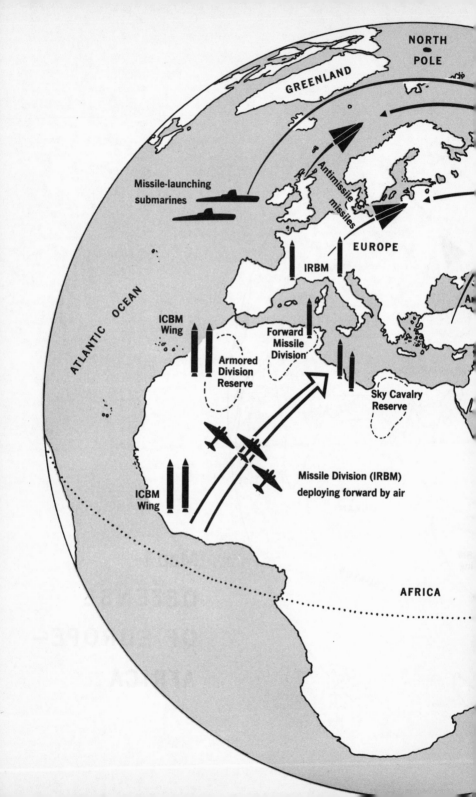

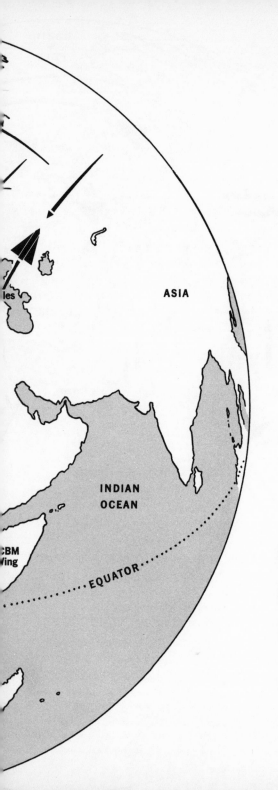

les

ASIA

INDIAN
OCEAN

CBM
Wing

EQUATOR

Map 1.
DEFENSE
OF EUROPE—
AFRICA

in the northern area where adequate land is not available to provide defense in depth.

Finally, in addition to the NATO requirements for forces committed to the immediate defense of Western Europe, there should be provided a local "fire brigade." This should be in the nature of a reserve and geographically placed so as to be available for air movement to any area in difficulty. A composite Battle Command consisting of at least one sky-cavalry division and two armored divisions, supported by several missile support commands would be adequate. Their general location should be in Western and Northern Africa with the divisions in the north and the missile units as far south as Liberia, for example. It should be evident from the foregoing, that the center of gravity of the effort of defending the European-African area has shifted far to the south. And while this very brief discussion has concentrated itself primarily with military forces, the political and economic implications of such a strategic concept are quite obvious and compelling. Technical and economic assistance must be provided the people of North Africa. The people of Africa must be given every opportunity to improve their living standards and they must become active in the community of Western nations. By 1965, it will become obvious, if it is not already so, that Africa is the key to the defense of Western Europe, and the Middle East with its great land bridge and economic resources is the key to Africa.

Asia

Let us now look to the Far East (see map 2). Here again we have a geographic situation in which the northern area of the Free Nations is shallow in depth, whereas the south is extensive. This, and a consideration of the prevailing west-to-east winds, places the offshore islands of the Asian land mass, Japan, Okinawa and Taiwan, in a hazardous atomic situation. By 1965, they will be "in the front lines" in every sense of that expression. They will be under immediate threat of Soviet and Chinese missile attack. Missiles used against the mainland in retaliation, if surface nuclear detonations occur, will create serious fallout conditions. This is true also of South Korea. It is important, therefore, that any tactical concepts developed to defend the Free World area in Asia be based upon: (a) maximum use of nonatomic force in South Korea and Japan, (b) surface-to-air nuclear missiles to provide an air defense, and (c) submarine-missile-launched support forces.

The southern portion of the area is highlighted by the Indo-China Peninsula that extends into the Malaya Peninsula, and then south to Singapore. Farther to the east is the Philippine Archipelago, and to the south Indonesia, Australia and New Zealand. Vietnam, Laos, Cambodia and Thailand, backed up by the Philippines, constitute the frontier of freedom in Southeast Asia. In a sense, the Philippines is the cornerstone of the area, physically and politically. Its dispersed islands, numbering over a thousand, provide numerous well-protected launching areas for retaliatory missiles in the event of aggression. In this area should also be located a local "fire brigade," a geographic reserve to back up the SEATO[28] area. SEATO is the key to the defense of the Asia-Pacific area. It should be anticipated that the Communists will make every effort to penetrate the area, through Indonesia and through member countries.

In the mid-thirties I served with the Philippine Scouts for two years. In late 1954 I went back for a brief visit. On the same trip I visited Vietnam and Thailand. I talked to Presidents Magsaysay in the Philippines and Diem in Vietnam about their mutual defense problems. They agreed emphatically on one point: if the

[28] The Southeast Asia Collective Defense Treaty (SEATO) was signed in Manila on September 8, 1954. In it members agree, among other things, to maintain by self-help, and mutual aid, their capacity to resist armed attack; to meet armed attack in the treaty area in accordance with each party's constitutional processes. A council to carry out this treaty has been established. Members of the treaty are: United States, United Kingdom, France, Australia, New Zealand, Pakistan, Philippines and Thailand.

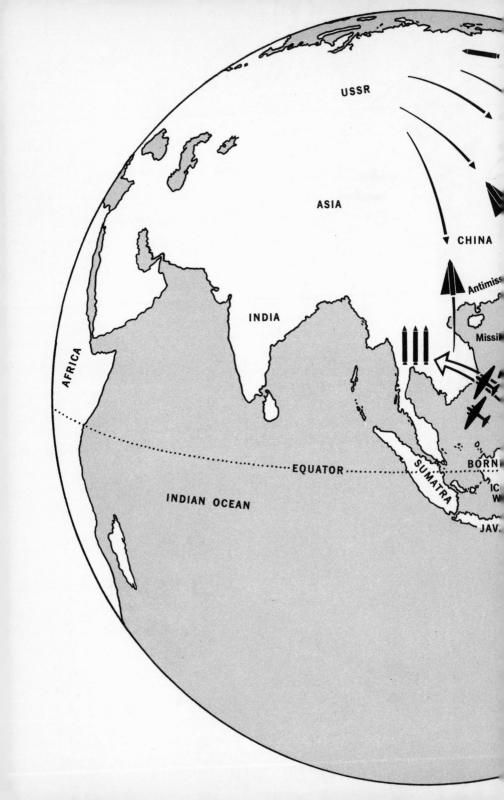

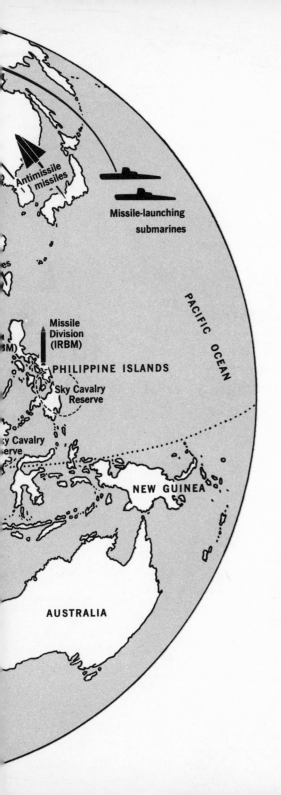

Antimissile
missiles

Missile-launching
submarines

PACIFIC OCEAN

Missile
Division
(IRBM)

SM)

PHILIPPINE ISLANDS

Sky Cavalry
Reserve

es

y Cavalry
erve

NEW GUINEA

AUSTRALIA

Map 2.

DEFENSE

OF ASIA

Communists were to establish themselves in the area it would be by way of the "rice paddies" and not by direct military force. These countries need our continuing economic and technical help. I believe that we have done wonders in the Philippines in the last fifty years. They stand as a monument to our generosity and dedication to the ideals of freedom. But much remains to be done, particularly in the Vietnam-Laos-Cambodia-Thailand area.

The two major areas of the planet just described contain, in effect, our Short Range Striking Forces. They are in immediate contact and would be engaged at once in the event of aggression. They should be adequate in strength to provide a defense of those areas for a prolonged period of time without reinforcement. It should be evident to an aggressor that they may not be taken over by military force without bringing upon himself unacceptable damage. The forces in being, and the geographically placed "fire brigades," should be able to deal effectively and rapidly with limited aggression in any form. Both of these areas should be backed by Long Range Striking Forces based in the North American area. Let us look at that area.

Viewed from the USSR (see map 3), the shortest route to North America and the United States is over the North Pole. Thus the Arctic area is of extraordinary significance. It has been considered impassable for military forces, except for aircraft and missiles, and like other once impassable areas, it may contain the key to our future survival. This is not to say that an army will cross the North Pole, but weapons with all of the power of an army certainly will. And furthermore an ability to operate in the Arctic—and in this area I would include Greenland—may be the key to the defense of the United States.

For example, the most critical factor in the defense against manned bomber attack and missile attack is time—time in which to react with defensive missiles. Reaction time depends upon the amount of warning one receives, and the amount of warning depends in general upon how far forward our observation may be. Theoretically, it is possible to be far enough forward in the North

Pole area to observe Soviet missiles while the engines are still burning in sustained thrust. From radar facilities in Greenland, one may track missiles long before the radar facilities in Canada can, and of course, long before those in the United States. At present we have an extensive line of radars across Northern Canada and Alaska. These were to protect the United States against manned bomber attack. Now we will require larger and more powerful radars, although fewer in number because of their increased range, to give us early warning of Soviet missiles. Their value to us is directly related to how far forward they are placed. Obviously such radars will be vulnerable to missile attack and raids by surface forces. They will therefore need protection. The ideal pattern of Soviet attack would be to destroy the early-warning radars, our eyes for defense, just prior to launching missiles. It is important, therefore, that we not only provide radars of adequate performance characteristics, but that we provide protection for them.

For a number of years Soviets have been living on ice islands in the Arctic regions. At the present time, three such islands are in operation. Recently one Soviet island was within two hundred miles of Canadian territory. Such an island, presumably conducting scientific studies, usually contains an airstrip, several aircraft and on the average one-half dozen helicopters. If we are to gain the scientific knowledge of the Arctic regions that we should have, we must embark upon a national polar research program as a matter of high priority. Next, we should be prepared to provide forces to protect our facilities in the Arctic regions. Briefly, this would involve all services: the Air Force operating the DEW line, the Army the missile defense and sky-cavalry type forces, and the Navy operating submarines. The entire undertaking should be integrated into a unified effort.

The defense of the United States, and the North American area, breaks down into several categories. (See opposite page.)

A Home Defense Force should be established to co-ordinate the

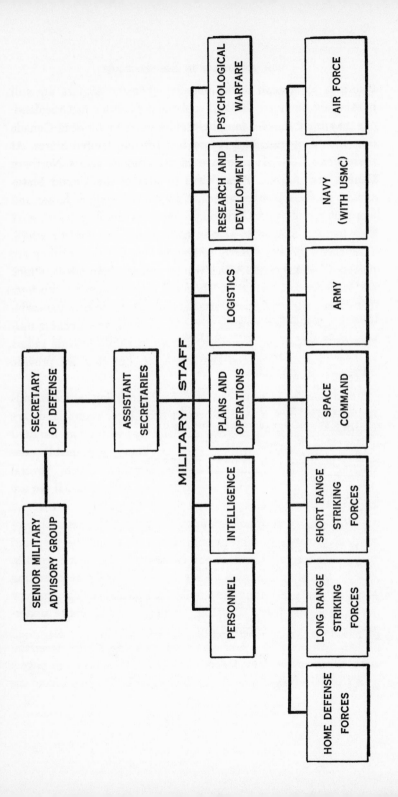

planning and operational activities of all the above categories. At the present time, the headquarters of the Air Defense Force is located at Colorado Springs, Colorado. It is a well-organized and effective organization. Its area is subdivided into a number of smaller areas. Information from the distant early warning is filtered through SAGE[29] and Missile Master Centers for transmission to the combat units that actually provide the defense. The Continental Air Defense Command is confronted with a tremendously difficult and challenging task. Originally organized to provide a defense against manned bombers, it now must be reorganized into a command adequate in its capabilities to the challenges of the missile-space age. Part of its reorganization is under way and its first surface-to-air nuclear missile, the Nike Hercules, is going on site. But to be up to the task it will face by 1965, it must fulfill procurement, equipment, personnel and training requirements without precedent, in my opinion, in our history.

Present responsibility for the defense of the United States against land attack is in the Continental Army Command located at Fort Monroe, Virginia. An operational echelon of this headquarters should be placed in the South and Middle West so that in the event of hostilities it would be free from immediate interference and thus able to do its job effectively.

The defense of the United States against submarine-launched missiles presents a most interesting technical problem. Our own Navy will do much to keep Soviet submarines at some distance from our shores. Unfortunately, it must be assumed that a number of them will be able to cruise within missile-launching ranges of both our coastal and inland areas. To deal with this threat a network of sonar pickets should be established as far from our shores as may be technically feasible, so as to give us warning of the approach of enemy submarines. These sonar pickets should be closely integrated with our air defense and with our coastal

[29] SAGE (Semi-Automatic Ground Environment) is a computing system designed to track an approaching enemy plane, figure out the most efficient way of shooting it down, and guide the defensive weapon to the kill.

missile defenses. Our missile defenses should consist of surface-to-air missiles, such as the Nike Zeus and Plato, to destroy enemy missiles in flight and surface-to-surface missiles, such as the Jupiter, Thor and Pershing, to destroy hostile submarines threatening our shores. Due to the range of our surface-to-surface missiles, it will not be necessary to man many missile-launching areas to obtain extensive coverage of the ocean areas. Such missiles, however, must be mobile.

The Department of Defense does not have direct responsibility for Civil Defense. The services should be prepared, however, to participate in that defense insofar as it may be necessary to assist in recovery following an attack on the United States. At the same time, we should keep free our Reserves and National Guard for deployment outside of the continental limits of the United States if this becomes necessary. Some states have organized "Home Guard" units consisting of older men with military background. Since disaster will not recognize state boundaries, a national agency should be prepared to assist in equipping and training such Home Guard units. The Department of Defense should support such a program in peacetime and be prepared in the event of emergency to back up the civilian-operated Civil Defense agencies. If directed by the President, it should be prepared to take over full responsibility. The proposed Civil Defense office, therefore, should be one of liaison. In the event the full responsibility were given to the Department of Defense, it would be appropriate to place this under the Continental Army Command, the headquarters responsible for the land defense within the Home Defense Force.

So far, I have described the three main tactical theaters, grouping the forces into functional categories, as Short Range Forces and Home Defense Forces. There is a third category, our Long Range Striking Force.

The Long Range Striking Force based within the United States consists of the Strategic Air Command, the Strategic Army Command and such Naval and Marine Forces as are available. They should be integrated into a unified whole. They should be highly mobile and prepared for immediate deployment overseas, preferably by air. In order to achieve this mobility, stockpiles of ammunition, supplies and heavy equipment should be established in key overseas areas, generally in the vicinity of the geographic reserves. By stockpiling in this manner, we can achieve maximum mobility with our Long Range Striking Force. Today this has been realized to a large extent in the Strategic Air Command. As manned bombers become replaced by missiles, the Strategic Air Command will depend to an increased extent upon firing its missiles from the United States. As the shift in the character of our air power continues, to an increased extent the Army and Marine Corps units of the Long Range Striking Force should move by air transportation. Once they have this capability, they should exercise it regularly. As we have flown bomber wings overseas on a regular training schedule in the past, as part of a global deployment plan, we should by 1965 be prepared to fly Army and Marine missile and ground combat units overseas with some frequency. In 1955, the Army and the Air Force carried out an exercise of this type. During the period July 12, 1955, to July 17, 1955, the Air Force flew the Army's 187th Airborne Infantry from Japan to North Carolina. The total lift consisted of 2,875 troops with their weapons, individual equipment and baggage. This is the type of tactical movement that we should conduct more often. To an increasing extent, as we enter the sixties, we must develop a capability of moving Army and Marine units equipped with an abundance of nuclear missile fire power into the areas most likely to be threatened.

Manned space vehicles will be in orbit by 1965. Equipment development and personnel training are under way now. It is past time therefore that we gave thought to an organization to conduct space exploration. We must not wait until science gives us the hardware to decide what is to be done. A command must be organized now to study the problems of space flight and the strategy and tactics of space combat. If this is done, then we

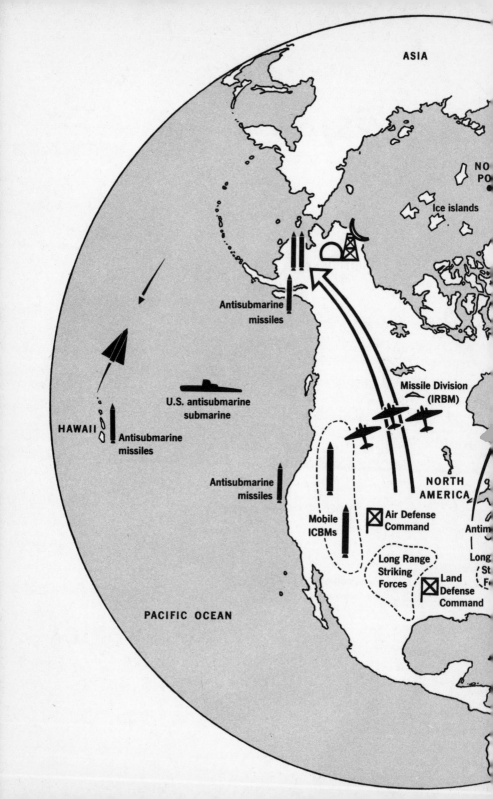

ASIA

NO
PO

Ice islands

Antisubmarine
missiles

U.S. antisubmarine
submarine

HAWAII   Antisubmarine
missiles

Antisubmarine
missiles

Missile Division
(IRBM)

Mobile
ICBMs

Air Defense
Command

NORTH
AMERICA

Antim

Long
St
F

Long Range
Striking
Forces

Land
Defense
Command

PACIFIC OCEAN

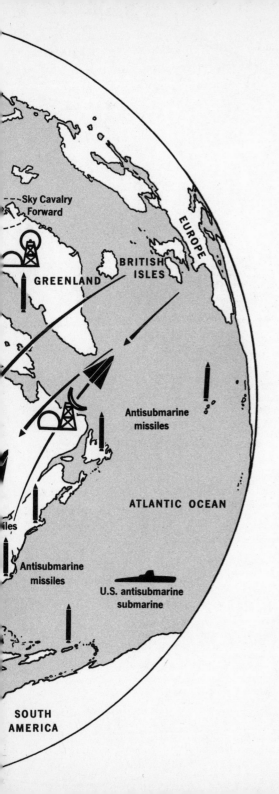

Sky Cavalry
Forward

GREENLAND

BRITISH
ISLES

EUROPE

Antisubmarine
missiles

ATLANTIC OCEAN

...les

Antisubmarine
missiles

U.S. antisubmarine
submarine

SOUTH
AMERICA

Map 3.
DEFENSE
OF AMERICA

may be assured that the demands made upon science will meet our actual needs. The proposed organization breaks down into: Plans and Strategy, Development, and Training. It should be noted that proposed functions of this command go beyond the present Advanced Research Projects Agency (ARPA) of the Department of Defense, which concerns itself primarily with research. The Space Command should be a unified command, with all services participating, reporting directly to the Secretary of Defense.

Recognizing that the effectiveness of weapons and their associated electronics systems, and of mobility, will reduce the earth to a tactical theater by 1965, the contributions of the Armed Forces to commands have been regrouped on a functional basis. Thus, integrated into unified teams, they will be capable of responding to any threat at once. This does not, in any way, diminish the present roles of the services as separate entities. Each service will maintain its present establishments as such, Army, Navy (including the Marine Corps) and Air Force. They will merely provide individuals and units to the unified functional commands when ordered to do so by the Department of Defense. Finally, it is important that we not create large headquarters establishments over the proposed functional groupings. Except for the Space Command, which must be created, the present headquarters are adequate to our needs. The important thing is the recognition of the need for functional groupings now, and giving this expression in the composition of the military staff that works for the Secretary of Defense.

Having examined the tactical tools, and the manner in which they are teamed to report directly to the Secretary of Defense, I believe it is obvious that the Secretary must have a competent military staff. He must have a staff that reports directly to him. It should be composed of officers of all services picked for their professional knowledge as well as their ability to work with the other services. After duty with the Secretary of Defense, the senior among them would very likely go on to higher command

and rarely return to their own service. It would be best to have the staff directly under the Secretary and his Assistant Secretaries. However, even if its operational and administrative functions were separated, as they are in the Department of the Navy, it would be far better than the present DOD-JCS arrangement.

The figure below illustrates the over-all organization proposed, both for the staff and for the commands. It should be noted that

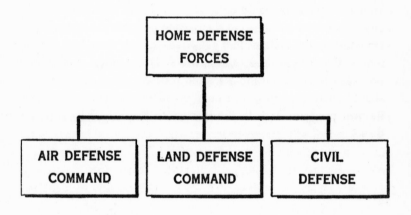

the Joint Chiefs of Staff become the Senior Military Advisory Group. The Chiefs of Staff and the Chief of Naval Operations become eligible for appointment to this group after completing their final tour of duty with their own service.

So far this discussion on the organization of our Armed Forces has dealt with just those—the Armed Forces of the United States and the Department of Defense. Actually, any military operations in the future should be conducted under the auspices of the United Nations. The United Nations is capable of maintaining the peace provided it is given adequate support by its member nations. Despite the difficulties that it has experienced so far— and it has done remarkably well in my opinion—in the space age it should be a fully effective instrument of peace. As soon as it can it should sponsor a space program. The International Geophysical Year will end on December 31, 1958. At that time, the United Nations should assume the burden of continuing that program. Its ultimate object should be the establishment of a United Nations Space Force that will have the capability of keeping the world under surveillance, thus keeping peace on earth. The exploration and use of space by its member nations should be co-ordinated through a Space Headquarters in the United Nations. It would be a tragedy for the Free World if the Soviets were so far ahead in their space program that they would flout the United Nations and go ahead on their own. It is for this reason that the United States, which is the other nation best prepared to contribute to a United Nations space program now, should spare no effort, no resource and no people in advancing its own program. It is in the interest of the Free World that it do so.

Summary

A Strategy for Peace

We have made it abundantly clear, by both our public statements and our behavior in international affairs, that we seek peace. Yet, despite this, we have suffered heavy military losses as victims of Communist aggression. Now we are in second place militarily and in second place in the exploration of space. The Soviet strategy continues to meet with success while the problems of the West multiply. If the present patterns continue the only peace that we will find will be the peace of Carthage.

It is past time that we revamped our strategy, from a strategy to avoid war to a Strategy for Peace. Since the object of strategy is to make physical combat unnecessary, we as a free people should be able to develop such a strategy. Our democracy has been for peace and for freedom since the Republic was founded and we should be assertively for them now.

First, we must be honest with ourselves, and clear-thinking in our analysis of our failures and our successes. Our national defense structure should be such as to minimize the harm that comes from the divisive forces present in the decision-making processes of our democracy. We cannot eliminate them, nor would we want to, but we can certainly organize and plan so as to reduce the harm that they do. Never should we tolerate a defense structure or a decision-making system that encourages, or even allows, the worst elements of our free enterprise system to cause delays and bad decisions. National defense is the most complex business in the world today and our Secretary of Defense should have available, directly, the best professional advice that it is possible for him to obtain. Our Defense Department, in co-operation with the other members of the National Security Council, should develop a national strategy, adequate in scope and objectives, to the needs of our growing democracy. Merely to choose a single strategy or tactic, and then announce it to the world, would be to surrender the initiative and thus to invite strategic failure and certain war. Our economic and technical assistance programs should be continued, closely co-ordinated with our strategic planning. Our stategic planning should reflect a full awareness of the crucial importance of space, of psychology, and of technology. Technology should reflect our awareness of the current economic situation, the need for careful planning in the use of resources and, finally, the compelling importance of lead times to winning in a technological race.

All of these things are possible with foresight and an energetic dedication to the task that now confronts us. With such dedication, and sacrifice on the part of our people, we can make the technological decisions that will restore to us the strategic initiative. We will then have a successful strategy, one that will make tactical battle unnecessary. It will be one to which free people the world over can aspire with confidence and hope. It will be a Strategy for Peace.

Index

Set in Linotype Caledonia
Format by Nancy Etheredge
Manufactured by The Haddon Craftsmen, Inc.
Published by HARPER & BROTHERS, *New York*